The International

THE SOCIOLOGY OF AN ENGLISH VILLAGE: GOSFORTH

Founded by KARL MANNHEIM

The International Library of Sociology

URBAN AND REGIONAL SOCIOLOGY
In 13 Volumes

I	An Approach to Urban Sociology	*Mann*
II	City and Region	*Dickinson*
III	The City Region in Western Europe	*Dickinson*
IV	English Rural Life	*Bracey*
V	New Dubliners	*Humphreys*
VI	The Personality of the Urban African in South Africa	*de Ridder*
VII	The Regions of Germany	*Dickinson*
VIII	Revolution of Environment	*Gutkind*
IX	Rural Depopulation in England and Wales 1851 - 1951	*Saville*
X	The Social Background of a Plan	*Glass*
XI	The Sociology of an English Village: Gosforth	*Williams*
XII	The West European City	*Dickinson*
XIII	Westrigg	*Littlejohn*

THE SOCIOLOGY OF AN ENGLISH VILLAGE: GOSFORTH

by
W. M. WILLIAMS

Routledge
Taylor & Francis Group
LONDON AND NEW YORK

First published in 1956 by
Routledge

Reprinted 1998, 1999, 2000, 2002 by
Routledge
2 Park Square, Milton Park, Abingdon, Oxon, OX14 4RN
Simultaneously published in the USA and Canada by Routledge
711 Third Avenue, New York, NY 10017
Transferred to Digital Printing 2007

Routledge is an imprint of the Taylor & Francis Group

First issued in paperback 2013

© 1956 W. M. Williams

All rights reserved. No part of this book may be reprinted or reproduced or utilized in any form or by any electronic, mechanical, or other means, now known or hereafter invented, including photocopying and recording, or in any information storage or retrieval system, without permission in writing from the publishers.

The publishers have made every effort to contact authors/copyright holders of the works reprinted in *The International Library of Sociology*. This has not been possible in every case, however, and we would welcome correspondence from those individuals/companies we have been unable to trace.

British Library Cataloguing in Publication Data
A CIP catalogue record for this book
is available from the British Library

The Sociology of an English Village: Gosforth

ISBN 978-0-415-17707-8 (hbk)
ISBN 978-0-415-86369-8 (pbk)

Publisher's Note
The publisher has gone to great lengths to ensure the quality of this reprint but points out that some imperfections in the original may be apparent

To
KATHLEEN AND JUDITH

CONTENTS

	PREFACE	*page* ix
	INTRODUCTION	1
I	THE ECONOMY	5
II	THE FAMILY	34
III	SOME ASPECTS OF THE LIFE CYCLE	59
IV	KINSHIP	69
V	THE SOCIAL CLASSES	86
VI	FORMAL AND INFORMAL ASSOCIATIONS	121
VII	NEIGHBOURS	140
VIII	COMMUNITY	155
IX	GOSFORTH AND THE OUTSIDE WORLD	168
X	RELIGION	178
	CONCLUSION	200
	APPENDICES	
	I Place of Birth of Occupiers, their Wives, and Parents	204
	II Size of Holdings	207
	III Male Labour on Farms	209
	IV Some Methodological Considerations in the Study of Social Class	210
	V Statistics relating to the Study of the Social Classes	215
	VI 'Familiar' Names as Symbols of Class Position	218
	VII Parochial Organizations	220
	VIII Part I. The Settlement Pattern of Medieval Gosforth	221
	Part II. Township, Vill, and Manor	221
	NOTES	223
	INDEX	243

MAPS AND TEXT FIGURES

1	Fragmentation of holdings	page	8
2	Kinship and the individual		71
3	Kinship in Gosforth		73
4	The social classes		87
5	Friendship configurations		101
6	Associations and social class		123
7	Office-holders and social class		125
8	Age, marital status, and social class of persons attending public houses		137
9	Co-operation among farmers		145
10	Gosforth in 1600		157
11	Gosforth in 1810		159
12	Townships		161

PREFACE

THE people of Gosforth found it difficult to understand why I had chosen their parish. The University of Wales, where I was working at the time, seemed to them remote, if indeed it existed at all. The answer is that I wished to carry out a study of a parish in North-Western England; a preliminary survey in West Cumberland showed that Gosforth was one of three parishes which were of the size of population and of a sufficiently remote location to seem worthy of full-time study over a period of about eighteen months. Gosforth was finally chosen because of its long history and because it contained both a village and scattered farms. The field-work took place between July 1950 and February 1952, and further field-work was carried out in the summer of 1953.

The success of the study is due in very large measure to the kindness and co-operation of the Gosforth folk. More often than not I arrived at their homes at the most inconvenient time; many of my questions were extremely personal; many of my requests for information involved considerable work. Throughout my stay, however, I found the hospitality which is so important and attractive a characteristic of the area. A great many people went to a great deal of trouble to help in the investigation. In particular I should like to thank Mr. Will Wilson, the Headmaster of Gosforth School, Mr. Harry Simpson, the Parish Clerk, Mr. Tom Moore, Mr. Matthew Singleton, Mr. Jacob Williamson and Mr. William Poole.

I owe a special debt of gratitude to my former teacher Mr. Alwyn D. Rees of the University College of Wales, Aberystwyth. His teaching first aroused my interest in rural sociology and his advice was of immeasurable help during the field-work and the analysis. Also I should like to thank Professor Shils of Chicago, Professor Homans of Harvard and Professor Gluckman of Manchester for their help and encouragement.

PREFACE

Most of all I record my gratitude to my wife, who made the field-work possible. Her help and encouragement have been invaluable always.

W. M. WILLIAMS

*University College of
   North Staffordshire.*
October 1955

INTRODUCTION

THE civil parish of Gosforth, covering an area of just over eleven square miles, lies on the western fringe of the Lakeland fells of Cumberland. About two miles from its western boundary is the Irish Sea, while to the north and east stand the moorlands and peaks of Copeland Forest and Eskdale, uninhabited save for hardy flocks of Herdwick sheep. The landscape of the parish reflects its position between the Lakeland hills and the undulating coastal plain, which extends from Millom in the extreme south of the county to Carlisle in the north. The southern half of Gosforth is a gently undulating plain rarely rising above 150 feet: the northern portion forms the seaward face of the western fells and the land rises north and north-east to over 900 feet on Bleng Fell and Hollow Moor. In common with all the western dales there are no sharp peaks, and the one valley which bisects the moorland is narrow and steep-sided, with a small development of flat land on the valley bottom through which runs the River Bleng.

Apart from a narrow belt of alluvium along both sides of the lower stretches of the Bleng, the 200-foot contour divides the parish roughly into a southern lowland of New Red Sandstone and a northern upland of andesite, with a small area of granite on the highest portion of Hollow Moor.

The intermediate position of the parish is also evident in its area, and in the size and distribution of its population. In Cumberland as a whole, small parishes with a relatively high density of population are typical of the lowlands and the North, while the moorlands are characterized by very large parishes with a few scattered farmsteads and cottages. Gosforth is much larger than the average coastal parish and much smaller than the fell parish. Moreover in many of the smaller parishes the population is concentrated almost entirely in nucleated settlements, while the inhabitants of the fell parishes live mainly in isolated farms. In Gosforth nearly two-thirds of the people live in the village, and

INTRODUCTION

the remainder in farmsteads and cottages dispersed throughout the parish.

In January 1951 Gosforth had 723 inhabitants,[1] most of whom were born in West Cumberland. Thus over two-thirds of the householders were born in the area within a ten mile radius of the parish, as were well over a half of their wives (see Appendix I, Table 1). The same proportions hold true for the parents of householders and their wives, and very probably a large number of the inhabitants of the parish are the modern representatives of families who have lived in this area for centuries. There are several people in Gosforth whose families have lived in the same place for four hundred years or more.

In addition a great many of the inhabitants were born in other parts of Cumberland, and a large number of these are only excluded from the proportions given above by the arbitrary nature of the chosen radius. Four out of every five of the male householders of Gosforth were born in the county, as were three out of every four of their wives, while only 28 per cent of their parents were born in other counties. Movement of families within West Cumberland has been common during the last hundred years, and therefore the proportion of householders (32·1 per cent) and their wives (23·5 per cent) and their parents (21·2 per cent and 16·1 per cent respectively) born within the parish is relatively small.

Like so many other counties in England, one of the marked characteristics of the modern history of Cumberland has been rural depopulation. In this area, however, the migration to the towns has taken place mainly within the county boundary, that is, from the rural parishes of the Lakeland foothills and plain to the industrial areas of the coast between Whitehaven and Maryport. For this reason there has been no decline in the population of the county as a whole (see Appendix I, Table 2(*a*)). The same is true of the Rural District of which Gosforth is a part, but when this unit is considered in detail, it is clear that the industrial parishes within it have grown in size at the expense of the rural parishes. Thus the population of Gosforth, in common with that in all the adjoining rural parishes, began to rise about 1810, after

INTRODUCTION

remaining relatively stable for over two centuries, reached a maximum about 1870, and has declined steadily ever since, so that its present population is just over half what it was eighty years ago. This decline has affected the isolated farmsteads, for as we shall see later, the village has grown in size since 1870, and there are numerous farmhouses and cottages now used solely as barns and byres, and many others which have decayed completely until they are little more than a heap of rubble.

The history of Gosforth is in many ways a reflection of its remoteness and isolation. It was for centuries part of the barony of Coupland, an area renowned for its backwardness and difficulty of access. In 1563 it was described as 'that little angle where I was born, called Coupland, the ignorantest part in religion, and most oppressed of covetous landlords of any one part of this realm to my knowledge.'[2] As late as the end of the eighteenth century, maps of this area showed the western Lakes hopelessly distorted and wrongly named,[3] while Ennerdale Water and Wastwater, the two lakes nearest to Gosforth, remained free from the 'Romantic Invasion' until eighty years ago.

The inaccessibility of Coupland, which lasted until the latter half of the nineteenth century, meant that, in comparison with much of England, the area around Gosforth was largely unaffected by developments of a national character. Largely as a result of this, many cultural features of considerable antiquity have survived until the present day.

The first record of man in the Gosforth area dates back to prehistoric times. Neolithic stone axes were discovered in the parish in the decade following 1880, and are now kept in the village school as a symbol of the immense length of time which has elapsed since human activity began in this area. The Norse Cross and the hogback stones in the churchyard, and the numerous Norse place-names and personal names which occur in the district, recall the Viking invasions of the ninth and tenth centuries, and part of the Church, which has survived from the time following the death of William Rufus, testifies to the presence of the Normans who succeeded the Norsemen in the control of Coupland. This area, however, does not appear in the Domesday Book,

INTRODUCTION

since what is now Cumberland was not regarded as part of England until the beginning of the twelfth century. Then during the reign of Henry I this portion of North-West England became firmly established as part of the Anglo-Norman kingdom, a change that brought with it the founding of the great monastries, one of which, at St. Bees, left a Chartulary that furnishes the first documentary evidence concerning Gosforth which is known to exist at the present time.

The centuries following the establishment of the St. Bees priory are only poorly documented until the beginning of the Parish Registers in 1571, and the Churchwardens' Accounts in 1697. These and other local sources are used extensively throughout this work and give an historical background to the sociological analysis.

CHAPTER I

THE ECONOMY

IN 1951, eighteen of the forty-one farms over fifty acres in Gosforth were freehold, twenty were farmed by tenants, and three were farmed by 'hinds' (i.e. estate managers) on behalf of owners living in the parish. Seven of the farms are part of an estate, the owner of which lives locally, four are part of an estate owned by an absentee landlord, and a further five belong to three estates which extend into Gosforth from adjoining parishes.

The history of land-holding in Gosforth is poorly documented and the limited evidence that exists is frequently conflicting. The earliest record is that of the Chartulary of St. Bees[1] relating to the late twelfth and thirteenth centuries, and this reveals that Gosforth, in common with other areas where the manorial system prevailed, was split up into demesne lands and holdings farmed by tenants of the Lord of the Manor. Little, however, is known of the detailed distribution of these medieval holdings, and it is not until the late eighteenth century that the evidence sheds any light on the evolution of the present farms.

The earliest document which lists all the holdings in Gosforth is the Glebe Terrier of 1778.[2] In this they are given together with their owners, and the amounts of modus in lieu of corn and hay which was payable in respect of each parcel of land. According to this document there were 137 holdings of land in the (then) parish, of which 15 are in the present parish of Seascale and 13 are unidentifiable, leaving a minimum of 109 holdings in what is now Gosforth. There was no large estate owned by one person. The Terrier names 99 owners, none of whom owned more than three farms. The Parish Award of 1815[3] shows that there had been little change in the intervening years. In this 111 holdings are listed, owned by 101 individuals. Again there is no indication of acreage, but from the maps which accompany the Award[4] and from the evidence of scattered farm deeds, it is possible to describe the system of land-holding at the beginning of the nineteenth century with some degree of certainty.

Before the Enclosure Act there were 2,708 acres of common land, out of a total of 8,565 acres in the old Parish. Nearly all this common lay within the smaller area which constitutes the present parish of Gosforth, accounting in fact for 38 per cent of its 7,124 acres (see Fig. 10). The remaining land was divided into 97 holdings, which included all the 41 present farmsteads and 9 of the present small-holdings. The remaining 47 holdings can all be identified and may be analysed as follows:

Former farmsteads now incorporated into other farmsteads	9
Former 'wheel-barrow farms' ,, ,, ,, ,,	11
Former small-holdings ,, ,, ,, ,,	27

The distinctions employed here are based on scattered farm deeds, and the size of the buildings which remain. For example, farmsteads were holdings roughly equivalent in acreage to present-day farms. A 'wheel-barrow farm' was the local term for an enterprise that was just large enough to support a family engaged in full-time farming. There is fortunately enough evidence to distinguish between the size of the three types; the farmstead varied between 40 and 100 acres; the 'wheel-barrow farm' averaged about 15 acres, and representative small holdings ranged from $1\frac{1}{2}$ to 6 acres.

There were, therefore, 50 farms in Gosforth in 1800, most of which must have ranged in size from 50 to 100 acres.[5] Interspersed among these were the wheel-barrow farms and small patches of land farmed by men who were also inn-keepers, farm labourers, and village craftsmen.[6]

Grazing rights on the waste land, which had been very important from medieval times,[7] were enjoyed by all farmers, and a great many of the farms were situated very near to stretches of common. There was a limited amount of squatting on the waste in the eighteenth century, and very probably there had been enclosure and improvement from time to time, a practice very prevalent in Cumberland.[8] The Enclosure Act at the beginning of the nineteenth century divided all the common in the parish between the landowners, with about 200 acres for the Rector in lieu of small tithes and moduses. In all, 299 allotments were made, ranging in size from 8 perches to 141 acres. Although in most cases some attempt was made to apportion the common so that the allotments were as near to their owners' holdings as possible, there were several patches of waste situated some distance away from the holding to which they were allotted, and occasionally farmers were allotted three or four patches of common in widely separated parts of the parish. The years following 1815 were marked first by a general increase in the size of the holdings, and then, as the bigger farms bought the allotments of the smallholders, by an increase in the size of the larger holdings, and a decrease in the size of the small ones.

During the remainder of the nineteenth century the pattern of holdings remained more or less unchanged, but the years from 1850 onwards were marked by the growth of large estates owned by *nouveau riche* people. These bought large numbers of holdings and substituted tenants for freeholders, without altering the amount of land attached to the farms to any great degree. Then after the first World War, economic factors of a national character forced estate owners to attempt to sell their property,[9] and when this failed, they amalgamated several groups of farms, so that there was an increase in the number of large holdings (see Appendix II, Table 1). The wheel-barrow farm vanished in these post-war years, and the number of small-holdings decreased considerably. In the past ten years there has been a partial reversion to the conditions of a century and a half ago. The number of owner-occupiers rose from 13 to 18 between January 1945 and June 1951, and a further four farms were unsuccessfully offered for sale to their tenants in May 1951.

One of the most striking features of land-holding in Gosforth at present is the high degree of fragmentation (see Fig. 1). Much of this resulted from the division of the commons, many detached allotments being improved and linked permanently with certain holdings, but occasional farm deeds and the limited evidence afforded by the Parish Award suggests that it was a feature of the landscape before the beginning of the nineteenth century.[10] Also typical are frequent changes of ownership, particularly of isolated

THE ECONOMY

plots, though there are some holdings which have remained virtually unchanged in the possession of the same family for centuries. These however are all owner-occupied farms; on tenant farms on the other hand there has been considerable change in ownership, particularly during the last fifty years, so that there are

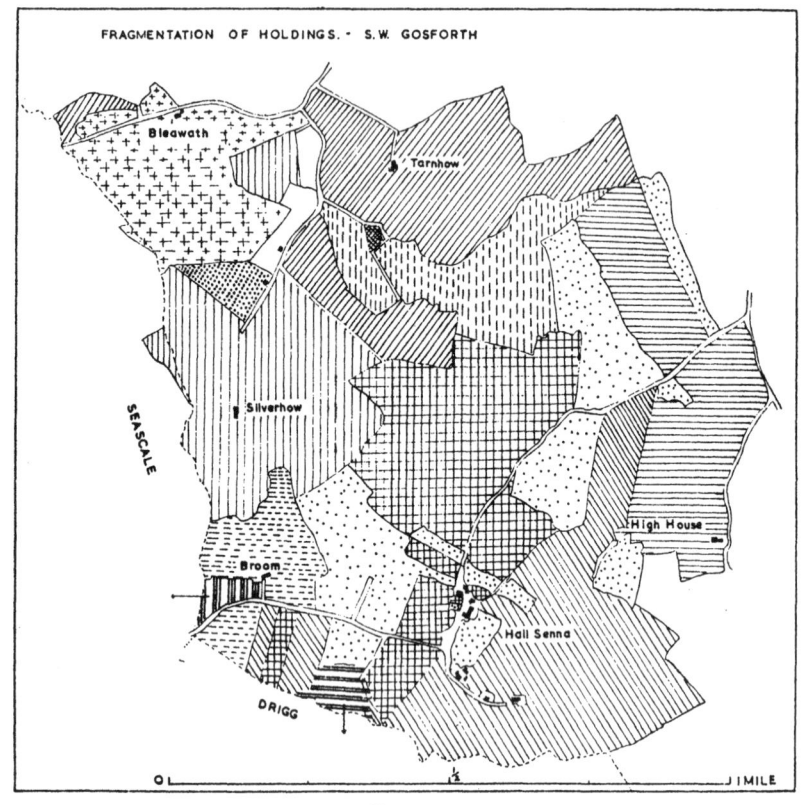

FIG. 1.

now very few leasehold farms owned by the same landlords as twenty years ago.

Little can be said of the history of farming in Gosforth as distinct from that of the remainder of West Cumberland, which has been fully described by several authorities.[11]

There is, however, a short eighteenth-century account of the agriculture of the parish which is of interest for the local detail, and also for the background it provides to the description of the present conditions given in the remaining sections of this chapter.

'The produce is chiefly oats and a little barley: but the proprietors in general seem negligent, as the soil is certainly capable of being employed to a greater advantage by proper culture. Would the occupiers sow turnips [12] (to which the ground seems peculiarly adapted), and dress them well, and the next year sow it with barley and clover or other artificial grass seeds, and so lay it down for a year or two, and then plow it out again for oats, and the next year work it in fallow for turnips, etc., they would certainly find a very great advantage; instead of which many of the farmers let several fields where the furze, with which the fences are in general, bearded and planted, had been suffered to spread their seed, and run all over the inclosure. There is an abundance of freestone but no limestone or coal. Upon the high commons to the east end of the parish, about 2,000 sheep are kept, which, with the other cattle [13] are of the same quality with those of the neighbouring parishes. Here is only one road of any note which leads from Egremont to Ravenglass. No river, some small brooks. The parish is situated rather high, but is not mountainous, though uneven; it is destitute of wood; the roads are good and dry; the buildings in general are good.'[14]

It has already been noted that Gosforth is intermediate in location, size and population. Its farming economy reflects this intermediate position, possessing features of both the highly specialized sheep-farming of the fells and of the arable and dairy farms of the immediate coastal lowlands, without, however, that sharp emphasis which characterizes these two extremes. In Gosforth there are no sheep farms composed entirely of vast expanses of rough grazing, while farms on which dairying and stock-raising respectively are the dominant occupation exist side by side.

The medial nature of the economy is seen to some extent in the size of farms and in the relative proportions of rough grazing and improved land. Of the 67 holdings the owners or tenants of which reside in the parish [15] 5 are over 200 acres, only one over 300 acres, while 28 are between 50 and 150 acres. Of the 28 holdings under 50 acres, only 4 are farmed as a full-time occupation. 19 out of the 41 farms in Gosforth are medium-sized, between 80 and 130 acres, but an analysis based on total farm acreage does not reveal the true pattern of land-holding. For example, the 3 farms which exceed 250 acres in area are composed respectively of 210 acres of crops and grass with 372 acres of rough grazing, 40 acres of crops and grass with 286 acres of rough grazing, and 250 acres of crops and grass with 27 acres of rough grazing. Again, of the 19 medium-sized farms, 13 have no rough grazing at all, 2 have less than a tenth in rough grazing and only one has more than half its area in unimproved land. This disparity in the relative proportions of cropland and rough grazing is, as we shall see later, closely related to differences in the actual economy of the individual farms.

Rough grazing occupies just over a quarter of the land held by Gosforth farmers, but its distribution is limited to a small number of holdings. Thus 8 farms account for over 82 per cent of the 'park' (the local term for rough grazing), the two biggest of these together occupying 39 per cent. Farm rents therefore vary not only according to total acreage, but also according to the proportion of the different types of land within the farm holdings. Further variations in rental result from differing accessibility of farms to main roads, the general state of farm buildings and the amount of repairs done by the respective landlords, altitude and degree of exposure, and the period of tenancy of the individual farmer. A few examples show how these factors interact:

(1) *Farm A.* A holding of 180 acres, of which 80 are rough grazing. The former tenant, who vacated in 1947, paid £95 a year; the new tenant pays £135 for the same acreage. The landlord was described by the occupier as 'very good' and all the repairs asked for have been carried out. The farm is situated near a main road, and milk for collection by the Milk Marketing Board has only to be taken about one hundred yards.

(2) *Farm B.* A holding of 84 acres, of which 6 are rough grazing.

THE ECONOMY

The last tenant, who vacated in 1948, paid £80 a year; the present tenant pays £120 for the same area. The farm buildings are in a good state of repair, but milk has to be taken over half a mile to the nearest main road.

(3) *Farm C.* A holding of 85 acres, none of which is rough grazing. The occupier, who has been a tenant since 1928, pays £57 a year, his rent having been raised by 20 per cent in 1950. It was said that no repairs have been made for a considerable time, despite frequent requests. The farm is about 350 yards from the main road.

The period of tenancy of the occupier and the policy of the landlord appear to be as important in determining the amount of farm rent as the basic factor of acreage and type of land. Most, if not all the landlords lowered rents by 10 per cent during the depression years of the early thirties and have raised them considerably in recent years whenever a change of tenancy allowed them to do so. The older tenants therefore pay much lower rents per acre than newcomers, but appreciable differences of rental occur even in the case of long-established tenants, since on one estate rents were generally raised by 20 per cent in 1950 by mutual agreement between landlord and tenant, while on the others this has not occurred.[16]

For this reason no average rent can be considered as really representative. On farms consisting of crop- and grass-land only, with soils of similar quality, rents vary from 13s. 6d. to 35s. an acre. A holding equivalent in acreage to Farm A, and with a similar amount of rough grazing, has a rental of less than £70 a year. Only for the rough grazing can any average be fixed; holdings of rough grazing have a rental of 4s. 6d. to 6s. an acre throughout the parish.

Factors determining the selling price of land seem to be even more complex, and the limited information available together with the enormous range in the selling price of farms make generalization difficult. Six farms have been sold in the last five years, all by private treaty; the details are on the following page.

THE ECONOMY

Farm.[17]	Total Acreage.	Rough Grazing.	Price. £	Date.	Price Per Acre. £ s. d.
1. Rowan Side	160	40	2300	Mar. 1950.	19 3 6
2. Low Beck	167	—	4650	Sept. 1950.	27 14 6
3. High Beck	40	—	1500	Feb. 1947.	37 10 –
4. Moor Gate	43	—	1740	Feb. 1948.	39 10 6
5. Black Bank	71	—	4700	Feb. 1950.	65 14 6
6. Bleng Hall	50	16	3375	May 1948.	67 10 –
7. High Beck	40	—	4575	Feb. 1950.	114 7 6

Even after full allowance has been made for such factors as accessibility and condition of farm buildings (particularly operative in the case of Rowan Side, situated well away from main roads and with very poor outbuildings), the prices realized in these sales vary considerably. Low Beck was bought by the sitting tenant at what were described as 'very reasonable terms'. Moor Gate, High Beck and Rowan Side were bought by experienced farmers who had spent all their lives in the locality, though not in the parish itself. Black Bank was bought by a former business man who had never farmed before, but who had always lived within fifteen miles of Gosforth. The second buyer of High Beck had no previous links with the parish and no knowledge of farming. Bleng Hall is now the property of a man with some farming experience, but no connection with Cumberland.

Despite these variations, all the buyers (in common with most of the other farmers in the district) have a well defined ideal pattern of farm purchase. The most desirable farm is a 'family holding', that is one that can be worked without the help of hired labour, and the payment of a high price for a comparatively small farmstead is justified by such rationalizations as 'It's cheaper than paying for a couple of hired men for the rest of your life anyway'. Low Beck, which is larger than the ideal 'family farm', is not considered to be exceptional because the occupier has three sons and a daughter and requires no hired labour to run the farm.

When describing their holdings, 11 farmers called them 'rearing farms', one 'stock-raising and arable', 27 said their farms were 'mixed' and 3 preferred the term 'dairy farms'. Classified by their main source of income, 30 are mixed farms [18] deriving their greatest income from the sale of milk and potatoes, with stock-

THE ECONOMY

raising as an important subsidiary, and 11 are stock-raising farms. Within this general framework four types of farm practice may be distinguished. These are:

(1) Mixed farms concentrating on milk production, with stock-rearing of minor importance.
(2) Mixed farms with milk production only slightly more important than stock-rearing.
(3) Rearing farms depending mainly on the sale of cattle.
(4) Rearing farms depending mainly on the sale of sheep.

(1) There are 10 farms of this type, each breeding either Friesians or Ayrshires for their milk-yielding qualities.[19] On these farms heifer calves are kept and bull calves sold shortly after birth, as a rule to local markets for veal.

(2) These farms, 20 in number, breed mainly dual-purpose Shorthorns, or Shorthorn crosses, animals valued for their beef carcase as well as their milk. In this case heifer calves and bull calves are reared, the former for calving at two years and nine months, the latter for sale, usually as stores, at 12–18 months—though a few are kept and sold as fat bullocks after a period of up to three years, dependent on the amount and quality of grass available on the individual farm.

This division in mixed farming is comparatively recent. Until about 1930 there were no Friesians or Ayrshires in the parish, so that the breeding of animals for their milk yield alone was not practised. Although cross-breeding with Shorthorns has been very popular in West Cumberland generally, to produce a milk animal that also has a moderate beef carcase, this has not occurred on the 'milk' farms in Gosforth, all of which have pure-bred herds. Despite this fact they cannot be classified as dairy farms, since they lack many of the features normally associated with true dairy farming, e.g. they do not sell cows that are not in 'profit' and their proportion of cows in milk is lower than that typical of a dairying district. More recently still there has been a change in the mixed farmer's calving programme. Until a few years ago buying and breeding was arranged so that the animals calved from September to Christmas, in order to provide the greatest yield of milk when it was at its maximum selling price. Nowadays the high price of feeding-stuffs more than counter-balances a low summer milk yield and calving is no longer confined to the latter months of the year. On all mixed farms calves are pail-fed.

(3) There are 7 farms in this category, none of which produce milk for sale. On these farms the main source of income is the sale of dairy heifers, for replacements in the lowland mixed farms. The sale of young store cattle is also important, while bull calves are often kept for two years before being sent to auction. These farms normally keep ten or twelve cows to breed a percentage of their own calves, or buy the remainder to make up their total young stock. Suckling is more important than pail-feeding, and a further difference between these and mixed farms is that calving takes place in the spring.

(4) On these 3 farms the breeding and sale of cattle follows the practice of those farms in category (3), but is subordinated to the breeding of sheep. These farmers depend mainly on the sale of shearlings and ewes in the fat market and only a few lambs that do not fatten are sold as stores to the lowlands. Draft ewes and wool are subsidiary sources of income.

Nearly all the cattle are bred locally; most farms have a bull for breeding, or use their neighbour's. Only three farmers utilize the facilities offered by the Artificial Insemination Centre. On mixed farms sheep have a minor role. More than half these farms have no sheep of their own, though most of them provide winterage for 80–100 Herdwick 'hoggs'[20] from the fell farms of Wasdale. The remainder have 20–60 Cheviot or Blackface ewes which are kept for fattening from autumn to spring and then sold, a new stock being bought annually as replacements. This is also typical of lowland cattle-rearing farms with little or no rough grazing, while those at higher levels breed their own flocks of 50–100 Cheviot or Herdwick sheep and sell fat lambs and ewes. On the hill farms the Herdwick is the only breed, the flocks ranging from three to five hundred in number. Farms with hill sheep differ somewhat from those with lowland breeds in their lambing programme, since Herdwicks do not lamb until they are two years old.

The part which sheep play in the economy has changed more drastically than that of cattle. Until recently many low-lying farms in the parish owned or rented expanses of rough grazing, each with its flock of 'heaf-gangin' sheep.[21] The practice then was to draft store lambs from the outlying park to the fields around the farm for fattening. The farms at higher levels with limited areas of lowland grazing concentrated on the production of store lambs for disposal by auction. Lowland farms without rough grazing or fell rights carried far larger numbers of sheep for fattening than they do at present. To-day there is only one lowland farm which has a stock of fell sheep. The remainder have either relinquished their grazing to hill farmers, or to the Forestry Commission which has covered extensive areas of fell with trees.

Pigs are important as a source of money income on four farms only, and most farms have only one pig for domestic use. Poultry is an important sideline on many farms (200–300 hens are quite common) and there are also two herds of Shetland and fell ponies, reared mainly for sale to collieries in Co. Durham (at Wigton in October).

In 1949, over two-fifths of the cultivated land was under permanent grass, a little less than a third in temporary grass and clover, and oats and rootcrops occupied a fifth and a twelfth respectively.[22] All crops are consumed on the farm, with the exception of potatoes which are sold in some quantity, and in most years considerable amounts of feeding-stuffs are bought in addition, particularly on mixed farms. In one case the cost of feeding-stuffs exceeded five times the rent paid by the tenant, and there were many instances in which it amounted to three times the rent or more. One result of the bad harvest of 1950 has been the introduction of silage on several farms. Crop acreages for four holdings representative of the different types of farming are as follows:

Type of farm.*	Total Acreage.	Oats.	Potatoes.	Roots.	Hay.	Rough Grazing.
Mixed (1)	100	17	11	4·5	20	Nil
Mixed (2)	80	15	4·5	3	17	Nil
Rearing (3)	120	13	3	2	28	40
Rearing (4)	200	5·5	2	1	10	140

* The numbers refer to the classification given earlier.

THE ECONOMY

In 1939 there were no tractors in the parish; power-driven farm machinery was confined mainly to threshing and milking, but since the early years of the war, tractors, and auxiliary machines powered by them, have become common on most of the farms. Here again the fourfold division in farm type becomes apparent:

	FARMS USING			FARMS WITH		
Type of farm.	Horses only.	Machinery only.	Machinery and Horses.	Thresher.	Binder.	Milking Machine.
Mixed (1)	Nil	2	9	8	9	8
Mixed (2)	5	2	13	13	13	11
Rearing (3)	3	Nil	4	4	4	Nil
Rearing (4)	3	Nil	Nil	2	3	Nil

Mechanization is most advanced on the 'dairy' farms and almost non-existent in the uplands, where equipment has remained almost the same for twenty years or more.

On the majority of farms in Gosforth the annual cycle of farm activity tends to lie between the two extremes of the mixed farm concentrating on milk production, with no sheep, and the high-lying sheep farm with its limited amount of cultivated land. Since these extremes are, numerically at least, of minor importance in the economy, the account that follows attempts to describe the yearly round on the large group of farms that lies between them.

When the calendar year begins, the days are short and the tempo of farm life is slow. Activity in the fields is confined to the trimming and repairing of hedges or stone walls,[23] while on the farm the feeding of livestock in the byres is the main task. Candlemas (February 2nd) is invariably mentioned as the date on which the ploughing for spring crops and summer fallow begins in earnest. Ploughing is followed by 'mucking' (manuring) and February and March are busy months, since to plough after Lady Day (March 25th) is to invite unfavourable criticism. In March also, land for potatoes is prepared and fields for cereals are harrowed. Late in that month and in early April oat seed and the first crop of potatoes are planted, and lambing has already begun on the low-lying farms in March, spreading to all the farms in the district by the early weeks of April. As April progresses, the tempo only slackens slightly on the lowlands, for although the animals have been brought out of their byres early in the month and the Herdwick hoggs returned to the fells, the farmer is busy sowing mangolds and preparing and rolling fields for the hay crop.

The planting of turnips and swedes in early May marks the beginning of a quieter period on the farm; lambing is ending and the time is devoted mainly to the weeding and thinning of green crops and roots. This task continues until the beginning of the hay harvest, which normally occurs during the first week of June and lasts two to three weeks. On some farms harvesting does not begin until the third week, a delay which results more from differences in farming method than from the weather.[24] The end of the hay harvest offers a respite to the farmer, but in late July and early August crops have to be cleaned and weeded and on many farms the lifting of 'first and second earlies' (potatoes) takes up much time. Hot days during the summer keep the farmer who has sheep busy in combating maggot-fly, and July is the month when 'dipping and clipping' marks a peak of activity if numbers of sheep are large. In mid-August the tempo is again at its quickest with the onset of the cereal harvest, the end of which is usually followed by the lifting of roots and the main potato crop on the lowlands, and the dipping and preparation of sheep for the autumn sales on the hill farms. By late September the cereal harvest has ended, cabbage has been planted on the few farms that grow it, and there is some lifting of root crops. This period, extending well into October, is one of quiet on the farm, although there are some very busy days when young hoggs arrive from the high fells of Wasdale. By early November the animals have been brought in, and the ploughing of stubble for winter fallow begins. This is completed by mid-December, to be followed by the annual task of preparing poultry for the Christmas and New Year market.

Candlemas, therefore, marks the change from the quiet of January to the bustle which characterizes farming until the end of April, and it is also the beginning of the farmer's financial year. More than half the tenant farmers pay six months rent and the year's rates at this time. (The remainder of the rent is paid 'between Gosforth Show and Martinmas', i.e. between the first Friday in September and November the fourteenth.) Also at Candlemas are the Horse Fair at Carlisle and the first of the big spring sales at Whitehaven and Cockermouth. Sporadic selling of dairy cattle and fat and store sheep in January is now augmented by the auction of store cattle and store sheep, and an important sale of young bulls. These sales continue throughout the spring, increasing in intensity as the farmers' supply of winter fodder comes to an end. On Lady Day those farmers who have not already done so at Candlemas, pay their half year's rent.[25] Few yearling calves are sold at this time, so that as farm activity slackens off after the spring sowing, so too on rearing farms does the money income diminish considerably. Those farmers who provide winterage for fell farms are paid in April,[26] and in the following months the main financial transactions concern the selling of potatoes, summer lambs, and a small number of yearling calves in May and June. As in the spring, the end of August is a time of hard work in the fields and of intensive commercial activity. The cereal harvest normally coincides with the beginning of fortnightly sales at Cockermouth at which the remaining lambs and wool are sold.[27] In early September there is an important sale of draft ewes at Cockermouth, 'Sucklers' and young bulls are auctioned in October, and some of the money thus obtained is used for the purchase of yearling ewes or the payment of the second portion of the farm rent at Martinmas. Unless the harvest is particularly bad, sales at Cockermouth end at Martinmas, and the only animals disposed of are small numbers of dairy and fat cattle, and some sheep at Whitehaven. Income from the sale of animals is generally small between Martinmas and Candlemas, but important sums are obtained from the Christmas and New Year poultry market.

In addition to this irregular pattern of financial outlay and return, during the past fifteen to twenty years mixed farmers have received a monthly cheque for milk sold to the Milk Marketing Board. More recently still, hired labour has been paid on a week to week basis. There are now only three youths in the parish who

THE ECONOMY

are paid half-yearly—at Whitsun and Martinmas—although hiring of labour still takes place at 'term-time' on nearly all the farms.[28]

The social life of the farming community forms a complementary pattern to that described above. Farm labourers have a week's holiday at Whitsun and Martinmas, and the school outing to Blackpool or Morecambe occurs in July, thereby allowing many of the farmers' wives to accompany their children. Autumn, however, is the time of greatest leisure and social intercourse for the farmer. All the big agricultural shows in West Cumberland are held then, while the two greatest social events in the life of the parish—British Legion Sports Day (August Monday) and Gosforth Show (the first Friday in September)—occur in the more leisurely periods that precede and follow the cereal harvest. On the Saturday nearest to the seventeenth of July and the third Saturday in December a Shepherds' Meet is held at Wasdale Head. The introduction of sheepdog trials in recent years has attracted many lowland farmers to this event, and it is now a social occasion of considerable importance.

This annual alternation of work and leisure, with certain important days as reference points, is a legacy that has descended in much of its original form from the early Middle Ages at least. In thirteenth-century England, Candlemas and Lady Day marked the beginning and end of spring ploughing, and then as now, cattle would be removed from the meadows at Candlemas and not allowed back until after the hay harvest. Whitsun and Martinmas have already been noted as holiday periods, and this too has been a traditional practice for centuries. Michaelmas is still the traditional time for the killing of geese, and eggs have a considerable importance in the ceremonies connected with the observance of Easter. In many West Cumberland parishes (but not in Gosforth) the plough is blessed at the altar on Plough Sunday, and ploughing competitions are held on the following day (Plough Monday). These and other holy days are landmarks to farmer and villager alike, and although their importance is not to be compared with that suggested by Homans in his superb description of the husbandman's year in the thirteenth century,[29] they still exert much influence on the patterning of work and leisure, and are a considerable factor in the outlook of the country-folk.

In almost every conversation with farmers in Gosforth, the phrase 'That died out when t'tractor came' occurred frequently, and this is symptomatic of the great technological changes that have characterized local farming in the past ten years. Rapid mechanization is, however, only one facet of the transformation from a highly localized and individual way of life to one of dependence on the outside world and of ever-increasing acceptance of a uniform national culture. Urban life was brought somewhat nearer to the inhabitants of Gosforth by the completion of a coastal railway from Barrow to Whitehaven in 1846–7, but its impact was small until the opening of a regular omnibus service in 1929 made a journey to Whitehaven a less noteworthy event. Easy communication with the towns soon influenced the economy and the material culture generally. When this century began, Gosforth had three blacksmiths and a full complement of village craftsmen, including a 'swiller',[30] basket-maker, clog-maker, watch-maker and saddler, who obtained most of their raw materials locally and produced finished goods in their own workshops. Clothes for men were made up by a tailor, a dressmaker catered for women and children, and in addition there were 'sewing women' who travelled from farm to farm making and repairing garments. Water provided the motive power for mills that ground meal or produced planks and sawn timber for the carpenter. At Boonwood Fair, held on the 25th of April and 18th of October, store bullocks and store sheep were sold by direct trading, outstanding debts were paid, lengths of cloth bought, and wool for the following year was sold in advance. In food and lighting the parish was largely self-sufficient. Rush candles were made from mutton fat, using a wooden mould resembling a test-tube in shape, examples of which are still to be found on occasional farms.[31] An important item in the diet was bread and cake made from oatmeal on the 'girder' or 'girdle', which in some houses was enclosed in a specially-built oven. A year's supply was made at a time and stored in air-tight boxes. This, unlike bread, which was baked once a week (usually in a brick oven), was not a household task, but was made by women who journeyed from farm to farm, normally in pairs, staying as long as a week at one place, bed and board forming the greater part of their remuneration.

To-day most of the old craftsmen have disappeared. The blacksmith devotes more and more time to mechanical repairs, and less and less to the shoeing of horses. The peripatetic sewing women, the tailor and the dressmaker competed for a time against the cheap mass-produced goods of the shops, brought within easy reach by motor transport, and then vanished. Oatmeal lost its importance in the diet soon after the turn of the century, and nowadays all the village and many of the farms buy bread and shop-made cake. Boonwood Fair declined and finally ceased in the mid-twenties as auctions at Whitehaven and Cockermouth absorbed more and more farm stock. The activities of the West Cumberland Farmers' Co-operative Society and the South Cumberland Farmers' Co-operative Society in many of the commercial aspects of farming, the beginning of the Milk Marketing Scheme in the mid-thirties, and the introduction of electricity and sewage a few years later abolished many traditional practices, while such wartime features as mechanization, compulsory ploughing, and control of labour reduced local and national differences even further. Changes, especially in the material culture, have therefore been great, but certain traditional crafts still flourish. The local mason still follows by hand the designs and precepts that have been a family heritage for generations, and his materials—red sandstone, Coniston slate, and Buttermere slate—are those his grandfather used. The joiner and wheelwright still make carts, a power-driven circular saw installed about 1950 constituting the only innovation for many years.

In the same way, many traditional practices flourish yet on farmsteads. Baking of bread, which died out very rapidly in the village when the baker's van started delivering from door to door, is still carried on in many farmhouses. On a larger scale, mechanization of farming has not been determined solely by the limits imposed by the natural environment and the purely economic

THE ECONOMY

aspect of farming. The various factors in the introduction of mechanized farming may best be illustrated by describing two farms, one considered locally as an extreme example of the traditional way of life, and the other a highly mechanized farmstead, whose owner, significantly enough, has been held to possess a 'King's College outlook'.[32]

(1) This is one of the more remote farms in the parish, owned and occupied by a man whose family have been there since the late eighteenth century at least. There are 44 acres of cultivable land and 16 acres of rough grazing. Sheep rearing and potato growing are the most important sources of money income; no milk is sold. Cattle are pure-bred Shorthorns, cross-breeds being considered inferior, and the very few purchases of animals that the occupier has made have been from neighbours. There is no power-driven machinery at all, and horse-drawn equipment is at the minimum required to run the farm. Until 1940 corn was bound by hand, but since that date a neighbour brings his binder when his own harvest is finished, and cuts and binds the crop himself since there is no one at the farm who is able to operate the binder. This is the only farm in Gosforth where the 'gin-ring' is still used for threshing. The occupier, who is unmarried, runs the farm with his brother and two sisters, and there is no hired labour. When asked if his was a mechanized farm, the occupier replied, 'It's nivver happened here and nivver will'. He has no car or bicycle and walks to Gosforth whenever the need arises.

The farm-house is one of the very few in the district with an open fireplace: bread is baked in a brick oven, butter is made weekly, and little food is bought. An oil lamp is used for lighting and water is obtained from a pump in the farm yard. Main contact with the outside world, apart from immediate neighbours, appears to be confined to occasional visits to the village and sporadic excursions to Whitehaven for the sale of livestock. The fact that there is no hired labour, that there is no delivery of food and that none of the occupants are married reduces the number of visitors to a minimum, and this was reflected in the occupier's attitude to being interviewed. There can be little doubt that changes on this farm have been few in the last fifty years, and that

THE ECONOMY

the occupiers' systems of values and standards of comparison are little removed from those of their father.

(2) The tenant of this holding of 277 acres, of which 27 acres are rough grazing, was a steel worker and hired man before coming to this farm in 1945, when he started farming on his own account. The rearing of Friesian/Shorthorn crosses, together with sheep fattening and the sale of potatoes, are the dominant farm activities, and make up the greater portion of the income. Milk was sold at one time, but this was discontinued some three years ago. Although there are three horses, almost all the work is done by tractor and there is a considerable quantity of equipment on the farm, including a modern type of potato-digger. The performance of the latter, the only one of its kind in the area, is known to almost all the farmers in Gosforth, and its owner is very often referred to as 'Agnew and his "tatie-digger" '. Threshing is done by a contractor, but such operations as mowing are done by auxiliary tractor equipment, and not—as is normal in the area—by using the tractor to draw the older type of horse-drawn machinery. The occupier is married, has five children, and employs three hired men. When interviewed, he described all his equipment in great detail, accompanying his description with photographs of himself operating the various machines. He travels rather extensively in his car and attends machinery demonstrations, agricultural films and talks, 'as often as possible'. Soil samples are taken by King's College and the occupier subscribes to a large number of agricultural journals and magazines. He is the only member of the Northern Seed Growers' Association in the parish.

The farmhouse is old, but a new bathroom and a large Aga cooker have added a note of extreme modernity. Bread and groceries are delivered weekly and butter is obtained from another farmer. Water is pumped from the mains to indoor taps. Visitors and tradesmen were said to be very numerous; the hired labour, and children attending schools at Gosforth and Whitehaven bring new ideas and behaviour patterns to the farmhouse. The occupier's outlook is highly coloured by his conception of technological advance and this is very apparent in his conversation and the way in which he runs his farm.

These two examples outline the disparity that can exist between the attitudes of different individuals to a complex diffused from without, even in such a limited area as Gosforth. An attempt has been made to select and arrange the facts to show how pre-existing conditions affect both initial acceptance or rejection of the complex as a whole, how the speed of the diffusion may vary once begun, and how certain traits within the complex may be accepted and others rejected, for example the use of the binder at the first farm. An examination of other farms would reveal other aspects of the process of diffusion, for example the use of a tractor to pull horse-drawn equipment. In abstract terms this could be described as an illustration of the way in which new items are adapted to integrate smoothly with the main body of the culture.

The growing dependence of Gosforth on the outside world, and something of the changes that have accompanied it, have been outlined. Some consideration must also be given to the results of this process in the present economy. Whitehaven and Cockermouth have already been mentioned in connection with the auctions held there, and the farmers buy and sell much of their cattle at these towns. There is still a great deal of private dealing, however, and since the establishment of the Milk Marketing Scheme, and the growth of pedigree Dairy Shorthorn herds, Penrith has become important as an additional centre for transactions involving cattle. Some yearling ewes are obtained from Kendal and Appleby, and large numbers of Cheviot stores are bought at Carlisle, Wigton, or at Scottish markets, particularly Hawick and Lockerbie. A few dealers travel around the farms buying stock, but the greatest commercial activity between farmers and travelling agents is concerned with the buying of lime and agricultural machinery, from firms in Kendal and Carlisle in the main. Those farmers who do not mill their own grain utilize a mill at Muncaster, while others have major economic contact with places as far apart as Perth, Lancaster and Driffield. Most of the remaining farm trade is shared between the Farmers' Co-operative Societies, with headquarters at Whitehaven, Egremont and Drigg. These supply virtually all the feeding-stuffs, most of the lime, some agricultural machinery and seeds, and buy most of the surplus eggs and potatoes. The West Cumberland Farmers' Co-operative Society has also established a grass-drying plant at Egremont, and is responsible for much of the farm insurance.

In general then, the greatest volume of commercial exchange is with Whitehaven, and this has been reinforced by its establishment as a grading station during the last war and the siting there of the local headquarters of the Cumberland Agricultural Executive Committee. Other economic transactions are spread over a considerable area, a fact of social as well as economic importance.

The distribution of the places where domestic objects (apart from food) are bought has little in common with that of the trading described above. The market for farm products is largely determined by availability; pedigree Shorthorns, for example, can be obtained conveniently only from Penrith. In the case of clothes, furniture, domestic appliances, etc., the determinants are rather more complex. Children's shoes, ribbons, smaller items of clothing and some articles of ironmongery are usually obtained from Gosforth, where there is also a chemist's shop, shoe repairer, and 'general' stores. The social status of the buyer and the type of article required largely determine the source of most other commodities. Thus shopping in Egremont is on a much smaller scale than at Whitehaven, and as a rule is confined to families who consider the dividend paid by the Co-operative Stores to be important as a means of providing an occasional 'nest-egg'. It is Whitehaven that supplies the farmer with his best suit, and his wife and daughters with clothes that fulfil the requirements of local 'fashion'.[33] It is the normal shopping-place for the more expensive domestic goods and furniture, and only a very small minority travel to Carlisle to obtain the more 'exclusive' styles. Day-to-day wear, dungarees and shoes are bought either in Whitehaven, or, more commonly, from travelling salesmen who visit the farms periodically.

Considerations of prestige do not apparently affect the buying of food, the only commodity which the farmer has continued to produce for himself to a large extent. Much of the diet consists of farm produce—eggs, bacon, milk, vegetables and fruit—supplemented by chickens, rabbits, pork, and meat products (e.g. 'black pudding' and sausage) from time to time. Enough butter for the family is made on many farms, but several farmers obtain their butter from stock-raising farms, usually in exchange for bacon or other forms of pig meat.[34] The village shops deliver almost all the additional food requirements, except to the most remote farmhouses. Bread, delivered once a week from Egremont to those families who do not bake their own, is probably the only foodstuff which is not bought locally.

Dependence on Whitehaven in commercial matters is therefore considerable, but the village has remained the centre for the banking and saving of money. The village bank handles sufficient business to justify normal urban opening hours, and the Bank Manager shares with the village schoolmaster the position of confidential adviser regarding financial affairs of all kinds. The recent Income Tax regulations which made the keeping of farm accounts compulsory altered the method of assessing the amount of tax a farmer pays, and also affected farmers' attitudes to money.

Before the new regulations came into force, the method of assessing profits on a fixed scale if rents were below a certain amount meant that only very few farmers in the parish were required to keep accounts at all.[35] Most of them apparently regarded payment of tax as something rather remote, leaving all details to be settled by the Bank Manager or Schoolmaster and 'yon laal feller from Whitehaven' (i.e. Inland Revenue official). The most common means of ascertaining total wealth or annual profits was to refer to the bank pass-book or the counterfoils of cheques, and these, together with a large pile of several years' invoices strung on a wire constituted the only 'accounts' kept on the majority of farms. In spite of his familiarity with the cheque book, the farmer's view of money was still far removed from that of the townsman. This is still true of those farmers who for one reason or another do not pay Income Tax, whereas many of those who do, have, in the last few years, begun to keep books and to have them audited by an accountant. The more prosperous farmers, therefore, have tended to adopt urban methods of managing their financial affairs, but the long established pattern of regarding 'experts' as the sole and ultimate authority on the calculation of tax and other monetary matters has still remained.

Some farmers do not bank their money, and apparently have little or no idea of their actual financial position from one year to the next. To support this view one informant, whose opinions on other aspects of farming proved to be very accurate, told the following story, which illustrates this point very clearly:

'During the war, an organizer of the National Savings Movement received a visit from a farmer's wife who wished to *donate* some money to help the war effort. He explained that National Savings were not a form of charity, but an investment on which interest was paid. A few days later the same woman returned carrying a battered suitcase, which she said she would leave with him while she went shopping, so that he could take what he wanted as savings. On discovering that neither the woman nor her husband knew exactly how much money was in the case, the official insisted on counting it. He found it contained well over a thousand pounds, all of which was eventually invested as savings. When he commented that it was unwise to keep such a large sum in the house, he was told that it had been hidden, together with another box, also containing money, in a "corn-kist" (meal chest) in the granary—"where no-one would think of looking for it".'

While this anecdote reflects some of the values held in regard to money, it must not be taken as typical of the amount of wealth possessed by Gosforth farmers. Since the farmer is normally not 'money-minded' and a conspicuous trait of most Gosforthians is a reluctance to discuss financial affairs, it is difficult to discover much about the wealth of the individual farmer.

The consensus of opinion was, however, that farming in the interwar period, and especially between 1923 and 1935, barely made enough profit to cover expenses, and several farmers stated that they farmed at a loss for several years in succession. Statements like 'It was a gay (very) bad time', 'We had to scrat along as best we could', and 'It paid if you worked hard and spent nothing' were frequently heard. Conditions on some farms were so bad that cattle and sheep were accepted from dealers and maintained for the payment of a small weekly sum, and undercutting in the price of winterage, in an attempt to gain this welcome source of income, was fairly common. Summer visitors were taken on almost all the farms that could accommodate them, and the money derived from this practice undoubtedly saved many farmers from bankruptcy. From 1937 there was a gradual improvement, and the outbreak of war marked the beginning of increasing prosperity which has continued until the present day. The Milk Marketing Scheme has been an important factor in this change of fortune. 'The "milk" kept West Cumberland farmers out of the bankruptcy court' and other remarks echoing this opinion were heard repeatedly. Many farmers even to-day, when economic conditions are generally conceded to be favourable, say they could not farm profitably without its help. Also it is probable that many of the present tenant farmers, who have progressed to holdings of their own after many years as hired men, found the quick returns of dairy farming an asset, in that they did not require the additional capital necessary for maintaining themselves while their stock were still young, as did those farmers confined to stock-raising.

Examples of the increase in income and turnover can be seen almost everywhere. Only two farms now cater for tourists, despite the numerous enquiries that are still received from town-dwellers, attracted by the scenery of the Lakes and the imagined joys of eating farm produce. It seems significant that only one farmer mentioned the impossibility of obtaining female domestic servants as the reason for this decline in the number of visitors; the others attributed it to travelling difficulties, or more often, remarked that 'they were not worth the bother' or that 'they got in't road' (i.e. they interfered with the normal working of the farm).

One tenant farmer, who started on his own account in 1939, gave his total capital at that time as £65; he now owns machinery worth about £3,000. Most farmers who possess tractors have in five to ten years spent the equivalent of fifteen to twenty-five years' rent on major items of equipment alone, and several have bought machinery costing from £2,000 to as much as £3,500 in the last four years. A few further examples show the same prosperous trend. A farmer who came to a holding of 95 acres in November 1948 made no profit in that year, £600 profit in 1949 and £2,300 in 1950. Another farmer who has only farmed on his own account for five years, after being a hired man for a long period, and who apparently received no capital from any other source, now possesses equipment worth £1,500 and made a profit of £855 (i.e. without the cost of machinery) in 1949.

While such examples cannot be claimed to be typical of all the farming community, they at least prove that the accumulation of wealth is possible. Furthermore the size of the sums involved in farm turnover, even on the least prosperous holdings, seems to indicate that recent years have been very favourable to the farmers.[36] On several of the 'milk' farms the annual cost of feedingstuffs exceeded £700; alternatively the income from the sale of milk ranged from £825 to over £2,500 in one case at least. Labour costs on some farms amount to £600 or more yearly, concentrates added amounts varying from £100 to £500, and when sheep subsidies were at their highest hill farmers received considerable sums in addition to their normal turnover. Of the 21 tenant farmers in the parish, 14 said they would buy their holdings if they were offered them, at least 5 have made repeated attempts to persuade the landlord to sell, and only 3 said they could not find the necessary capital for purchase.[37]

It is, however, impossible to equate both turnover and profits with urban conditions. Much of the farmer's food, both for his family and for his animals, is produced on the farm, and is generally not thought of in a commercial sense at all. Less than a third of the farms employ hired labour, and eight of the twenty-eight hired men are either relatives or work on those farms which are run by an agent. So on most farms labour is a theoretical expense only, since a farmer 'pays' his sons or relatives in accordance with the official scales solely for income tax purposes, and in practice does not consider this an item in any way separate from normal family expenses. Similarly rent is conceived as a payment for land alone. Farmers describing how their rent was made up would quote prices per acre for rough grazing and improved land respectively, which when calculated equalled the total rent paid: there was no allowance made for house rent. Although groceries as well as farm commodities are usually paid for in cash, there are still many exchanges in kind. Butter has already been noted in this context, and in addition a horse or a calf may be bartered for a load of turnips, or the services of the mole-catcher may be repaid in eggs or bacon.[38] The borrowing and lending of machinery and of man-power is carried on without any question of money payment, indeed there are very strong cultural prohibitions on the use of money in this respect. Generally therefore, the urban idea of exact payment in money for all commodities and services is absent.

So during this century farming has been characterized by general hardship, interrupted by two periods of prosperity, by very far-reaching changes in the methods of farming and sources of income, and by increasing dependence on the surrounding district. The economy of the remaining section of the parish, the village, must next be considered, and the effects of these and other changes outlined.

The economy of the village, reflected in its occupational structure, has been changed very drastically in recent years by the development of new industries in parishes adjoining or near Gosforth. Until about twenty years ago virtually the only occupations open to men living in the village (apart from a minority of village craftsmen and tradesmen) were agricultural labour, estate work, and iron-ore mining. The latter involved a journey of 10–15 miles every day—an important consideration prior to the opening of the omnibus service in 1929. Therefore during the first three decades of this century agricultural labourers formed by far the largest occupational class in the village, followed by a much smaller number of estate workers[39] and iron-ore miners, and a few postmen, carters, road men, clerical workers, etc. Nearly all the women in full-time occupations were domestic servants, although a few were employed in shops and offices.[40]

The relative importance of agricultural occupations decreased rapidly after the early thirties as a result of very extensive planting by the Forestry Commission, the opening of an Ordnance Factory in a nearby parish in the early years of the war, and finally the building of the Atomic Energy Station at Sellafield in the adjoining parish of Seascale. By 1951 the number of agricultural labourers, excluding farmers' sons working at home, had shrunk to 6·7 per cent of the total working population of the parish, as compared with 20·3 per cent employed in 'modern' industries (see Appendix II, Table 2).

Accompanying this change there has been a growth in the number of people employed in the distribution of goods and in services. In January 1951 the total working population was divided into four primary producers to every six people engaged in secondary and tertiary occupations. These proportions are almost certainly the reverse of what they were in the early years of this century, and very probably the proportion of primary producers was formerly even higher.

This change of emphasis has resulted mainly from the attractiveness of the new industries, which pay higher wages for shorter hours of work than agriculture. Moreover, the opportunities for advancement are much greater in industry and many young men in the village now speak of agricultural work as 'a dead end'. When the constructional phase of the Atomic Energy Station is ended, the fact that nearly all the inhabitants of the parish employed there are unskilled or semi-skilled workers will mean that probably many of them will be forced either to return to agriculture and forestry, or to leave the parish in search of work in another area.

The effect of 'Sellafield' on the life of the parish extends far beyond its purely economic aspects. The men and women who work there associate constantly with people from all parts of the British Isles, most of whom are urban by background, and as a result the adoption of urban values has become very much more rapid in the village. One of the most striking features of employment at the Atomic Energy Station has been the tendency for unskilled and semi-skilled employees to work long hours, in order

THE ECONOMY

to profit from the increase in wage-rates for overtime. Consequently the parishioners who work there have become accustomed to relatively high wages and a day that is divided rigidly into a period of work and a period of leisure. This concept, which is highly developed under urban industrial conditions, contrasts very markedly with the traditional attitude of regarding work and leisure as overlapping. The farmer and village craftsman do not think in terms of 'overtime', 'time and a half' and 'shifts', and neither do they look upon work as a necessary evil to be endured for so many hours each day.

Furthermore, as we have seen in an earlier part of this chapter, money payments have not yet intruded into many of the economic exchanges between farmers, or farmers and craftsmen. And when the majority of villagers were farm labourers much of their remuneration was in the form of food, shelter and other necessities, and most of the single men were paid in money only twice yearly.[41] The arrival of new industries brought the payment for services in money alone, a practice that also symbolized the impersonal nature of the urban conception of the employer-employee relationship. As a result many villagers have become familiar with an economic structure which minimizes the obligations between master and men, thereby considerably increasing the potential mobility of the individual. This is in marked contrast to the relationship between, say, a farmer and his hired labour, where mutual rights and duties are strongly emphasized.

High wages have brought about a rise in the standard of living of many village households and one of the results has been an increase in the number of people who own the houses they live in, or who are saving to do so. During the short period from July 1950 to September 1951 the number of freeholders in the village rose by as much as 11 per cent, and informants' statements suggest that, if no significant change occurs in economic conditions, the proportion will increase as rapidly as the number of houses available for sale will allow.

The distinction between the economy of the village and that of the farmsteads is not, however, as sharp as the occupational analysis suggests. There are, for example, many retired farmers and farm-

THE ECONOMY

labourers living in the village and several of these give part-time or periodic assistance on farmsteads. Also there are several villagers who are 'spare-time farmers', that is who own or rent small-holdings which they farm in addition to their normal occupation (see Appendix II, Table 3).

At present, therefore, the village is in a state of transition from an economy in which goods and services were an important medium of exchange to one in which money is the sole medium. In the future one or two trends seems possible: either that general economic conditions remain more or less as they are, in which case the transition is almost certain to progress further; or that a decline in the opportunities for unskilled and semi-skilled labour in the new industries will bring about at least a partial reversion to the occupational structure of thirty years ago, in which case the transition may be retarded—to what extent, and for how long, it is impossible to say.

CHAPTER II

THE FAMILY

THE primary unit in the social structure of Gosforth, as in all Western communities, is the conjugal family, and no discussion of this or that aspect of the life of the parish can be worth-while unless viewed in relation to this basic grouping.

THE HOME

Almost all the houses in Gosforth are built of red sandstone, or 'freestone', obtained from a quarry near the village or from others in adjoining parishes. There are also a few houses built of other kinds of stone and six prefabricated dwellings of wood and steel erected in 1947. All the stone houses, the small cottage as well as the large farmhouse, are very substantially built, and some of the walls are three feet thick or more. The common building material gives a uniformity of appearance that is interrupted only occasionally by plastering or some other form of surface treatment and the few houses not built of freestone stand out as landmarks in the surrounding countryside.

The homes of most of the inhabitants were built in the period 1700–1900. Many of the farmhouses were built before 1800 and most of the houses in the village after 1850. Houses vary a great deal in age, size and ground-plan, but essentially most are composed of a 'parlour', a 'kitchen' (or living-room) and 'back-kitchen' on the ground-floor and several bedrooms above.[1]

Generally the family lives in the kitchen. Meals are often prepared and normally eaten there and this is the room in which the casual visitor is most likely to find the family when he calls during the day. As one opens the door, the features that first strike the eye are the fireplace and the large oak or deal table. The fireplace is most often filled by an enormous black iron 'range', complete with oven, boiler for hot water with a gleaming brass tap, and a large 'crane' for hanging kettles or other utensils above the fire. In some houses there is also a 'brick oven' at the side of the fireplace. This is built into the wall and made of stone (not brick); it is used for making bread after raking out the ashes of the twigs used to heat it. More often however this is to be found in a corner of the back-kitchen.

In the smaller houses and cottages the range very often occupies the entire width of one side of the kitchen. Chairs are grouped around the hearth and I was invariably asked to 'come and sit by t'fire'—which burns even on the hottest days of summer. In a few remote farms peat is still cut to feed an open fire, which, in winter at least, is kept alight day and night.[2]

The long table, which is the other prominent feature of the kitchen, particularly on farms, usually stands near the wall opposite the hearth, with one end near the kitchen door. In most farms this table is big enough to seat twelve or fifteen people, and—like the fireplace—it is a relic of former days and conditions. Within living memory almost every farm had at least one maid-servant: several farms had fourteen farm workers, all 'living in' and many more had as many as eight resident servants. For the past hundred years in Gosforth servants have normally lived and eaten with the farmer and his family. At the table the occupier sits at one end and his wife at the other. The occupier's children sit at his end of the table, on benches along each side, and the farm servants at the wife's end.[3] Probably this has always been the custom in the parish; the practice of having a round table near the fire, at which the occupier and his family sat, while the servants were seated at the long one near the wall, appears to be unknown.[4]

Also it has apparently never been the custom on farms for the back-kitchen to be used for meals, either for the family or the servants. On most farms the back-kitchen is a single storey building used for washing clothes and similar domestic tasks, and in a few cases for cooking. This absence of distinction between master and man has its counterpart in the sleeping arrangements of the household. Servants have always slept in the dwelling-house and not, as in many parts of Britain, above the back-kitchen or in the outbuildings.

Other articles of furniture common to most kitchens are a

long-case clock, often of local manufacture, an arm-chair or two near the hearth and a large open dresser filled with crockery. On the mantel-piece there are usually a pair of candle-sticks, a metal tea caddy which originally held biscuits or sweets, an alarm clock and sometimes a gleaming pair of polished shell-cases, a relic of the first World War. The stone floor is often covered by a strip of rough matting or a home-made 'rag-mat' in front of the fireplace. In farmhouses the kitchen ceiling is festooned with hams and strings of sausages hanging from hooks, and, in a prominent position, the neatly plaited 'last cut' from the last harvest, bound in a bright ribbon.[5] On the walls are several calendars showing agricultural or rural scenes (supplied normally by firms which sell fertilizer or machinery) and very often the illustrations from these calendars are kept and used as pictures for many years. Other pictures show family groups or a scene in the Lake District painted in water colour.

Most of the families in Gosforth live in the kitchen all the time, leaving the parlour free except on rare occasions. However, many farmers use the kitchen during the day and retire to the 'living-room' at night and at week-ends, or possibly at week-ends only. When this is the case the house has a 'living-room' and a 'parlour', the latter being rarely in use. In the smaller houses and cottages there is no parlour, and the back-kitchen is normally too small to be lived in: when this is so the occupants have no alternative but to make the one large room a kitchen and parlour combined.

The parlour contains those items of furniture most highly prized in the household and is obviously not intended to be lived in. A typical parlour contains highly polished oak furniture, several arm-chairs and often a few old straight-backed chairs of local design and craftsmanship. There is often a china cabinet and a piano. The former is a repository for such highly valued articles as a rum-butter bowl handed down from one generation to another for a hundred and fifty years or more,[6] a tea-set and dinner-service, and one or two jugs or pieces of china bought by a member of the family on a visit to London or some other place far outside the normal range of travelling. The piano is often simply an article of furniture. Many people who possess pianos consider music lessons for their children as 'a waste o' good money'. More often than not the fire-screen and some of the pictures on the wall contain samplers or tapestry representations of Biblical scenes, beautifully executed, some of them dating back as far as the seventeenth century. Photographs of family groups, marriages and baptisms are also common.

In Gosforth the parlour is not used as a sick-room in cases of serious illness and it is not the usual practice to lay out a corpse there before burial. Visitors, either friends or strangers, are rarely asked into this room and it therefore remains uninhabited for long periods of time. Wills and inventories of earlier centuries make it clear that the 'parler' has always performed the function of linking the existing members of the family with those of the past through the symbolism of heirlooms. It has also been an ornament for the maintaining of prestige. In the village its prestige value has largely superseded its other function. This state of affairs is consistent with the decline in kinship ties which is (as will be shown in a later chapter) characteristic of the village.

Since the parlour is nearly always in the front of the house and the kitchen in the back, the front door is not very much used.[7] As a result, a knock on the front door is taken to imply that the caller is a stranger.

THE ECONOMIC UNIT

Among farmers, and to a lesser extent in the village, the family is the unit of economic production. The role of the family as the basic unit in the farming economy is clearly illustrated by the fact that in 1950 73 per cent of the male labour on farms in Gosforth was provided by farmers, their families and relatives, and 95 per cent of the female labour by farmers' wives, daughters and their relatives (see Appendix III, Tables 1 and 2). This is another example of the intermediate position of the parish between upland and lowland. Hired labour is rare on fell farms and becomes increasingly more common with decreased altitude. Since the family farm is considered the most desirable form of holding, the severe shortage of farm workers in post-war years has enhanced the importance of the family in agriculture.

The predominance of the ideal of a farmstead which can be run without paid assistance is such that it appears to over-ride purely economic considerations. The general decline in the size of the family in Gosforth has meant that, on most farms, the conjugal family is only able to provide sufficient man-power to do all the work comfortably for a very limited period of its existence. Where there are, for example, only two or three children, family labour operates at a maximum solely from the time the sons or daughters leave school until they marry and leave home. In spite of this, only eleven of the farmers in Gosforth hired labourers who were not relatives and on farms of a hundred acres or less only one farmer in six employed hired workers. There can be no doubt that on a great many holdings this failure to hire workers imposes a great burden on the occupier and in many cases considerably impairs the efficient running of the farm. Agricultural officials confirmed that several holdings are deteriorating in quality because the amount of labour available is insufficient to maintain the land in good condition (see Appendix III, Table 3).

There are many reasons for this failure to hire labour. There is a shortage of man-power due to the opening of new industries. Many farmers lack the capital necessary to pay the added expense of hired workers for the period up until the extra man-power pays for itself in increased profits. Also important is the shortage of accommodation for married farm workers, and the difficulty of attracting young men to remote farms far removed from the bus routes. In addition there is the divergence between the farmer's conception of a working day, determined by the needs of the farm, and the increasingly prevalent concept of a day's work fixed by the clock.

Whatever the reasons, there is no doubt that the shortage of farm workers greatly increases the functional importance of the family as an economic unit, and makes necessary a high degree of co-operative effort among its members. This in turn emphasizes the cohesiveness and solidarity which exists between parents and children.

The conception of the family farm is extended in many ways

beyond parents and children. It is expressed to some degree in the preference given to the sons of other farmers when hiring men, and in the concept of the farm servant as a member of the family. The single farm labourer in Gosforth lives with the occupier and his family, eats with them at meals, and shares in the conversation as a member of the group. If he falls ill, the farmer's wife gives him the attention she would to any member of her family, while in the running of the farm the employer-employee relationship typical of urban areas is reduced to the barest minimum. It is very significant that the only farmer in Gosforth who has attempted to establish himself as an employer in the urban sense finds the greatest difficulty in hiring workers and has not in his period of tenure yet succeeded in keeping an agricultural labourer for more than one 'term'.

Farm labourers address their employers by their Christian name more often than not, but this minimizing of the social distance between them implies an obligation on the part of the hired man to work, irrespective of hours, to suit the needs of the farm. This conflicts with the recent legislation which fixes the hours of work and rates of pay for agricultural workers and there is evidence that the informal relationship between master and man which formerly prevailed is now breaking down as more and more farm workers adopt urban standards. On the majority of farms, however, the hired man still adjusts his work to fit into the pattern established by the farmer and his family. In turn he is rewarded by payment for periods of inactivity and by permission to leave the farm to participate in various social events, for example a football match or a visit to friends, without any deduction in his wages.

A few farm labourers are still paid at Whitsun and Martinmas in accordance with traditional practice; and although occupiers are now obliged by law to pay their employees according to their hours of work, on most holdings it is customary for the farmer and hired man to come to an agreement about wages when the latter is initially engaged, and then to 'tak things as they come'. This arrangement is excellent from the occupier's point of view, since the hired worker is fitted into the pattern of family co-operation with a minimum of friction and can be relied on to work continuously for days if the occasion demands. It is equally desirable from the labourers' viewpoint since their wages are often considerably more than the minimum fixed by law.

The perpetuation of the traditional relationship between master and man is materially assisted by the fact that many of the hired men are farmers' sons themselves who eventually become 'hinds' or tenants of holdings of their own. Despite a general decrease in the size of families there are still several farmers in the district who have more children than they need to farm their holdings; these are usually sent to other farms in the area, not always those of relatives or friends. In 1950, of all the sons of occupiers aged over 16, 50 per cent worked at home, just over 22 per cent worked for other farmers, 5 per cent farmed on their own account and the remainder were in non-agricultural occupations. As for the occupiers themselves, 55 per cent of those who were farmers' sons worked as farm labourers away from home before they began farming on their own account. The occupiers and their sons are therefore accustomed to the practice of sending their children to work for other farmers, and nearly all of them regard this as an advantage to a would-be farmer and not in any way a token of inferior social or economic status. Moreover it so happens that the occupiers of the largest holdings in Gosforth are tenant farmers who have worked as labourers in a variety of places before coming to the parish; there is thus no tendency for 't'big farmers' to keep their sons at home for prestige purposes.

The remaining hired men are drawn from the village and the surrounding parishes. Male agricultural workers are of all ages and a fairly high proportion of them are married. The only female agricultural workers (hired) are three 'Land Girls' who remained in Gosforth after the disbandment of the Women's Land Army.

Farm workers are sometimes engaged to fill a specialized post, such as that of tractor-man or head cowman, but in most cases the hired man is expected to do any task which may arise, from milking to ploughing. On farms where there are several sons there is a fairly rigid division of male labour, but the allocation of duties varies a great deal from farm to farm. Thus on one holding the eldest son is responsible for the cattle, helped by a younger brother after school hours and at week-ends. Another son does ploughing and a third takes care of the sheep and horses, while the occupier varies his responsibility from day to day according to the work to be done. On another farmstead the father does the ploughing and takes care of the horses, his eldest son feeds and milks the cows, and another assists the hired man in the management of the sheep. On a third holding, where the occupier has three sons working at home, the division of labour was said to be changed about once every two years— 'to give t'lads a chance to learn summat'.

When a hired worker or farmer's son has a special aptitude it is employed to full advantage. One farmer, for example, said that his hired man was a 'gay good hedger' and during the autumn he was employed solely in trimming and repairing the 'dykes'. In several families one son displays mechanical skill and is made responsible for the driving and maintenance of the tractor and its auxiliary equipment.

There is also a fairly clear division of labour between the sexes, but on many of the smaller farms, particularly those which have no hired labour, farmers' wives and daughters work in the fields during the two harvests, and frequently help in the milking and in the preparation of food for the animals. Generally, however, the activities of the women are confined to domestic duties and to the care of poultry and pigs. On all the farms in Gosforth, poultry and eggs are the particular province of the farmer's wife, assisted possibly by a daughter. The money for eggs and the proceeds of the seasonal poultry sales are always the wife's property, and this 'pin money', as it is called, is used for the maintenance of the farmhouse and in buying clothes for the adult females in the family. The occupier is expected to pay for clothing for himself, his sons and young children, and usually he has little or no idea of the amount of money his wife obtains from 't'hens'.

The wife is therefore largely independent, and may indeed have inherited sums of money from her parents (often farmers) so that she may be more wealthy than her husband. Moreover, on a great many farms the farmer's wife handles all the money and it was common to hear her referred to jocularly as 't'Chancellor of the Exchequer'. This practice has been customary as far back as the older farmers are able to remember and there is a general belief that 't'women-folk' are able to keep accounts better than men. In some families separate accounts are kept, but as a rule the wife handles all the bills and money, while the farmer signs the cheques and visits the bank.

When discussing this matter, farmers seemed very anxious to justify the role of the wife as accountant. The impression I gained was that they considered her dominance in financial matters as a threat to their position as head of the household, at least in the eyes of outsiders. On many occasions during the field-work a farmer was heard to have a hurried consultation with his wife about the payment of a bill, before opening the door to a visiting tradesman. In the ensuing conversation the farmer made every effort to appear as if he alone was responsible for all money matters, (not always very successfully), while his wife remained in the background. Other farmers are not as concerned about the possibility of losing prestige and leave their wives to deal with all outsiders in financial affairs.

Farmers' sons working at home are 'officially' paid wages similar to the hired workers, but in practice they rarely receive more than small amounts at irregular intervals. However, many farmers were of the opinion that the present younger generation were becoming more and more anxious to receive regular pocket money 'like t'lads in t'village'.

PARENTAL AUTHORITY

One farmer remarked on one occasion 'I worked till I was near forty afore ivver I was paid owt' and this seems to have been the experience of most of the present occupiers who were brought up in the area. The subordination of farmers' children was said by many informants to have been so marked until very recently, that several farmers' sons in the district had killed themselves rather than submit to further repression. One of the few suicides in Gosforth was described as due to this type of treatment.

Apparently the man concerned was friendly with a group of farmers' sons and farm labourers who were generously supplied with money, and his constant failure to emulate their behaviour, together with their remarks and taunts, drove him to this extreme act. It is, of course, difficult to judge now much truth there is in this account, but there can be no doubt that the present occupiers of farmsteads were completely dependent on their parents during their youth, and often for many years after they had become adults.

This state of complete dependence is almost as well developed at the present time and has been brought sharply into prominence by the regular weekly wages received by some farm labourers and the majority of the younger workers in the village. Nowadays, farmers' sons and daughters usually ask their parents for money when they require it, and, as far as one could tell, their requests are normally granted. It should be remembered, however, that their demands for money are on a much more modest scale than those typical of people of their own age in urban areas. The material possessions of most farmers' sons in their twenties would seem very meagre indeed to a town-dweller of the same age, while several farmers' daughters considered my wife's wardrobe to be very lavish and extravagant, although by urban standards it would arouse little comment.

The younger members of farm families accept this state of dependence without any overt sign of resentment. They are often completely ignorant of the family's financial affairs, even when they are old enough to be parents or possibly grandparents. Thus many people in the parish mentioned one family where the three sons, all in their thirties, encountered many obstacles in running the farm for several months after their father's death because he had maintained strict secrecy in all financial matters during his lifetime. However the cohesiveness of the farm family is such that sons and daughters are well aware of their position as heirs to their parents' property, and obtain far more satisfaction from any increase in the wealth of the family as a unit than is characteristic of more urbanized areas where personal gain tends to be emphasized.

Farmers' sons are, therefore, accustomed to paternal dominance until they marry; and since their position of dependence lasts often until they are over 30 years of age they are frequently little removed psychologically from a state of adolescence when they assume the responsibility of a holding. This was very apparent from many conversations with those farmers who had inherited the family farm and with tenants who began farming on their own account after a period as agricultural labourers removed from parental dominance. The former seemed comparatively immature and their general attitude was described excellently by a very observant villager who said of them 'Every time I meet the farmers from really old families, I get the feeling they want to run away and hide when I speak to them. My eight year old grandson has more about him than most of them.' It seems likely that this delayed maturity is responsible for the practice (mentioned earlier) of entrusting financial matters to the farmer's wife. Farmers' sons are accustomed to being kept completely ignorant of their parents' financial affairs, while on the other hand the farmer's wife very probably confides in an unmarried daughter concerning these matters.

Unlikely as it may seem at first, the recent mechanization of farming appears to be influencing the structure of parental authority, at least in respect of sons. While farming remained unmechanized a farmer derived much of his position as head of the family from the fact that he was the sole authority on all matters connected with farming. His accumulated experience made his word law. Since the arrival of the tractor the tendency has been for farmers' sons, rather than the farmers themselves, to be responsible for the farm implements and machinery. Sons usually know a great deal more about this branch of farming than their fathers, and their total dependence is thereby decreased to some extent. It should be added that, as yet, this change does not seem to have greatly undermined the father's position: on the other hand the way in which a technological change may have completely unforeseen effects on the social structure is of considerable interest and importance to students of society.

THE FAMILY

MARRIAGE

Farmers' sons and daughters cease to be dependent on their parents either when they marry or when their father dies. The age at which children of farm families marry is shown in the following table, which is based on the marriages entered in the Registers between 1900 and 1950:

AGE AT FIRST MARRIAGE (*percentage*)

Group.	−21	21–4	25–9	30–4	35–9	40–4	45–9	50–4	55+
Farmers' sons	1·7	16·7	44·5	24·5	6·7	4·2	1·7	—	—
Farmers' daughters	9·4	31·9	37·5	17·9	3·3	—	—	—	—
Others' sons	3·7	17·5	36·5	27·0	7·9	3·7	1·6	2·1	—
Others' daughters	16·9	46·8	17·9	13·4	2·0	1·5	—	1·5	—
Total sons	2·9	17·1	39·7	26·0	7·5	3·9	1·6	1·3	—
Total daughters.	14·3	41·7	24·7	14·9	2·6	0·9	—	0·9	—

It will be seen from this that the peak age of marriage of farmers' sons is between 25 and 30, and that a considerable number are married between 30 and 35. The average age of all farmers' sons married in Gosforth between 1900 and 1950 was 28·3. The peak age of marriage of farmers' daughters is between 25 and 29, the majority marrying between 21 and 35.

The contrast between the ages at which farmers' sons and daughters marry and the ages at which children of villagers marry, and with the averages for England and Wales, is striking. The peak age of first marriage for men in England and Wales is between 25 and 29 (36·8 per cent), with a slightly smaller proportion between 21 and 24 (35·3 per cent), followed by a very considerable drop after the age of thirty (21·6 per cent for all males 30 +). The peak age of marriages of women is 21 to 25, with much less between 25 and 30 and comparatively few after the age of 30. The majority of other occupiers' sons in Gosforth marry between the ages of 20 and 35, the average age of marriage being a little higher than that for farmers' sons. This apparently anomalous state of affairs can partly be explained by the fact that among villagers are included a certain number of farmers' sons who 'retire' to live in the village when a brother inherits on the death of their father. These men are generally in the 35–45 age group and thus push the average age of marriage 'up'. Other occupiers' daughters tend to marry before they are 25 and quite a large proportion marry before they are 21; they therefore compare more closely with national trends than do farmers' daughters.[8]

The delay in the age at which farmers' sons marry must be attributed to filial loyalty and the role of young men in the family economic unit. Loyalty to parents means that sons do not willingly withdraw their much needed support after only a comparatively short period of repaying the debt they feel they owe to their parents for their upbringing. The fact that farm tenancies have become increasingly difficult to obtain in recent years has, if anything, raised the age of marriage even higher than it was a generation ago and, as can be seen from the table, some farmers' sons do not marry until they are over 35, or even 45. The last marriage of a farmer's son which occurred during the field-work (in September 1951) took place when the man was over 60. This is an extreme case, but one which local informants attributed directly to the desire to farm the family holding for ageing parents.

The average age at which farmers' sons in Gosforth marry is, however, lower than that to be found in parts of rural Wales and Eire, the latter in particular being characterized by a very high percentage of unmarried adult males. This probably results from the custom in Gosforth whereby farmers' sons from families with several boys marry and live in cottages or village houses and continue to work on the family holding as long as this is necessary. Only in the past three or four years has the housing shortage become so acute that farmers' sons have to delay their marriage unduly because there is no accommodation available near to the family farm. There are several farms in Gosforth still with two or three sons living in different parts of the parish who arrive daily to help their father.

Although they do not live at home, these married sons remain completely loyal to their parents and in every case where this arrangement prevailed one son remained at home unmarried. This is in keeping with other features of the family organization. Farmers' sons rarely, if ever, bring their wives to live on the family farmstead while both parents are alive. There was only one case of this in Gosforth (newcomers from an urban area), and the consensus of opinion was that 'folks hereabouts don't do that; it would never work out likely'.

There is no marriage bargain, so common in other European countries, but frequently the families of the young couple come to an informal arrangement which has much the same effect. In one instance the two sets of parents contributed the money to buy a freehold farm. In other cases the bridegroom's parents bought the land and the bride's parents some of the stock and machinery. There seems to be considerable variation in the amount and nature of the respective families' contribution, but in general the bridegroom's family spends most, usually on land, stock, equipment, etc., while the bride's family confines itself largely to household goods. In recent years the inflated value of small freehold farms has meant that most farmers have to rely on placing non-inheriting sons (at least) on leasehold properties. In this case it is usual for them to buy as much livestock and machinery as they can afford.

Although this is the normal pattern, there are a great many variations in the sequence, depending on the size and wealth of the family farm, the number of dependent children, the marital status of sons and so forth. To quote but a few actual examples; in one case the youngest of two sons married in his early twenties and obtained the tenancy of a farm in an adjoining parish. Although this deprived the family homestead of much needed labour, the parents assisted him in buying stock and implements, and then hired an agricultural worker to fill the gap made by his departure. In another case three sons remained unmarried until their parents' retirement. The youngest son inherited the farm, but married and went to take up the tenancy of another farm about four miles away, leaving his two brothers to farm the family holding for as long as they chose.

Farmers' daughters, like their brothers, tend to marry later than villagers, or than is usual in England and Wales as a whole. The delay in the marriage of daughters is, however, less than that of farmers' sons, probably because they have a much less important role in the economic unit. The farms in Gosforth are generally too small to need the help of a large number of females and the decline in the number of daughters per family in recent years has to some extent been compensated by the introduction of mains water, electricity, and other improvements which greatly lessen the burden of the household routine. Farmers' daughters are therefore free to marry at a much younger age than sons and the proportion who marry before the age of 21 is more than five times the number of males. However, family loyalty is equally characteristic of daughters and the rather high proportion who marry after the age of 30, together with those who remain unmarried to take care of ageing parents or to act as housekeepers to middle-aged bachelor brothers, is an expression of this sentiment.

Remarriage appears to be rather common in Gosforth and is recorded fairly frequently through the period covered by the Marriage Registers. Only two of the present occupiers of farmsteads have remarried, as compared with three who have remained widowed; but each of the latter was over 60 when their respective spouse died. Corresponding figures for present occupiers' parents (i.e. while they still occupied holdings) are nine remarriages as compared with sixteen who remained widowed, of whom eleven were over 60 when their respective spouses died. From this limited evidence and from a general impression gained in analysing the entries in the Parish Registers it seems to be customary for men and women who are widowed before they reach the age of 45 to marry again within two to five years.

Little can be said with certainty of the factors underlying remarriage, but it seems very probable that it is closely linked with the role of the family as an economic unit and the desire to retain the holding within the family. The two cases of remarriage of present occupiers occurred when a wife was widowed while her children were still young. Remarriage replaced the most important member of the economic unit, but the holding has remained the wife's property and passes to her children by her first marriage when she dies. The second husband, therefore, does not gain possession of the holding and, as we shall see later, this principle of continuity is fundamental to the family structure.

THE FAMILY

Since farmers' sons usually marry at a later age than farmers' daughters, and farm families tend to inter-marry, there is normally some disparity in the age of spouses. An analysis of all the marriages of farmers which took place in Gosforth between 1900 and 1950 shows that:

Wife is older than husband in	19	per cent of marriages.
Husband and wife are roughly the same age in	10·8	,, ,, ,, ,,
Husband is older than wife by 1–3 years in	32·4	,, ,, ,, ,,
Husband is older than wife by 4–7 years in	24·5	,, ,, ,, ,,
Husband is older than wife by 8+ years in	13·5	,, ,, ,, ,,

In over a third of the marriages, therefore, the husband is four or more years older than his wife. This reinforces the position of the farmer as head of the household and, together with the difference in the life expectancy of the two sexes, largely accounts for the high proportion of widows as compared with widowers (see Appendix I, Table 2(*d*)).

CONTINUITY AND FAMILY STRUCTURE

The normal practice for the transmission of family holdings is for the occupier and his wife to retire to a house they have bought in the district, leaving the farm in the hands of the son who inherits. Therefore a farmer's son who is unable to find a cottage while his parents remain in control delays his marriage, if he is heir, until he is able to do so or until his parents retire.

Marriage then is closely linked to methods of inheritance, and the cohesive family organization ensures that farmers' sons take the 'long view' of marriage in comparison with the members of those families which are not also economic units. Where both parents are alive, they very rarely retire before they are 65, which means that the inheritance of the family holding often occurs when the heir is well over 30 years old. There is no fixed pattern of inheritance, as the following analysis of 19 farms which have been occupied by at least three successive generations shows:

Youngest son inherited	6	cases
Eldest son inherited	18	,,
Only son inherited	9	,,
Joint inheritance by two sons	8	,,
Joint inheritance by other siblings	4	,,

THE FAMILY

In addition the present occupiers in Gosforth stated their holdings would be inherited as follows:

By eldest son	9 cases
Jointly by two sons and a daughter	2 ,,
By youngest son	1 case*
By second eldest son	1 ,,
By the only daughter	1 ,,

* The only son unmarried and living at home.

It will be clear from this that there is a preference for the eldest son, in accordance with the custom in many parts of England, but that partible inheritance—similar to that found formerly in Wales and Ireland [9]—is also fairly common. This absence of a rigid pattern of inheritance appears to have been characteristic of Gosforth from at least the middle of the seventeenth century. An examination of old farm deeds, some dating back to 1649, revealed that in addition to the types of succession listed above there were examples of a daughter inheriting when there were sons at home and of joint inheritance between daughters. (Therefore the generalization found in so many histories that Cumberland, as an area of early enclosure, was characterized by partible inheritance is disproved, at least as far as Gosforth is concerned.)

In the majority of cases, where the eldest son inherits, he remains at home unmarried until his parents retire. He then assumes control and is free to marry, and the limited information available suggests that marriage follows inheritance within a very short period. The remaining sons are free to marry more or less when they choose, subject to the labour requirements of the holding. Where there is a superfluity of man-power, the parents attempt to establish one or two sons as freeholders or tenants in their own right when they marry, and when this is possible the parents' contribution is thought of as absolving them from any future obligation to these children.

The reduction in the size of families in recent years has meant that there is often only one son, or only one child, so that the pattern of inheritance is simplified.

Whatever the variations in practice, the underlying principle is the maintenance of the family group as a relatively self-sufficient economic unit and the retention of the holding within the family.

These cardinal values apply equally to instances where the normal pattern of retirement and succession is interrupted by the death of one of the parents. When the father dies the inheriting son remains at home unmarried during his mother's lifetime, since the prohibitions against a daughter-in-law still obtain. In such cases the son may often remain a bachelor for the rest of his life. Again, if the mother dies first and the father remarries, the heir is still not free to marry. On the other hand, if the widowed father retires to a small cottage, possibly with an unmarried daughter to take care of him, or if he remains at home and does not remarry, the heir is then free to marry.

From these examples it will be apparent that the heir to the family holding is bound by loyalty to adjust or postpone any decision he may make concerning marriage to suit fluctuations in the family circle. Among the families on holdings over 50 acres in Gosforth were the following:

(a) Widowed mother (86)
Bachelor brother (82)
Bachelor nephew (67)
Hired man (50)

(b) Widowed farmer (84)
Widowed daughter (54)
Grandson (25)
Grandson's wife (24)

(c) Widowed mother (88)
Bachelor son (45)
Spinster daughter (52)

(d) Widowed mother (60)
Married daughter (28)
Daughter's husband (32)
Daughter's child (2)
Daughter's child (8)
Spinster daughter (21)
Bachelor son (18)

(e) Widowed mother (78)
Bachelor son (49)
Bachelor son (45)

(f) Widowed mother (74)
Bachelor son (47)
Spinster daughter (37)

(g) Widowed father (91)
Spinster daughter (52)
Spinster grand-daughter (29)

These examples speak for themselves; in addition, in all three cases of holdings occupied jointly by unmarried siblings at present, the mother survived her husband without remarrying for a comparatively long period. As a result the sons who remained at home to provide the necessary labour were middle-aged before the surviving parent died.

When parents die or retire, they provide for unmarried daughters either by a sum of money or by stipulating that the heir provides them with a home and an allowance. In the few cases where there were unmarried siblings of both sexes, it has been the custom to leave the family holding and possessions jointly among them—a practice recorded in several eighteenth and nineteenth-century wills.

When a farmer is survived by a widow, she normally inherits the holding. It remains her property until she dies or, much less common, until she transfers it to the inheriting child. It seems customary for the heir to be chosen during the occupier's lifetime, so that the wife's period of widowhood is in fact one of possession for life, and many wills have special clauses designed to ensure that the widow does not change the succession favoured by her husband. Occasionally the inheriting child receives possession of the holding immediately on the death of his father. When this happens the new occupier is obliged to provide for all the wants of his mother for as long as she lives, provided she does not remarry.

The whole complex of inheritance customs has been handed down from one generation to another during the period covered by the Registers, and indeed is clearly derived from practices common in early medieval times. Almost all the variations which have been described were to be found in different parts of England during the thirteenth century, for example, inheritance by one son, either the youngest or the eldest; provisions for non-inheriting sons and daughters, and for retiring or widowed parents; arrangements designed to keep the land in the family, such as the reversion of a holding to children in the ancestral line when a widow remarries; customs of wardship and widow right.[10]

Since it is usual for retiring parents to move into another home, elementary families are the most common type on farmsteads. Thus of the 43 families occupying farms in 1950, 32 were elementary families, 3 were composed of unmarried siblings, 1 of a widow and her unmarried brother, and 7 are three-generation families. Two of the latter are actually elementary families with unmarried daughters who have illegitimate children, and four are families composed of a widow or widower with a married son or daughter with children. The absence of such customs as the 'West room' of Ireland,[11] the '*Altenteil*' of Germany,[12] and the 'East room' of medieval England,[13] whereby parents retire into a part of the house instead of to a separate dwelling, implies that true three generation families are atypical in Gosforth.

It has already been noted that the general decrease in the size of farm families has simplified the pattern of inheritance and reduced the need of parents to make enough money to help establish children who cannot be provided for at home. In the parish as a whole the average size of a household in January 1951 was 3·2 persons; in 1931 it was 3·9; in 1901 it was 4·8; in 1891 it was 5·0; and in 1821 it was 6·4. This decline is to some extent due to the decrease in the number of hired workers on farms, but it is clear that families are much smaller at present than they were in previous centuries. In Gosforth in 1950 there was only one family with ten children and only five families with five or more. An analysis of the Parish Registers showed that in 1801 and 1601 there were (at a minimum) the following:

NUMBER OF CHILDREN IN FAMILIES IN SELECTED YEARS

Year.	\multicolumn{6}{c}{Number of children.}	
	9	8	7	6	5	4	
1801	1	2	5	8	12	22	families
1601	—	1	3	5	4	12	,,

It must be borne in mind that the number of children given here are those that I was able to trace in the Registers. The movement of families in and out of the parish, which was moderately common in both years, may well mean that families were much larger than the figures above suggest and that the number of large families was greater than shown. Even so, the total population in 1801 was only 652, so that the 50 families together accounted for over half the total. Other evidence confirms this general picture. Five of the occupiers of holdings in Gosforth in 1755 had families of at least twelve children, and this is by no means unrepresentative of the period. Again, three of the occupiers in 1950 had one parent who was one of a family of 20 or more children.

THE FAMILY

Most of the inhabitants who are old enough to remember families of eight to ten children as a fairly common feature in the parish described the decline in family size as being due to 'folks having more sense' or 'parents being more sophisticated', and usually economic reasons were cited as the main cause of the decline. These informants were usually very reluctant to discuss family limitation, but, as we shall see later, there is no reason to suppose that the decrease in family size is due to the introduction of modern methods of contraception.

CRAFTSMAN FAMILIES

The fundamental importance of retaining the allodial land within the family, so strikingly expressed in the statement of the farmer's son who said 'When you're born to a spot you're married to it,' is found in modified form in the few village families who function as economic units. These are the families of craftsmen and tradesmen, particularly the former, who inherit the possessions of their parents and, more important, the processes and muscular skills which have been the particular property of ancestors for generations. The life history of one village craftsman shows how closely the organization of these families resembles that of the farm family.

This man's family can be traced back in the Registers to 1768, when an ancestor is recorded practising the family craft in the parish. Since that date the eldest son, and often one other, replaced his parent, so that the son of the present craftsman will represent the seventh generation in an unbroken line. This craftsman said of himself: 'I worked for me father till I was married (i.e. until he was 30) and he nivver paid me nowt. I only had yan holiday in that time and I had to work gay hard for that, I can tell thee maister. I went to relatives in L—— for a week, and when I asked me father for money he gave me twenty-five shilling, and the train fare were twelve and six. If me father thowt I wasn't working right I'd get half yan egg for breakfast. Them were t'good old days all right; the lads now don't know they're born. I gives me lad fifty shilling a week, and more off time in a month than I got in ten year. When me time's past he'll get me business o' course, but till then he works for me like I did for me own dad.'

From many hours spent at this man's place of work it was clear that his son was virtually as dependent upon his father as the latter had been in his own day, and the son's wage, though very generous in comparison with the father's experience, seems little enough when equated with the earnings of young men of the same age living in other households in the village. The craftsman obviously regarded payment to his son as a privilege to be viewed in the light of his position as heir, and the son himself was apparently more than satisfied with his position. When asked if he was courting, the son agreed with his father that 'There's time enough for thinking on that when I'm working for meself'.

Village craftsmen's families closely resemble those of farmers in the pattern of retiring to another house and handing over the home and place of work to the inheriting son, and there is plenty of evidence in the Parish Registers that this has been customary for several centuries. In the same way, there is little or no difference in the provisions made for unmarried daughters, widows, and non-inheriting sons. In this case the latter are either established on their own account, if the father is relatively prosperous, or are apprenticed to another craftsman elsewhere.

VILLAGE FAMILIES

The family organization of the remaining inhabitants of the parish reflects the absence of the fundamental principles described above. The average village family is not a productive unit and there is rarely a transference of inherited property, be it land or special skills, from one generation to another.

For this reason the patterns of inheritance and the associated family structure are somewhat different from those characteristic of farmsteads, although filial loyalty is usually sufficiently strong to ensure the stability of the family. Villagers' sons, for example, marry at a later age than that typical of England and Wales as a whole, and the fairly high proportion who are married after the age of 30 or even 35, can only be explained in terms similar to those already cited for farmers' sons. The shortage of houses and of sufficient capital to start married life may possibly be contributory factors, but, obviously, similar conditions apply to an even greater degree to urban areas, where the average age of marriage is much lower.

In the village, therefore, loyalty to one's parents is instrumental in delaying the marriage of sons whose wages help support the family, since there is rarely the incentive of possible inheritance to be considered. In the same way, daughters are free to marry at an earlier age than sons, since their economic contribution is much smaller and their marriage frequently eases the burden on the wage-earners. But the number of villagers' daughters who marry after the age of thirty is high enough to point to the loyalty which they feel towards their parents, for example in those families where there are no sons, or where a daughter's assistance is much needed by ageing parents.

Unlike the farmsteads, however, village youth are rarely tied to the home as heirs, and this partially accounts for the fairly high percentage of widows and widowers who live alone, though not unsupported by their married children living elsewhere in the village. Sons are free to marry and leave home when they consider they have repaid their debt to their parents. More often than not they go to live in houses nearby when they marry and are therefore available and willing to offer support should the need arise. Marriage transfers the individual's responsibility from his own family to the new family of which he is the head, but the transference is not a complete one and numerous villagers with children of their own help—in some degree at least—to support widowed or ageing parents.

The composition of village families reflects the features of family organization just described. The details are as follows:

Elementary families	115
Three generation families	20
Unmarried siblings	5
Persons living alone	33*
Widowed siblings	3
Widow and child(ren)	5
Widow(er) and other relative	2

* Including retired farmers.

THE FAMILY

The absence of land as a factor in inheritance means that parents' property, which is for the most part 'movable' (since only one in five villagers own the house they live in), can be subdivided among children. Partible inheritance is therefore much more characteristic of the village than of farms. In contrast with farmers, very few villagers make wills and therefore there is little documentary evidence concerning past conditions. Statements collected during the field-work indicate that there is considerable variety in the apportionment of a villager's property after his death. About fifty years ago, when families were larger than they are to-day, typical procedures were:

(i) Where an unmarried son or daughter remained at home, he (or she) inherited the tenancy and all the household goods. Any money was divided equally among the other children.

(ii) Where all the children were married or living away from home, the household goods were auctioned and the proceeds divided equally among the children. In this case, family heirlooms were retained, the choice depending on seniority as a rule, and allowances were made in the distribution of the sum realized on the remainder.

(iii) Where a widowed parent sold the household goods and went to live with a married son or daughter, this child alone inherited all the parental property in return for the additional assistance given to the parent.

Nowadays families in the village are much smaller and there are rarely more than two children in the family, so that problems of inheritance have decreased considerably in recent years. Thus of the married couples living in the village:

26·3 per cent were childless.
35·4 per cent had one child.
19·6 per cent had two children.
9·9 per cent had three children.
8·8 per cent had more than three children.

Villagers are far less dominated by their parents during their youth and early manhood than farmers, although my impression was that filial obedience is demanded to a much higher degree than is typical of most urban families. Most villagers' children begin to work for their living at the age of sixteen and their position as wage-earners, together with freedom from parental control for much of the day, contribute to increasing their independence. Many children in the village are given regular amounts of pocket-money every week, usually on Friday or Saturday evening.

In many families where the parents are young, the housewife's position is much less subordinate than that of the farmer's wife. Most of the middle-aged parents in the village were farm labourers and maids in their youth and many are farmers' sons and daughters. In these families the traditional family organization found on farms has persisted to a much greater degree than is to be found in households where the parents (usually in their twenties or early thirties) have absorbed urban values, and there is an obvious contrast between these two groups in the freedom of action given to children. Indicative of this is the fact that in families where the old standards persist parents usually had very definite opinions on what career their children should choose when they grew up. Those parents who have adopted urban standards almost invariably stated that their sons and daughters 'can decide for themselves'.

CHAPTER III

SOME ASPECTS OF THE LIFE CYCLE

IN Gosforth, as elsewhere, the welfare of a baby before its birth is a matter of considerable concern to the family, relatives and friends of the mother, and numerous beliefs are held about the consequences to the child of the mother's behaviour during pregnancy. For example, horrible tales are told of expectant mothers who stood on bridges over a river, or who did too much 'brain work', actions which are said to result in the birth of an idiot child. The unborn child is referred to as 't'babby' very much as 'living' children are, and a birth is therefore thought of as a transition from one state of existence to another.

Within living memory almost all babies were delivered by aged women in the village who possessed no medical qualifications, but who were locally considered to be very highly skilled in midwifery, and even to-day many people say they would prefer these villagers to 'proper doctors'.[1]

Following a period varying from a few days to two or three months, the child is baptized, an event attended by a gathering of relatives from far and near. After the ceremony there is a feast at which 'Cumberland ham' and rum butter are prominent dishes, and before they leave guests 'cross the baby's palm with silver'.

It was very difficult to obtain statements of the reasons why people had their children baptized. Most people could give no reason at all. Some said it was because they 'believed in the Church of England'; others because they 'believed in God'; and a few because they 'wanted their children to go to Heaven'. Everyone, however, agreed that to bury a child without baptism was a terrible and shocking thing, to be avoided at all costs, and in commenting on this many people who had found it impossible to say why they had their own children baptized were stimulated into expressing opinions. A village craftsman, for example, said,

'If tha didn't get kiddy baptized by t'parson, it would have to be put in a box and stuck in t'ground like some sort o' animal.' Other characteristic remarks in this context were 'It wouldn't be right, like a proper babby, 't'would be just like burying a dog or a sheep', and 'Tha's got to get a babby baptized, because if it died, it would be too late then'. It was said that at least once in recent years an unbaptized child was buried by its father in a box somewhere on the fells, but in the vast majority of cases children who have died before baptism have been buried without any ceremony in the graveyard of the church, as close to the wall as possible.[2]

Clearly, therefore, baptism is believed to be the sole means by which a baby may be transformed into a human being from its previous state of existence, which is thought to be very similar to that of an animal. Closely connected with this is the belief that a baby will not thrive unless it has been baptized, and the speed with which the Rector's services are sought when a child appears unlikely to live.

There are a certain number of beliefs concerning the early years of a child's life which apparently, do not apply to older children. These are rigidly put into practice to an extent which would seem fantastic to the more 'sophisticated' town-dweller. Babies born in the seventh month of pregnancy are expected to thrive, but those born in the eighth month are believed to have little hope of a healthy childhood. Washing a baby's head, cutting its nails, allowing it to look in a mirror and placing it too frequently on its left side are thought to be 'terribly unlucky' in the first year or eighteen months of a child's life.[3]

As it grows older the child's immediate environment extends beyond the four walls of its parents' house. At the age of five most children in Gosforth begin to attend the village school, where the great majority of them will remain until they are old enough to start work. The subjects taught at this school and the methods of teaching differ little from those found in schools all over the country, and there is comparatively little effort to instruct the children in matters of local interest. Although all the teachers in the school are Cumbrians, none were born in the parish, and only

SOME ASPECTS OF THE LIFE CYCLE

the school-master is a permanent resident there. In effect, therefore, formal education in Gosforth does little to assist the child in assimilating the more individual aspects of local culture. It is difficult to generalize upon the ultimate effects of such an education, but it seems probable that, to some degree at least, the lessons taught at the village school serve to increase the attractiveness of urban life in the eyes of the children, and correspondingly to lower the prestige of rural conditions. Such an education may be said to increase the potential mobility of the individual and in turn, to endanger the stability of the community.

Adult opinions on education varied widely, but most people thought of attendance at school merely as an unavoidable prelude to working for a living. In particular, education for girls beyond the elementary level was thought to be a waste of time, and there were several cases of parents refusing to allow children to attend the local grammar school after passing the necessary examination. Only a negligible proportion of parishioners have been educated beyond the grammar school level.

Outside school hours there are a few associations which may be attended, for example the Girl Guides, the Girls' Friendly Society, the Wrestling Academy and the Young Farmers' Club, but these are very poorly patronized. The history of organized activities for the youth of the parish is one of short-lived associations which have failed through lack of support or the inability of the organizers to discipline the members. The youth of Gosforth are markedly apathetic and even hostile to 'clubs', a phenomenon found in other rural areas [4] and which, according to some authorities, is characteristic of societies where familistic control of children is highly developed.[5]

On summer evenings the youth of the village are to be found on the playing field, where the boys play cricket and the girls either watch them or play tennis. Bicycle rides to the surrounding lakes and walks on the fells are also very popular during the fine weather. Farmers' sons spend most of their leisure time 'following the gun' or rabbiting, and are very rarely seen on the village playing field. In winter the main attractions are the football matches on Sunday afternoon, table-tennis at the Public Hall, the weekly dance, and the mobile cinema at Holmrook in an adjoining parish. There is no youth group of either sex, and in winter the majority of the younger people spend most of their time at home or, if they live in the village, visiting their close friends. Farmers' children in particular spend most winter nights at home.

Friendship between young people of the opposite sex usually begins about the age of 15 for girls, and a year or two older for boys. Boys and girls aged 15 to 18 are seen frequently together in summer, sometimes in pairs but more often in groups of six to eight. For much of the year when the weather is inclement these friendships remain in a state of 'suspended animation'. Apart from the few organizations mentioned above, younger adolescents can offer no reasons to go out in the evening, and since their parents look on friendships between boys and girls under 18 with considerable suspicion and displeasure, courting before this age is virtually a seasonal activity.

Similar restrictions of opportunity apply after the age of 18 but parental disfavour tends to diminish fairly rapidly after the age of 20, especially in the village. Boys are generally much less restricted in their movements than girls, and it is the limitation of the latter's freedom which determines the age at which courting begins. It is very difficult to generalize on the age at which courtship is sanctioned by parents. One family may accept the rumour of their 20-year-old son's attachment to a girl with equanimity, while another may forbid a son of 23 to go 'making a fool of himself'. Attitudes to courtship appear to have changed in recent years. Most of the people who were 35 or older agreed that 'in t'old days' courting was a matter to be kept from one's parents as long as possible, and courting couples went to great lengths to appear casual in each other's company in public. Several people mentioned a copse not far from the village as a favourite meeting-place of lovers, and apparently it was customary for both the girl and her suitor to steal out of the house after their parents were asleep for a rendezvous there. In recent years, however, it has become fairly common for the courting couple to visit each other's homes after they have been 'keeping company' for a month or so. If the parents approve of their child's choice, these visits become a regular event. This is, of course, an urban practice and is confined mainly to certain of the village households. Nearly all the farm families and a great many of those in the village have retained the traditional method of courtship, except that recent building has caused a change in the meeting place to 'Guards Lonning'.

This new rendezvous is a lane leading to three farms which is normally little used at night. Since it stands at the top of the steepest hill in the parish it is open to conjecture whether its popularity is due to the fact that it is immune from interference by all but the most athletic of 'Peeping Toms', or whether, as it is locally maintained, the journey up the hill is sufficiently strenuous to discourage the 'flirts'. Whatever the reason, it is significant that nearly all the adults in the parish are aware that such a meeting-place exists, and it is usually referred to with amused tolerance. It appears therefore to be an example of the well-known phenomenon whereby a society has patterns of behaviour for those aspects of its culture which are generally viewed with disapproval, just as there are recognized methods of committing suicide.

'Bundling', once common in West Cumberland, is now unknown in Gosforth, and there is no evidence that it ever existed.

Since parental control of children is strict, and since the family is still to a large extent an economic unit, courting is considerably influenced by the attitude of kindred. Among farm families, and to a lesser extent among villagers, economic considerations are very important in choosing a spouse, and the courtship between two young people is very much less restricted when their families consider their choice to be economically suitable. Prestige is also important, particularly in the upper class, and the friendship of a son or daughter with someone of a markedly lower social status is likely to arouse a great deal of parental opposition. Quite a number of informants mentioned courtships ended and marriages prevented by family interference. Despite this, the choice of a spouse is left entirely to the individual. The *mariage de convenance* seems to be unknown. Family loyalty is apparently strong enough to ensure that in most cases a person chooses someone of comparable economic and social status. Farmers' sons tend to marry the daughters of other farmers in the locality, and often when this is not the case the girl's family is closely linked by ties of kinship to several farming families, or her grandparents were once farmers.

The period of socially unrecognized courtship ends at the formal 'engagement'. Normally the partners ask their respective parents for approval, and once this has been granted regular meetings at each other's home are considered to be appropriate. Local opinion is united concerning the length of time a couple should be engaged before marriage. Anything less than three months is considered as bordering on the indecent; three months to nine months is thought to be much too short for 'decent folk', and while a year to eighteen months is the usual period at present, engagements of three years or longer are not unknown nor are they considered in any way unsuitable or unusual.

The number of pre-marital pregnancies, and more important, the amount of time that elapses between marriage and the birth of the first child indicate that sexual intimacy is quite common during courtship. An analysis of 247 first marriages [6] yielded the following result:

%	Time which elapsed between marriage and first birth (Months).
		−1	1–2	2–3	3–4	4–5	5–6	6–7	7–8	8–9	9–12	12–24	+24
Marriages.													
All		7	1	4	10	3	6	6	3	6	4	24	26
Farmers		11·1	2·2	4·4	13·3	4·4	6·7	6·7	4·4	8·9	2·2	17·9	17·8
Others		3·6	0	3·6	7·3	1·8	5·4	5·4	1·8	3·6	5·5	29·2	32·8

First child born.	0–4 months after marriage. %	0–8 months after marriage. %
All marriages.	22	40
Farmers.	31	53·2
Other occupiers.	14·5	28·9

(39 of the 247 marriages were childless—11 farmers and 28 others.)
In addition 18 illegitimate children were born in the parish between 1900 and 1950, giving an illegitimacy rate of 57 per thousand live births.

Comparisons on a regional or county basis tend to be very misleading because Cumberland has been characterized by large-scale population changes in the last hundred years, largely as a result of rapid industrialization and the entry of many thousands of immigrants from Ireland which accompanied it. Thus Ennerdale Rural District, of which Gosforth is a part, is by no means completely rural in character. Indeed, three-quarters of the inhabitants are concentrated in industrial parishes, and a large proportion of them are Irish Roman Catholics whose way of life contrasts sharply with that of the native Cumbrians. It is, however, interesting to recall that at the beginning of the nineteenth century, when Cumberland was still mainly rural in character, the illegitimacy rate for the county was the highest in England. In 1842 it was 114 per thousand live births as compared with 67 per thousand for England and Wales as a whole. Twenty years later the corresponding figures were 113 and 63 respectively.[7] By 1887 the county rate had dropped to 72 per thousand, and in 1949 it was 49. Of course this does not mean that there is a simple correlation between the number of illegitimate children and the degree of industrialization. On the contrary, demographic studies have shown that no simple explanation is possible for the regional variations in the illegitimacy rate in Britain and Western Europe.[8]

The evidence afforded by the Parish Registers suggests that Gosforth resembled the remainder of the county in having a high illegitimacy rate in pre-industrial times, and added to this is the fact that a great many of the legitimate children were born very shortly after the marriage of the parents, often within a matter of days.[9] This is in keeping with the present practice of regarding illegitimacy with considerable tolerance, while at the same time every pressure is brought upon the couple to marry before the birth takes place, especially if the putative father is a native of the district. Unmarried mothers are regarded as unfortunate, but more often than not their status is said to be due to the father of the child being, say, a farm-hand who had moved to an unknown part of the country, or a stranger who vanished when the results of his conduct became known. In short the onus is rarely, if ever, placed on the mother.

Many people in Gosforth were of the opinion that pre-marital sexual intercourse had increased during recent years owing to the introduction of modern methods of contraception. However, nearly all of those among them who were willing to discuss this matter in personal terms admitted that they did not use mechanical or chemical methods of contraception themselves. Enquiries throughout the parish indicated that the use of such methods is limited to a very small minority of the parishioners, a conclusion borne out to some degree by the number of first maternities occurring within the first eight months of marriage.[10]

Marriage in Gosforth retains few of the customs which were typical of the early nineteenth century 'bidden wedding' or 'bride-wain' of Cumberland.[11] Those that survive—tying the lych-gate and decorating it with flowers and branches, throwing pennies to children, holding the married couple 'to ransom' with a rope tied across the road, firing guns, etc., are general in rural England and Wales. As elsewhere in Northern England, marriages almost invariably take place in the afternoon. Those which occur in the morning are described as 'for them folks who want it to be private'. The wedding 'breakfast' which follows the ceremony is therefore usually held between three and four o'clock in the afternoon. The Public Hall is normally hired for this purpose, since the number of guests is far too great for even the largest house in the village. The celebrations continue long after the newly wed couple have departed, and when all the food is eaten the tables are cleared away for a dance which often lasts until the early hours of the next day.

Nowadays most of the marriages are followed by a short 'honeymoon', usually in Morecambe or Scotland. This is a very recent innovation, and it is still fairly common for the bride and groom to remain at the wedding feast until it is time for them to go to their new home or to that of a parent or relative. This appears however to be dying out very rapidly and normally every attempt is made to save enough money for a honeymoon, no matter how short its duration or how near the place. Failure to do this entails some loss of prestige and often evokes charges of niggardliness or of being 'old-fashioned'.

The life-cycle of the countryman ends very much as it began, with a large gathering of friends and relatives, a church ritual and a feast. The death of a parishioner is made known by the ringing of the church bell and often 'mourning cards' are sent to the deceased's kindred and neighbours inviting them to the funeral. The corpse is almost always 'laid out' upstairs [12] and when the pall-bearers arrive it is customary to give them each a glass of whisky or rum before they bring the coffin, made by the local joiner, down from the bedroom. What follows is best described by a villager: 'Then all t'folk lines up behind t'coffin, and most on 'em is wearing bowler hats: to see some on 'em you'd think they'd just come out o't'Hark. They all walks to t'Church, and after service and such they all goes to t'Globe for a funeral tea. Funeral teas is very like weddings. Ivverbody sits down to plenty o' food, wid rum butter and funeral biscuits, and plenty to drink, and most o' t'folks nivver go yam (home) till t'place closes. If tha wants to know who folks' friends and relations is, maister, tha'd best wait on 'em being buried.'

The importance attributed to burial is reflected not only in the fact that the number of people present is much larger than at any of the other ceremonial occasions in a person's life, but also in the wealth of stories that exists about burials in the past. Many of these, for reasons which are rather obscure, are characterized by a macabre humour. For example one tells of a funeral procession which paused at the Wellington Inn for refreshment after a journey from a distant farm, and continued to the Church where it was discovered that the coffin had been left behind on a wall near the public house.

Another, related with much graphic detail, describes the occasion when a coffin, while being brought by horseback over the fells, was accidentally jolted against a rowan tree; the shock revived the apparently dead woman inside the coffin who was taken home amid great excitement. Some time later she died again, and was once more carried over the fells. As the procession neared the tree the widower was heard to call out anxiously to his son, who led the horses carrying the coffin, 'Take care o'yon rowan, John!'[13]

In addition to these stories there are numerous beliefs widely held in the parish relating to death and burial. The most common is that 'you can always smell death in a house', and another is that Sunday is the most propitious day of the week on which to be buried. To drop a coffin is regarded as an omen of another death in the near future, and animals, particularly dogs, are believed to be aware of the approach of death long before this is apparent to human beings. Most of the parishioners also believe in ghosts, and the parish is said to have three 'boggles'. One is stated to have been seen by several people, and the strength of the belief in these apparitions is reflected in the fact that one farmhouse, which is reputed to be haunted, was untenanted for over thirty years because of its evil reputation. There are many people in the parish who say they would not live in it 'for all t'brass there is' despite the fact that it has now been occupied for some considerable time without any misfortune to its occupants.

Birth and death are, therefore, events to which great significance is attached in Gosforth, and they are distinguished by beliefs relating to the supernatural which are present to a much lesser degree in the marriage ceremony. For the greater majority of the inhabitants birth and death are occasions on which religious beliefs become temporarily of great importance, and, as we shall see in a later chapter, there are very few other times in the lives of most people when this is the case. Marriage does imply a religious service but seemingly the ceremony is principally regarded as an accepted means of achieving social approval for cohabitation. Of the great variety of reasons which were given for marriage in church as compared with a civil marriage, none were mentioned which related to the sacred nature of the church service. The two religious events are, of course, those at which the beliefs promulgated by the Church are brought most forcibly to the attention of the individual, since they invariably imply far-reaching changes in his immediate social environment, and introduce elements which cannot be explained in terms applicable to the material world. This probably accounts for the perpetuation of the sacred content of the ceremonies which accompany birth and death as compared with, say, the marriage rites in a parish which is largely peopled by 'indifferent' believers.

CHAPTER IV

KINSHIP

UNTIL recent years the physical isolation of Gosforth was very marked. The Turnpike roads, which had such a profound effect on social life in other parts of Cumberland, did not run through Coupland until the Napoleonic Wars had ended. The coastal railway between Maryport and Barrow was not completed until the middle of the nineteenth century. A regular bus service in West Cumberland was not established until the nineteen-twenties. This absence of rapid means of communication, together with a lack of immigration into the area,[1] have meant that a very high proportion of the inhabitants of the parish and their ancestors were born locally and married into local families. The resulting high degree of physical consanguinity which is characteristic of Gosforth provides a biological basis for a complex and important network of social relationships, some aspects of which will be described in this chapter.[2]

The maximum extent to which most of the inhabitants 'claim their kin' is shown in Fig. 2. This attempts to give a generalized diagrammatic representation of the relative closeness of the ties between one man and his kindred. It will be seen that the total relatives the average person recognizes are divided into four main groups. Clustered around him are 'the family', who may or may not share the same house. Less close are uncles, aunts, stepbrothers, etc., who are known as 'close relatives'. Second cousins, 'half-cousins', father's first cousins and others are in a group, not designated by any collective name, which lies between 'close relatives' and those persons known as 'distant relatives', who, as their name implies, are least close in ties of kindred.

The complexity of the kinship system, however, far exceeds the rather simple arrangement shown in the diagram, and moreover the ties which unite relatives are not always fixed. The relationship between an individual and, say, his brothers, half-brothers, and first cousins involves sentiments and associations which are extremely difficult to analyse and which cannot be verbalized by the persons themselves more than in exceptionally vague terms. It is, for example, possible to classify half-brothers equally well with brothers, and in some cases with first cousins, with almost as much justification as in the arrangement given in the diagram. Relationships on the periphery of the system are especially fluid in their relative positioning: the average Gosforthian often makes little or no distinction between the closeness of the ties that bind him to, say, his grandfather's first cousin and his father's second cousin.

One of the most important factors in determining the closeness of the association between relatives is physical location and its duration. When a person has kindred scattered all over Great Britain and other countries, it is usual for those he meets most frequently to become regarded as tied more closely within the kinship framework than others with whom contact is sporadic, even when the latter are biologically linked much more intimately. One man, for example, frequently mentioned his grandmother's sister (who lives nearby) as a 'close relative', and did not mention his mother's sister, who lives in Southern England, at all. The existence of this aunt was discovered by cross-checking with the kindred listed by his siblings and parents. As the youngest son of the family he had never seen her, while his contacts with his great-aunt were frequent.

There are many instances where a person's close relatives have moved from Gosforth to a distant part of the country. Fig. 2 is, therefore, based on the assumption that there is equivalence of possible social relations between the 'central' individual and his kindred. If, for example, one of his first cousins migrated to Australia, this relative would in course of time 'progress' towards the periphery of the kinship system. Conversely, if an aunt returned from abroad after a long absence to live in the parish, she would probably move rapidly from the class of 'distant relatives' to that of 'close relatives'.

Generally however, the relative positions shown in the diagram hold true in the parish and the surrounding district. Needless to

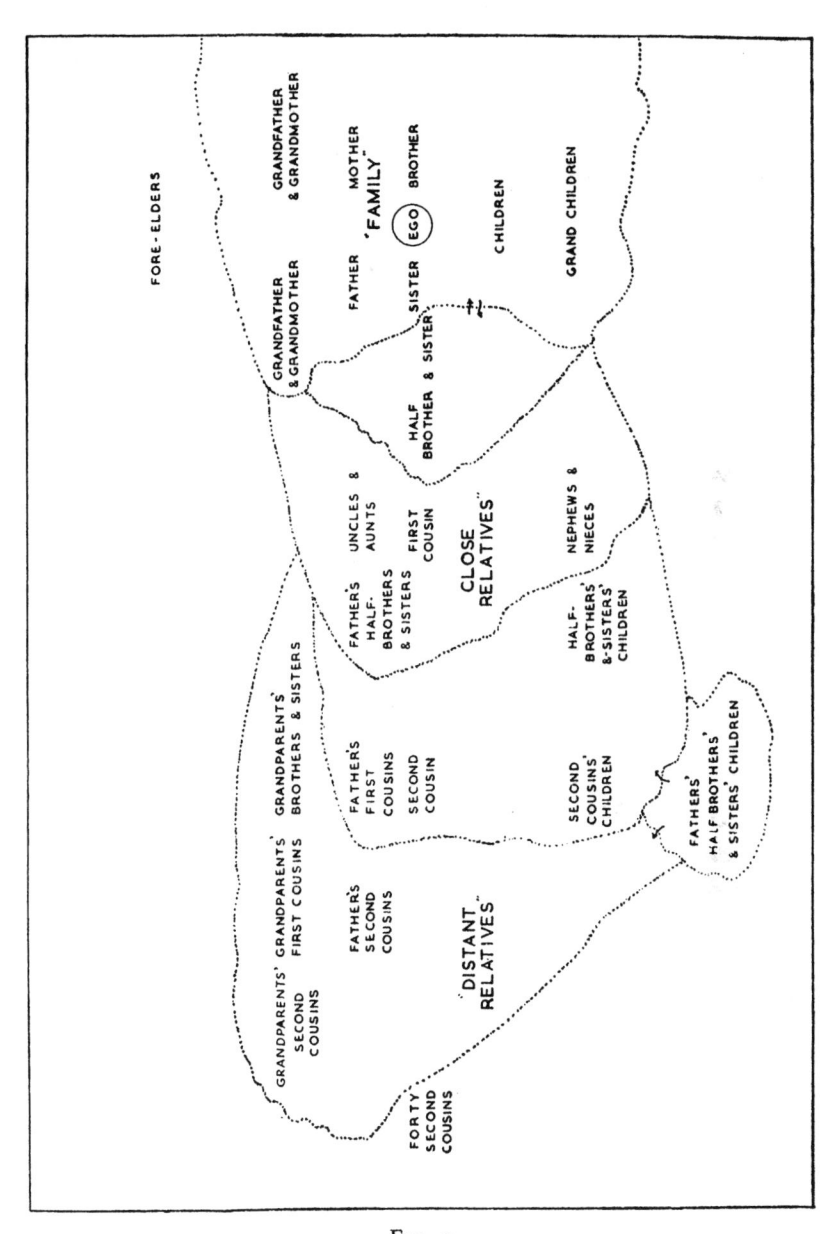

FIG. 2.

say, improved communications in recent years have tended to increase the number of 'close relatives' at the expense of the remainder.

While a sharp distinction is recognized between the 'father's side' and the 'mother's side' in 'claiming kin', there is no overt difference in the ties that unite the respective parents' kindred to the individual. (For this reason, and to prevent the diagram from becoming too complicated, only the 'father's side' of the individual's kindred is shown.) The householder's wife was almost invariably the genealogical expert and in the collection of kinship data it was very often found that the amount of material obtained concerning the wife's kindred greatly exceeded that of her husband's. Often indeed the occupier's wife knew a great deal more about her husband's kindred than he did himself. One farmer summed up this difference by saying, 'Tha'll have to ask t'womenfolk about claimin' kin. All I've ivver bothered about is me brothers and sisters and them who lives in t'district.' Generally, relationships as far as second cousin are traced in detail, but among younger villagers the exact relationship of more remote kindred is a matter requiring reference to older members of the family. The term 'forty-second cousin' is used to describe any relative too distantly placed to be identified exactly, but the degree to which kindred are recognized makes the use of this term relatively rare. Some indication of the ramifications of the kinship system may be obtained from the fact that in the cases of four individuals who named other parishioners as their 'forty-second cousins', the relationships had to be traced (in the Parish Registers) over five generations, and in one case over six.

Just under half the occupiers and their wives in Gosforth have 'family' relationships with at least one other household in the parish, and many 'families' extend over six or more households (see Fig. 3). Over 80 per cent of occupiers or their wives are 'closely related' to at least one other household in the parish, and nearly 65 per cent are 'closely related' to two or more households. In several cases the network of 'close relatives' extends over ten or more households. While the diagram shows the linkage between households related by 'families' and by 'close relatives', the

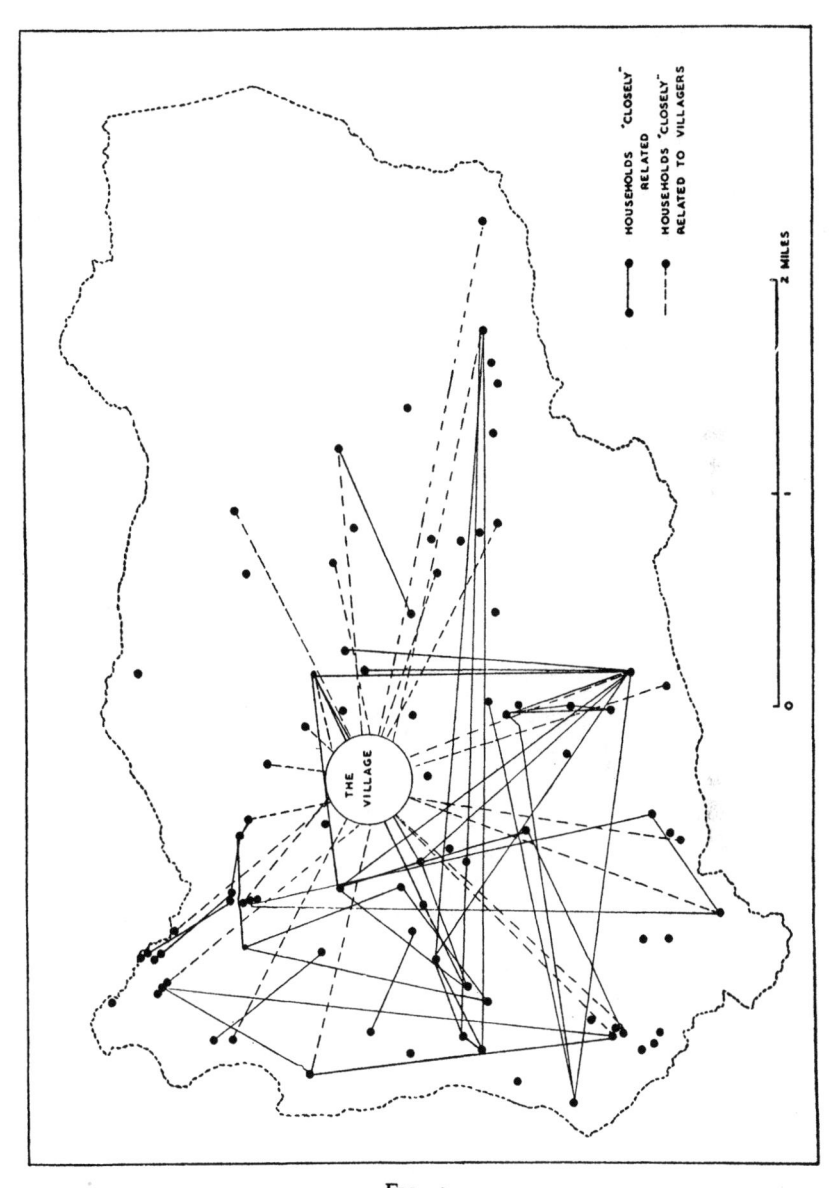

Fig. 3.

number of ties illustrated would obviously be increased a great deal if more remote relationships were to be traced. For example, a great many of the households shown as unrelated may have second cousins living in the parish, while many more recognized relationships have been omitted because these involve people living outside the parish boundary, who are not shown. Moreover distant relationships were often omitted by informants and came to light from time to time during subsequent conversations. The blacksmith, for example, remarked casually that a farmer who had brought a horse for new shoes was a relative 'on my mother's side—some mak o' forty-second cousin', although he had not mentioned this fact when questioned previously on his kindred. Later investigation in the Parish Registers revealed that the farmer was a descendant of the blacksmith's mother's great great grandfather.

Relationship by marriage is also recognized in Gosforth, but most people distinguish between kindred and 'in-laws'. When informants listed their relatives they invariably left out their 'in-laws' and when this was pointed out the answer was almost always to the effect that 'He (or she) isn't one o' my kinfolk, he only married my cousin', etc. When a person's married sibling dies the latter's spouse is no longer regarded as a 'relative' in any way, although children of the marriage are. Nevertheless, ties by marriage are the basis for social relationships and in some cases these ties are closer than those existing between individuals and their more remote kindred. If links by marriage were plotted in the diagram, then the number of households completely unrelated to any other in the parish would be very small indeed.

The following examples show the extent of the kinship system in the parish:

(*a*) Mrs. ——, a housewife, has three sisters and one brother, all married, living in the village. She has two first cousins in the parish and thirteen other 'close relatives' there also. Her husband has a widowed mother, a brother and two sisters in Gosforth, and four other 'close relatives' in different households. This couple also has a married daughter living in a house of her own, and the

KINSHIP

household is therefore 'closely related' by blood to twenty-seven other households in the parish.

(b) Mr. ———, a farmer, has three brothers in the parish who are farmers and a sister who is married to a farmer. He has one first cousin who farms in Gosforth and an aunt and first cousin living in the village. His wife's mother also lives in the village, and his wife has three aunts, two first cousins and three nieces living in different parts of the parish. This household therefore has sixteen 'close relatives' living in separate households in the parish, and there are also a further nine 'distant relatives'.

The families of these two people and of their 'close relatives' total sixty-five and forty-two persons respectively. If the ties by marriage and blood of the two households are traced out fully they are found to embrace sixty-nine homes with a membership of two hundred and forty seven people—over a third of the population of the parish.

The extent of such kinship ties was widely recognized in Gosforth, and it was common to hear it said that 'You've got to be very careful what you say about folks in Gosforth, because you don't know who is related to who half the time, and it always gets back to them'. Farmers, although united as a group by as many ties of kinship to other households in the parish as villagers, spoke of the village as 'a rabbit warren', while the parishioners generally believed the nearby district of Eskdale to be characterized by a far higher degree of physical consanguinity than Gosforth. In the local view, Gosforth was intermediate between Eskdale, where 'If one of them Tysons claimed all their kin, there would be nobbut a knuckle-end of four or five left ower' and Whitehaven, where, it was believed, blood relationships were almost completely lacking.

During his childhood the Gosforthian learns the names and specific relationships of his kindred, and as he grows older assimilates the kinship details of his friends and neighbours. The relatively high degree of physical consanguinity provides a means of identifying an individual by his or her relationship to other people and also emphasizes the solidarity and stability of the community.

For example, it was said of one family, who have no known kinship ties in the parish, that they were by no means 'offcomers' (strangers) because there were dozens of old grave-stones in the churchyard to prove that they were members of what was once a large and important local family, and were therefore in all probability related distantly to 'a whole lock (lot) o'folks in t' parish now'. Again, it was very common during the field-work for a man or woman whose name was unfamiliar to me to be identified by an informant as, say, the second cousin of the man who lived in a nearby house, or as the husband of his wife's first cousin.

The kinship system, however, is much more than just a framework of reference points which helps the individual to identify other people. It emphasizes the stability of the community by linking its present members with those of the past. People talk of a 'father's brother' rather than of an 'uncle', and of a 'father's mother's sister' rather than of a 'great aunt'. It is generally believed in Gosforth that in 't'old days' the inhabitants of the parish were far more closely tied by kinship than they are to-day and that the further one is able to trace back one's ancestors the greater will be the links with the parish and its present inhabitants. In tracing back these connections, the terminology used reflects this belief. One farmer, when talking of a local farmstead, said, 'The folk that built that place, the Dixons, were distant relatives of mine. Mrs. Dixon was a Briggs, she was me father's father's mother's sister.'

The use of surnames and place names, usually together, is the normal practice in Gosforth, and epitomizes several of the more important aspects of the social relationships based on kinship. There are Buchanans Bolton Head; Sherwens Tarnhow; Pooles Hall Senna, Souty Harry Benn,[3] and so forth. The identification of a surname with a holding may possibly have arisen to distinguish between several families with the same surname.[4] Whatever the reason, at present the name of the ancestral holding is usually used when referring to a kin-group, to the exclusion of the names of any other holdings belonging to its members. The Sherwens, for example, have farmed Tarnhow for several centuries, and when speaking of them collectively the term 'Sherwens Tarnhow' is used, although brothers of the occupier of Tarnhow farm at Town End, Bank End and Kemplerigg. Farmers are known by the names of the family holdings long after they have retired and gone to live elsewhere. This identification of a kin-group with a particular holding reflects the high value placed on land which has been the property of past generations [5] and also symbolizes the close attachment between a man and his 'fore-elders', that is the past members of his kin-group.

This attachment was illustrated in rather a remarkable manner recently. Two farmers, whose kin-groups [6] had occupied their present holdings continuously since 1806 and since the latter part of the eighteenth century respectively, said that it was a tradition handed down from one generation to another that their original ancestral holdings were two farms now occupied by tenant farmers who were not related to them in any way. Neither farmer could produce any evidence to support this belief. Later investigation of local documents showed that in one case an ancestor of one of the farmers had moved from the homestead mentioned to the present one in 1806, and that in the other case the farm specified was occupied by yeomen with the same surname as the present farmer for several generations during the seventeenth and eighteenth centuries. [7]

The use of a surname as the sole designation for a kin-group is very widespread in Gosforth. A man may be 'one of the Bunkers' or 'a Tyson' for example, and underlying this usage there is an extensive body of values and beliefs. A kin-group is thought to have physical and emotional attributes which distinguish it from other groups and individuals. The Sherwens are said to be tall and well-built and to have a marked degree of facial resemblance within their group of kindred. [8] Another group is characterized as 'coarse', a third as 'stupid and stubborn', and another as 'gay good folk who always make you welcome, and the whole lock on them is the same too'.

This belief in collective attributes is strong enough to affect the behaviour of people sharing the same surname, and also the attitude of other people towards them. Moral lapses and anti-social acts are explained frequently as the type of behaviour to be expected from a man solely because he belongs to a group which is characterized as immoral and anti-social. The reputation of a particular kin-group is often so widely recognized that unrelated men and women with the same surname are considered to share the attributes peculiar to the group. When this was pointed out to informants it was usual for this practice to be explained by postulating a remote biological relationship 'by his fore-elders yance ower'. Thus one family, which settled in the parish early in this century and which has a reputation for dishonesty, is linked with a kin-group of the same surname which was formerly strongly represented in the parish and was attributed with this same characteristic, although there is no traceable relationship between them. One farmer said of this family, 'That mak o' folk is all the same. I can remember me father saying that them as lived on t'next spot to him would have stole t'barn if they could have carried it.'

This collective kindred reputation is also extended to include women who marry into the group, and so assume its surname. The wives of two members of a kin-group locally thought to be eccentric and extremely unsociable were pointed out by several people as 'gay queer' and 'daft as a brush'.

Marriage between people with the same surnames is recorded fairly often in the Parish Registers, but it is very difficult to judge how many of these are consanguinous. Of the married couples living in Gosforth to-day, at least twelve married within their own kin-group and seven of these married their first cousins. Marriage to 'close relatives' is nowadays generally frowned upon and is believed often to bring unfortunate results. Much more common is the practice of intermarriage between sets of siblings. I found one case of three brothers marrying three sisters, one of two brothers and a sister marrying two sisters and a brother, and five cases of two siblings marrying a pair similarly related. Such marriages obviously serve to form firm alliances between kin-groups, and in time to increase the complexity of kinship ties in the parish as a whole. There is also one example of a widow marrying her husband's brother.[9]

KINSHIP

The difficulty of analysing the relationship by blood between the people mentioned in the Parish Registers largely results from the system of naming children that prevailed in this area. From the time when the Registers begin in 1571 until the middle of the nineteenth century, it was customary to name either the first or second male child after the father or paternal grandfather. One of the first female children was normally named after the mother or paternal grandmother. The remaining children appear to have been named after closely related members of the kin-group, so that, since the number of surnames was relatively limited, there are plenty of examples of five or more persons living in the parish at the same time with exactly the same Christian name and surname. For example, there were twenty-nine boys baptized in the years 1598–99; fourteen of these were named John and five Nicholas. An analysis of all the baptismal entries with the surname Moscroppe between 1710 and 1810 gives the following result:

John	11	Elizabeth	5	Esther	5	William	4	Matthew	2
Sarah	7	Joseph	5	Thomas	4	Charles	3	Sally	2
Jane	7	Clement	5	Bridget	4	Henry	3	Nelly	1
Mary	5	Hannah	5	Ann	4	Isaac	2	Peter	1
Moses	1	Nicolas	1	Eleanor	1	Bella	1	Edward	1

This method of naming has been so persistent that it is very common to find people living in the parish at present with exactly the same names as those found in the earliest years of the Registers. For example, John Nicholson, Thomas Benson, John Moore, William Poole and Elizabeth Sherwen occur almost continuously from the sixteenth century until to-day. Moreover, it is often found that certain Christian names are more closely associated with one surname than with any other. Andrew, for instance, is common with the surname Herbert, but very rare otherwise; there is only one Clement Mossop in the parish at present and this Christian name occurs only once or twice with any other surname in local records.[10]

About the middle of the nineteenth century, in addition to the traditional method of naming children, a new custom appeared very suddenly. This was to give as baptismal names those that had previously only been used as surnames, and in the years following 1850 such names as John Noble, William Wilson, and James Tyson are accompanied by such combinations as Noble Tyson, Tyson Noble, Wilson Tyson, Noble Wilson, etc. Towards the end of the last century this practice had developed so much that names like the following are to be found in the Baptismal Register: Joseph Edward Wilson Tyson, Henry Dickinson Mawson Clements, John Sharpe Dixon Hinde, and Noble Wilson Tyson.[11] The most common method of choosing these Christian names seems to have been to use the wife's maiden surname. For example, a child of the marriage of William Steele and Dinah Braithwaite was named Braithwaite Steele. When more than one Christian name was given, it was common to use one or more of the maiden names of the parents' mothers as well. This custom declined in popularity after 1930, but examples still occur, as it does throughout most of West Cumberland.

The whole practice of naming children has been described in some detail to show that it symbolizes the close tie between the youngest generation and those that have gone before.[12] The importance of this symbolism is emphasized by the introduction of Christian names previously unknown in this district, which are rapidly becoming more and more popular among the younger married couples in the village. These 'new' names, which are apparently inspired by motives of prestige,[13] are, very significantly, confined almost entirely to those families who have absorbed urban standards the most, that is those people who are characterized by social mobility rather than loyalty to a stable grouping and who place little importance upon the ties of kinship, particularly those with previous generations.

The custom of naming children after their grandparents is less prevalent now than it was formerly, but the close ties between alternate generations appear to be very strong still. People are very interested in the names given to their grandchildren and exert all their authority to have them named either after themselves or other members of the family.[14]

The people of the parish do not consider that to give a child the name of a deceased member of the family is unlucky,[15] but also

KINSHIP

there is no evidence of the contrasting practice of favouring the names of deceased relatives, as in parts of Wales and Ireland. In families of large numbers of young children, some of whom die young, the same name is often used several times, although this was more typical of the parish before 1900, when large families were much more common than they are to-day. The Registers record the use of the same Christian name for successive children, who have died, three or four times in as many years. Very occasionally one finds examples of two living children being given the same Christian name. The most striking example of this in the Gosforth Registers occurs in the late seventeenth century, when twin girls are entered with the name Margaret for both of them.[16]

The method of naming children, therefore, reflects the solidarity and persistence of the kin-group, and the same is true of the local custom of continuing to call women by their maiden surnames after they are married. To refer to the mother of a large family by her original surname emphasizes the fact that she is still regarded as a member of her kin-group, however closely she may be tied to her husband's kindred through her children. It also symbolizes the recognition of the fact that blood ties are of much greater importance than those brought about by marriage. Occasionally an unmarried mother retained her maiden surname for herself and her children after marriage, and cases occur of married women who have borne a child before being wed having their maiden name inscribed on their grave-stone and entered in the Burial Register when they died. The last known example of this practice occurred in 1928, when a woman who had been married for twenty-three years was buried: her son is still known by his mother's maiden name. Even when a mother changed her name on marriage, the child often retained the family name.

It seems likely that in the latter case the absence of a father caused the child to be regarded as a full member of its mother's kin-group, and that her subsequent marriage was not considered to affect the status of the child. However, this custom was not universal, as the following entries in the Parish Registers show:

Nov. 6 1609.   John Mawson, putative son of Robert Mawson and Elizabeth Priston. (Buried.)
June 24 1634.   John Dickinson, alias Biby, the son of John Dickonson (sic) and Ellen Biby. (Baptized.)
March 22 1639. Alice, putative daughter of John Hunter. (Baptized.)

The strong kinship values attached to names were clearly illustrated during the field-work on the occasions when children were born who appeared likely to live for only a few hours. When this happened, every effort was made to have the child baptized at once. Several informants explained this in the following terms: 'A lock on these old families is very proud o' t'family name, and they keeps Bibles and such with all their kin folk in. They knows all about Parish Registers, and if they are t'real old families like Pooles their names will be in them a whole lock o' times likely. So they has the laal thing baptized by t'parson, and then its name goes in t'Register like t'rest o' t'kin.'[17]

The solidarity and continuity of the kin-group is not, however, by any means confined in its expression to symbolism such as that described above. Considerable attention has been paid to the importance of names since they provide detailed documentation of kinship values that are otherwise difficult to analyse, but there are other social expressions of kinship sentiments of great significance. Each kin-group is an association in the sense that its members tend to associate more among themselves than with non-members except where considerations of distance make this inconvenient. Kin-groups in Gosforth are not territorial groups. Biologically related individuals are scattered all over the parish, but this does not materially affect the relationship between them.

For example, a group of related farmers who occupy holdings in widely separated locations co-operate amongst themselves in the borrowing and lending of machinery, and in so doing bypass farmers outside the kin-group whose farmsteads are situated nearby (see below and Fig. 8). 'Clippin' Day' at Fleming Hall, the only lowland farm in the parish where sheep-shearing is still a major event once a year, was described as 'a family affair' to which come relatives from all over the district, some from parishes over twenty miles away. Co-operation between relatives in major and minor matters of everyday life is continuous in Gosforth and is emphasized in such crisis situations as serious illness. This underlies the remark of a man who, when asked if people in the village knocked at the door when visiting a neighbour, replied, 'No, but most on them is related and tha doesn't knock on a relation's door tha knows, maister.'

The internal solidarity of the kin-group, so evident at funerals, when as many as a hundred members may collect from widely scattered parts of the country, imposes a series of obligations and rights on the individual member. Kindred have an *esprit de corps* which implies that each member is expected to uphold the prestige and status of the group, and continued failure to do this may result in the ostracism of the offender. During the collection of genealogies in one group of kindred, full details of a distant relative who has become a noted cattle-breeder were given by all the heads of member households, but no mention at all was made of two less distantly related individuals. One of these is certified as insane and the other has twice married women whom the group as a whole considered highly undesirable. The members of the kin-group were very surprised when I mentioned the existence of these two people (discovered from the Parish Registers) and were obviously annoyed and reluctant to discuss them. Such instances were not uncommon.

The values based on consanguinity appear to be very different from those held in relation to the social class system of the parish. Loyalty to one's relatives, which is a *sine qua non* of the kinship system, is strained when, for example, a member of a kin-group rises to a class above that of most group members, or when another marries someone who is thought to be socially inferior. Occasionally informants made such comments as 'She's become a real snob now and she won't come to have a crack with us now like she used to. You'd not think she was a close relative the way she carries on, and if she's not careful she'll find she's jumped right out o' bed into t'beck. If me father was alive he'd have told her a thing or two.'

KINSHIP

Blood ties seem, however, stronger than considerations inspired by social class as a rule, and the social relationships arising from the former are apparently not normally disrupted to any great extent by the differing standards of the respective social classes. Symptomatic of this was the reluctance of people to pass adverse judgments on those members of their kin-group who were generally regarded as 'snobs'. It is also very significant that an informant never credited any one of his kindred with a lower social status than himself, even when many other people assessed them at different social levels.[18]

The solidarity of the kin-group is a potent factor in controlling the behaviour of its members. Natives of the parish and others who have lived in the district for some time are well aware of this cohesiveness, and many stories are told to illustrate the dangers of offending a member of a large kin-group. A newcomer to the parish who has no kinship ties there rapidly becomes aware of his position outside the close networks of the kin-groups which comprise the greater part of the population of the parish. If he should by chance offend a member of one of these groups, he is very likely to find that he has, in effect, offended the whole group and probably other groups related to it by marriage. This was very evident from the statements of several people from urban areas who had settled in the parish. They described their new neighbours as 'clannish' and constantly drew comparisons with the towns, where they had never experienced the influence of a close-knit system of personal relations.

Kinship finds expression in few overt forms, but, as we have seen, it has a great influence on much of the social life of the parish. It links farmer and villager, and parishioner and non-parishioner, thereby assisting in the integration of the parish as a unit, and at the same time as a part of the countryside as a whole. When a Gosforthian goes to an Agricultural Show at Millom or an auction sale at Wigton he is certain to meet either members of his own kin-group or others he knows as relatives of people in the parish. A visit to a distant town or village, for whatever purpose, invariably implies a visit to relatives in that area. Indeed many of the longer journeys by the inhabitants of the parish are made with the express purpose of calling on kindred. At Gosforth Show, where farmers from all over Cumberland gather together, men and women from as far away as Carlisle or Penrith will be identified as, possibly, a second cousin or nephew of someone living in Gosforth or one of the adjoining parishes. Those that cannot be identified in this way are very often dismissed as 'offcomers'.

In this chapter the Parish Registers have been cited frequently to indicate that extensive kin-groups have existed in Gosforth for four hundred years at least. Furthermore, some surnames which occur in the late sixteenth century Registers often enough to suggest large groups of kindred at that time are mentioned in the few surviving documents which relate to an earlier period. For example, Poole, which is a surname prominent in the parish from 1571 until the present day, is mentioned several times in 1500. Other surnames which have been common in Gosforth for an equally long period, and which are mentioned in documents much older than the Parish Registers, are Kechyn in 1466 [19] (i.e. the modern Kitchin); Postylthuayt in 1472 [20] (i.e. Postlethwaite); Kyrkeby in 1466 [21] (i.e. Kirkby); Jonisson in 1365 [22] (? i.e. Johnson); Skelton in 1387,[23] and Rossel in 1303 [24] (i.e. Russell).

Unlike much of England,[25] therefore, Gosforth and West Cumberland generally have been characterized for many centuries by a high evaluation of blood ties. It seems almost certain that this is a heritage from early medieval times at least, and even possibly from the days of the Norsemen and of the Celts before them. Both Norseman and Celt placed a high value on biological relationship, and large kin-groups flourished in both societies.[26] The far-reaching effects of the Norse invasion of Cumberland upon the life of that area are described by many authorities, some of whom state that when the manorial system was introduced it was adapted by the Vikings (many of whom became lords of the manor) to their particular way of life.[27] If this were so, and the evidence is very convincing, then a society where kin loyalty is all-pervasive has persisted in West Cumberland from the tenth century (if not earlier) until the present day, and this would be the reason why this area is so different from the 'champion' country.

CHAPTER V

THE SOCIAL CLASSES

IT was soon obvious from the behaviour and conversation of the people of Gosforth that, apart from personal likes and dislikes, their attitudes towards certain parishioners, both as individuals and groups, tend to vary along well-defined lines. In a chance encounter—on the village street, or at an auction sale—the behaviour of any two or more people will depend largely on whether they think themselves members of the same group or not; in the latter case it will depend further on what is locally regarded as the 'correct' relationship between the specific groups involved. This division of the parish into groups of people became more apparent with time. There were men who were 'a different type from the village' and others were 'people who won't acknowledge you'. There were 'better class folk who make you feel awkward' and 'people who are different because of the way they carry on'. These groups or classes [1] are also believed to possess qualities which make them 'better' or 'higher' than another class. Gosforth has its 'Upper Ten' or 'Top Class' and there are 'people you look up to' and 'people you look down on'.

Since the same people were always mentioned in connection with a particular class, and never as belonging to another class, it became possible to divide the parish up into a number of classes, each with a comparatively fixed membership, and arranged in a graded series. Two methods were used to determine the nature and membership of each class [2] and the results showed that the people of Gosforth believed themselves to be split up into seven social classes (see Appendix V and Fig. 4).

Each class is thought by members of other classes to have special attributes and modes of behaviour. The seven classes will be described in turn, as more or less separate entities. Although this is in keeping with the local belief that a class has definite limits and a social reality of its own, it must however be borne in

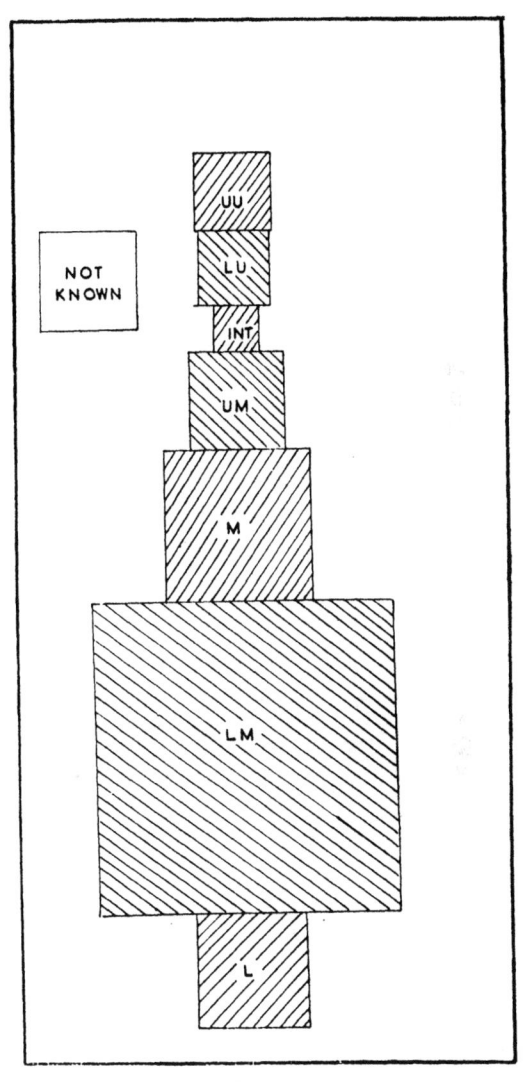

Fig. 4.

THE SOCIAL CLASSES

These classes can be arranged in tabular form as follows:

Assigned Class Name.	Local Class Names.
Upper Class — Upper-Upper	Upper Ten.* Top Class. Think themselves so. The Nibs. Better class people who make you feel awkward. Our social level. Upper Class.* A different type to the village. Higher class. People whose family counts. People who don't mix. Old school tie folks. People who won't acknowledge you. People who talk more posh. People who are a higher class than we are. Them posh folk. The gentry. The higher-ups. People you can look up to.
Upper Class — Lower-Upper	Folks that would like to be gentlemen but aren't. Haven't arrived yet. The money maker class.* Those who have ambitions of climbing and who are always boasting, but who will never make the grade. Aren't Upper Ten but like to think they are.* Ought to be in the Upper Ten but aren't. Not in the Upper class but different from the village. In a class of their own. One foot in heaven and t'other in hell.
Intermediate	Neither here or there.* Don't know where he is. In between and not very comfortable. In between because of education. In a class of their own. In betweens.* On their own. Barrack-room lawyers.
Lower Class — Upper-Medial	Class who never talk to anyone.* People who keep themselves to themselves. People who think they are a class better than anybody else.* People who fancy themselves. Big snobs.* Old snobs. Bloody snobs. People who think they got good jobs. The village aristocracy. People who have class distinction. Classy people. Social climbers. People who try to run the village. Flaming Nosey Parkers.
Lower Class — Medial	Farmers.* People with good jobs. Decent folk with good jobs and farmers.* Farmers and tradespeople. Decent bodies with better jobs than us.
Lower-Medial	The rest of the village.* Real nice folk. The village.* Decent folk.
Lower Class	Lower Class.* People who are different because of the way they carry on. Scruffy people. Roughs and toughs. People who got plenty of brass but they're dirty. The semi-submerged class. The Bob Prettys. Sort of people whose mentality is lower. Untidy people.

(Those local class names marked with an asterisk are the ones most commonly used as class designations in Gosforth. In the assigned class names the term 'medial' is used in preference to 'middle' in order to avoid confusion with the body of ideas that is inseparable from such phrases as 'Upper Middle Class'. The Upper-Medial class in Gosforth is not 'Upper Middle' in the sense that the term is usually understood, but in fact spreads over the 'Lower Middle' and 'Working' classes.)

mind throughout this chapter that each class has position only in relation to other classes, and that the characteristics of any one class become meaningless when divorced from the total system.

The Upper-Upper class is the most clearly defined in that its membership is acknowledged throughout the parish by everyone, regardless of age and sex, its members tend to associate more with themselves than with people from other classes, and its limits are locally recognized as the most rigid of all class 'boundaries'. This class also has what may be called a high degree of 'social visibility'. The 'A' family is a typical example of this class. Mr. and Mrs. 'A' were both born outside Cumberland and were educated in a public school and a boarding school respectively. When they came to live in Gosforth, their only connection with the district lay in the fact that they had spent several weeks on holiday there over a period of years, usually staying at one of the larger houses.[3] The house they bought on their arrival is situated outside the village and stands in its own grounds, well away from the main road. Until 1939 all their domestic work was done by servants and the grounds were maintained by a staff of gardeners who lived in the village. To-day there is only one resident servant, and most of the work in the house is done by women from the village on a part-time basis. The gardens however are still as carefully tended all the year round.

Mr. 'A' has no occupation and is believed by the parishioners to be very wealthy. His daughter, who was educated in a series of boarding schools, is judged by the villagers to be 'lonely', since most of her age-group in this class do not live at home. An attempted friendship with a villager of a lower social class was the subject of a great deal of comment. It was 'very surprising' to a number of people and was generally regarded in the village as 'wrong'.

Mr. 'A' knows, and is known to, almost everyone in the parish and is referred to usually by the initials of his Christian names. (For a discussion of the sociological significance of names see Appendix VI.) He is on 'speaking terms' with a large number of people, but the only ones he visits 'socially', and who have ever eaten with him in his own home, are those of the Upper-Upper class. The ancestors of one member of this class have lived in the parish for generations, but the others—including Mr. 'A'—are newcomers whose antecedents are relatively unknown outside their own class. Yet, within the Upper-Upper class, pedigree is an important determinant of rank, and Mr. 'A' is well aware of the fact that Mrs. 'B's French name is of Huguenot origin, and that Mr. 'C' has 'old records' illustrating the antiquity and importance of his family in the South-West of England. The Upper-Upper class, however, considers pedigree to be confined to its own social level. One of the 'Upper Ten' who professed deep interest in genealogy was unaware that there were several families in the parish whose ancestors could be traced back for five centuries, and dismissed this fact by saying 'but that class intermarried with all sorts of odd people anyway'.

Among the Upper-Upper class it is believed that 'other people' do not understand 'pedigrees and that sort of thing' and there is a 'tabu' on discussing pedigree with anyone of a lower social rank. Nevertheless, people from other classes take it for granted that the 'Upper Ten' are of necessity 'posh' in origin, and none of them mentioned pedigree when listing the factors that make a member of the Upper-Upper class what he is.

All the members of the Upper-Upper class are not considered wealthy, although only one of them has to work for a living. Their economic standing varies from that of Mr. 'A', who owns a large estate and many houses in the village, to that of Mr. 'D', who occupies a cottage smaller than a great many ordinary houses in the parish, and 'who lives very modestly and does most of the housework himself'. A highly observant villager described the importance of wealth as a rank determinant as follows —'The big nobs have got enough brass to live on, although there's a big lock o' folks in t'village have got more. It isn't only brass with them (i.e., the Upper-Upper class). If it was, Mrs. "T" would be one on them.' (Mrs. 'T', the widow of a prosperous farmer, lives with relatives in a small house in the village.) Money, therefore, does not of itself qualify a person for a place in the Upper-Upper class, but at the same time this class must have enough money to behave 'like gentlemen'.

When we come to discuss the Lower-Upper class it will be seen that considerable wealth alone is universally thought to be insufficient for membership of the topmost class. The Upper-Upper class itself considers the discussion of its members' wealth by an outsider as 'very bad taste'. Ideally, an individual could remain in the 'Upper Ten' even if his financial position were of the lowest standard.

In addition to pedigree and wealth, education is important in determining rank among the Upper-Upper class. All its members have been educated at public schools or boarding schools, and express this fact in a mode of speech which is noticeably different from the local dialect. This difference serves to affirm the unity of this class, and to emphasize the social distance between it and the rest of the community. As with occupation and the training that leads up to it, there are minute gradations of rank, which depend almost entirely on the place one was educated and the status given to that place. Education beyond the public school level is a social asset only if it is obtained at Oxford or Cambridge. Two members of this class asked me if I possessed a University degree. When answered in the affirmative, both asked 'Oxford or Cambridge?'—the implication being that nowhere else could matter. One (if not both) of these men had never heard of the University College of Wales, Aberystwyth.

. Occupations too are important for prestige purposes. Mrs. 'D', when asked if she had ever visited any of the farms in the area, replied, 'No. There aren't any gentlemen farmers in Gosforth.' Later, when discussing the owner of a small farm in the parish, she remarked, 'He comes from a very good family, and so does his wife, but we don't know him very well.' Mrs. 'D' regarded this farmer's antecedents, education, financial position and much of his behaviour as socially acceptable, but the fact that he farmed the land himself and catered for tourists made him unacceptable as a social equal. There are two doctors in Gosforth, one Upper-Upper class, the other Lower-Upper. Their occupational status would admit both to the upper-most class but other factors exclude one of them. Occupation, like education, cannot alone confer sufficient prestige for membership of the Upper-Upper class, but it is important enough to exclude people who would otherwise qualify.

Immediately below the topmost class and often coupled with it as 'upper class' is the Lower-Upper class. The 'F' and 'G' families are examples of this social level. Mr. and Mrs. 'F' are Cumbrian by birth, born near enough to the parish to be known to its inhabitants as 'local folk'. After an elementary and secondary school education, 'F' entered business and rose eventually to be an independent operator earning a considerable income. Their house, occupying a prominent site near the village, resembles the houses of the Upper-Upper class, but the garden is small and no gardener is employed. They employ a 'daily help' who does not live in the parish. They have no children. 'F' knows very few people in Gosforth and is rarely seen in the village. His friends are his business associates in a nearby town. Mrs. 'F' knows more people in the district and is more well known than her husband, but her social orbit is nevertheless a very small one. They are known in the village as Mr. 'F' and Mrs. 'F', and the parishioners know very little of their life before they came to Gosforth, despite the nearness of their former home.

The 'G's are also Cumbrian in origin and both their families are known to the older parishioners. Both were educated in independent schools, and when he was old enough 'G' entered his father's business and eventually became a director. He resigned from this office some time ago and now lives on his income. Their house, which is one of the largest in the parish, is generally regarded as being in the village, though it stands in its own grounds and is sheltered from the road by banks of trees on either side. The gardens are known in the district for their fine display of flowers. They have one son who attended a well-known public school and is now being trained in estate-management. Both are known throughout the parish, and their acquaintances are correspondingly widespread. 'G' is known locally by a diminutive form of his Christian name, while his wife is always referred to as 'Mrs. G'.

The position of these two families in this class obviously does not depend on the same factors. The Lower-Upper class is not as homogeneous as the class above it, but is rather a heterogeneous collection of families whose position results from the fact that they are credited with a rank that is sufficiently high to make them 'upper class', but not high enough to qualify them as members of the 'Upper Ten'. The farmer mentioned by Mrs. 'B' is one example. 'E', on the other hand, is Lower-Upper because his wealth (which is locally thought to be very great) and occupation alone qualify him for a socially superior position. One of the Upper-Upper class said of him, ' "E" has great ambitions of becoming higher class, but hasn't the ghost of a chance. He's always boasting of his business deals. There's nothing in the world to him but money and he'll never be satisfied with what he has.' Typical Medial and Lower-Medial remarks about 'E' were, 'He likes to think he's a gentleman, but he nivver will be', and 'He thinks he's the Lord Almighty because he's made his pile'.

The position of the 'G' family is more complex. Everyone regards 'G' and his son as Lower-Upper class and Mrs. 'G' as Upper-Upper. Mrs. 'G' was often referred to as 'a real lady', or more specifically as 'much higher class than him' (i.e. her husband). Of 'G' himself a typical Upper-Upper class evaluation was 'He likes to be on good terms with everyone, and he can be far too convivial at times. He would resent it very much if we "declassed" him.' People in socially inferior classes described him variously as 'The only one who really ought to be in the "Upper Ten" but isn't', 'Definitely not a gentleman and nivver will be either' and 'He talks to you like anybody else, but he wouldn't ask you in for a cup of tea'. Largely the same judgments are passed regarding the son—'He likes to be like his father. He'll talk to you like a proper Cumbrian, but when he's with them posh folk he talks the same as them. He's not one thing or t'other.'

This characteristic of altering one's accent according to the type of people present is found in several persons in the Lower-Upper class. It suggests that such people are aware (consciously or otherwise) of their position in relation to the 'Upper Ten' and that they are attempting to 'make the best of both worlds'. In other words, they know that the majority of people class them as socially superior and at the same time as inferior to certain men and women; they therefore modify their mode of speech (unlike the 'Upper Ten') to make themselves more acceptable to everyone—or so they believe.

Apparently then the rank of members of the 'G' family is determined by their behaviour, particularly by the people with whom they associate and by their mode of speech. The behaviour of Mrs. 'G' is socially acceptable to the Upper-Upper level, and is recognized as such by members of other classes. The husband and son possess most of the qualifications necessary for membership of the Upper-Upper class, but do not behave consistently in the manner considered natural to that level.

Other people in this class exhibit the same characteristic of 'just failing to make the grade'. 'H' has great wealth and high occupational status, but he has not fully assimilated Upper-Upper class mannerisms, and lacks a socially acceptable background of family and education. His married daughter has succeeded in absorbing Upper-Upper class behaviour, and also possesses a University degree, but is prevented from inclusion with Mr. 'A' and his group by her family connection. She is ' "H"'s daughter' to her neighbours and until that is forgotten she will stay at her present social level.

The Intermediate class is numerically the smallest group. The 'J' family may be taken as an example of this class. Mr. 'J' was born in the West Country and educated in state schools and Training College. He entered the teaching profession and came to Cumberland over forty years ago. He has lived in Gosforth since his retirement in 1940. Mrs. 'J' is a clergyman's daughter; they have no children. The house they own is one of the most recently built in the parish, standing on its own, with a small garden which occupies much of 'J's time. 'A woman from the village' comes in once a week to help in the cleaning of the house. 'Mr. and Mrs. J', as they are called locally, are known from one end of the parish to the other, but little is known of their life before they came to Gosforth.

This family is described at all class levels as 'in between' or 'neither here nor there'. Other members of the Intermediate class

THE SOCIAL CLASSES

are held to be 'betwixt and between and not very comfortable' or 'in a class of his own'. Despite the apparently indeterminate position of members of this group, it is sharply defined, both as to its membership and its position in the social scale. 'It is', one informant remarked, 'in between the high class folk and the rest of us.' One of the 'Upper Ten' stated that 'They are neither one thing nor the other because they are educated people. The attitude of people around here is a relic of the old Cumberland days, when there was no contact with large numbers of educated people. The villagers and farmers had no dealings with the intelligentsia; the only upper class they knew was the squirearchy. It's disappearing now, but the average Gosforthian still does not know what to do with them' (i.e. the Intermediate class). A Lower-Medial housewife said in the same context, 'People around here are peculiar. They have an idea that education creates a wide gap and that educated people aren't natural. They are frightened of "J", that's what it is.'

Members of this class own their own houses, possess cars, and feel it necessary to wear 'the right clothes' on the 'right occasions'. They are therefore considered more 'well off' than the majority of people. But there are many other people lower in the social scale who own houses and cars. The one factor which distinguishes this class and isolates it from the common people is 'education'. It is true that the Upper-Upper class also is educated. Indeed, several of its members have received advanced professional and academic training, but this class has many other distinctive qualities, and it is very significant that its members are seldom referred to by their inferiors as 'educated people'.

Below the Intermediate class is the Upper-Medial class, the uppermost level of the 'lower classes'. Mrs. 'M' and Mr. 'N' are typical examples. Mrs. 'M' was born in the parish and educated at the village school. A member of a fairly large family, she has several brothers and sisters and other relatives living nearby, and details of her family and its history are generally known in the district. The house in which she lives is no different from the majority of village houses. It is rented on a weekly basis but Mrs. 'M' hopes to buy a house in the near future. She and her family

THE SOCIAL CLASSES

are normally referred to by a Christian name and surname together.

Mr. 'N' was born and grew up within twenty miles of Gosforth and came to the village when he married a local girl. He has no relatives in Gosforth and details of his kin are not widely known in the village. Although he has lived there for twelve years he is still an 'offcomer'. Like Mrs. 'M' he was educated in a village school. He now lives with his family in a rented house. In common with a great many villagers he works at 'Sellafield' as a clerk.

The class to which 'M' and 'N' belong is unique in that it is only vaguely recognized by the Upper-Upper class, more clearly by the Lower-Upper, and very distinctly by the remaining classes. A member of the Upper-Upper class thought, 'There might be one or two social climbers in the village, but I'm afraid I don't know who they are.' People in the Lower-Upper class referred to members of this (U.M.) grouping as 'Village bigwigs' and 'the village upper-crust', while most of the parishioners described them variously as 'Big snobs', 'People who fancy themselves', 'The class who never talk to anyone', 'People who think they are a class better than anyone else', and 'Old snobs'. Of Mrs. 'M' it was said, 'She'd fall ower and dee afore she'd have a crack wid you.' Mr. 'N' evoked the comment, 'Who does he think he is, the way he carries on. If he held his nose any higher when he passes you his hat would fall off.'

The note of hostility characteristic of these remarks is not confined to these two people, but is typical of most, if not all, lower class comments on the Upper-Medial group. Also such comments are often accompanied by a corollary which explicitly excludes other members of a person's family from this particular class. Thus Mr. 'M' is not Upper-Medial, but his daughter is—'She is just like her mother.' Mr. 'N's wife and children are 'the same as the rest on us' or 'not the same class as him at all'. This class then, more than any other, cuts across family lines. In several households one member is singled out as belonging to this class, while the others are placed in the Medial or Lower-Medial categories.

As the descriptions show, pedigree, place of birth, education, occupational status and material possessions are not prominent in determining class position. What has been written about 'M' and 'N' could apply equally well to dozens of people who would unhesitatingly be placed by common consent in the Medial or Lower-Medial classes.

The overriding determinant of position in this class is the behaviour of the individual. This takes the form of emulating the Upper-Upper class as much as possible. Upper-Medial men and women make every effort to own the house in which they live, and in one case a family in this class moved from a house let at an exceptionally low rent to another identical in size, which they bought by borrowing a sum of money that can only be repaid by considerably lowering their standard of living.[4] Upper-Medial people speak the local dialect which is often camouflaged by an accent borrowed from the Upper-Upper class. This affectation causes much comment among members of other classes from time to time.

The position of these people between a largely hostile lower class and an upper class which regards them with indifference or contempt has two very striking results. Firstly, Upper-Medial folk tend to adopt a defensive attitude towards other people. Men and women at this social level almost invariably went to great lengths to justify certain aspects of their behaviour which would pass without comment in other classes. Expensive domestic alterations, for example—the installation of a bathroom, or the purchase of a carpet for the sitting-room—are explained as being 'cheaper in the long run'. A modern grate to replace the old-fashioned range in the kitchen always 'pays for itself in the coal it saves' or 'makes the house much easier to run'. Secondly, when an ambitious individual of this kind has unassuming parents or brothers and sisters there are frequently family conflicts. The standards the child was taught, and by which the parents still live, are now believed to be vulgar, outdated and cheap. Time and time again indignant villagers described graphically how a sister or niece had become 'too good for her father and mother'.

The classes so far described have been numerically small. The Medial and Lower-Medial classes, which lie next in the social scale, contain more than four-fifths of the population of the parish (see Fig. 4 and Appendix V, Table 2). While there is general agreement in Gosforth that there is a social division between Medial and Lower-Medial, the dividing-line is the most tenuous and uncertain of all the class divisions. Many people, particularly those at the Lower-Medial level, conceive the classes to be aligned laterally rather than vertically; for example, 'He's not the same class as us like, but he don't look down on us.' Others, believing the alignment to be vertical, qualify this belief by such statements as 'X and Y are different class, but not different the same as us and the Upper Ten is'. The differentiation between the two classes is based almost entirely on economic and occupational factors. The Medial class is composed of all the farmers, owners of the larger shops and businesses, the bank manager and a few other people whose occupation or financial position singles them out from the majority in the village.

(The status of the bank manager is rather exceptional. When he first came to Gosforth he was regarded as Lower-Upper class like his predecessor. Since then, his insistence on 'equality' and his participation in activities which are regarded as below the dignity of the Lower-Upper class have resulted in his being placed at his present social level.)

That there is a division between the two classes is very clear. Many farmers, for example, described the villagers as 'always on the scrat' (i.e. always begging) and none of the farmers would like to live in the village, usually because 'I like folks to mind their own business' or 'Folks are ower nosey there, and a lock on them is too standoffish'. Many villagers, on the other hand, describe farmers as 'mean', 'primitive', 'clannish', 'sharks' and 'twisters'. Within the village itself the dichotomy is equally clear. A Lower-Medial householder, describing a Medial class family, said, 'Money hides a lot, but they don't mix a lot. They aren't exactly looked up to, but they are a different class from folks like us. They have got good jobs and more money than us.' Very significantly, it is widely assumed in the village that the children of Medial parents receive preferential treatment in the village school. It was alleged, for example, that children of Lower-Medial class families were made to peel potatoes in the school canteen, while those of Medial class families were not. (This was untrue.)

At the bottom of the social scale is the Lower class, the 'roughs and toughs' or the 'people who don't try to lift themselves'. Membership of this class is sharply defined, the same families being mentioned by everyone without hesitation. Comments about this class were usually derogatory and often highly slanderous. They were the 'people who are different because of the way they carry on', 'You can tell them by the way they live', 'They've got plenty of brass but they're so dirty', 'A pig is happiest in its own muck' and so on.

This lowest level is distinguished mainly by the behaviour of the people rather than by their possessions, and in this respect it may be compared with the more pretentious Upper-Medial class. Some Lower class families are 'better off' than many Lower-Medial class households. But any suggestion that a Medial or Lower-Medial class person was of equivalent rank to a member of the Lower class provoked a reaction sharp enough to prove beyond all doubt the existence of a considerable social distance between them. It was generally believed that the mentality of this class was well below average, if not sub-normal, and that drunkenness and sexual immorality were rife. There was no evidence of this, and such allegations are, of course, typical class judgments in a large number of communities. Symptomatic of the low social ranking of this class is the common practice of obtaining obedience from children by threatening 'to send you to "Z"'s' (a Lower class household).

People in the Lower class are usually well aware of what other people think of them,[5] and either make a show of indifference or criticize the other classes very strongly. Lower class comments on neighbours were nearly always hostile in tone and characterized by the very frequent use of swear-words and obscenities. One of the mildest remarks was 'Gosfer' is full of bloody Nosey bloody Parkers and bloody snobs.'

It seems probable that much of the behaviour of people in this class resulted from an unconscious attempt to 'Live up to their bad name'. Several times during conversations with young men from this social group it was very noticeable that whenever a villager joined us, they raised their voices, swore much more frequently and became far more outspoken in their opinions.

In the description of the Upper-Upper class it was mentioned that Mr. 'A' confined his choice of guests at meals to members of his own class. In the 'Upper Ten' intimate friendships are almost entirely limited to Upper-Upper class families, an exclusiveness that is unique in Gosforth. Fig. 5 is an attempt to show how the pattern of intimate social relationships (i.e. 'close friends') is influenced by the social class system in Gosforth.

In the Lower-Upper group, Mr. 'G's close friends live mainly outside the parish and are in fact all former business associates. Within the parish boundary he is friendly with one member of the Upper-Upper class (who is not, significantly enough, to be found in Mrs. 'B's circle) and with two other men not of his own class. This is typical of the Lower-Upper class. People who visit each other regularly are the exception rather than the rule in this social group. It is a status stratum rather than a social group bound by close ties between its members (see Appendix IV). It would seem that this is due in part to its heterogeneous nature. 'G' is Upper-Upper class by family and background and is only rated Lower-Upper because of his personal behaviour. The 'E' family have risen from Lower-Medial beginnings and have only recently arrived at their present rank. 'G' feels at home with Upper-Upper people and regards 'E' as a 'social climber'. The 'F's are constantly on the defensive when in contact with the Upper-Upper class, but feel that a friendship with 'G' could be of little use to them in their upward climb, now that they have attained equivalent rank.

This highly developed sense of rank is found otherwise only in the Upper-Medial class. The configurations show that people in the other classes range above and below their own social level in their friendships. Upper-Medial people, on the other hand, associate most closely with members of their own or superior social levels, or with those members of the Medial or Lower-Medial classes who are in the process of moving upward in the

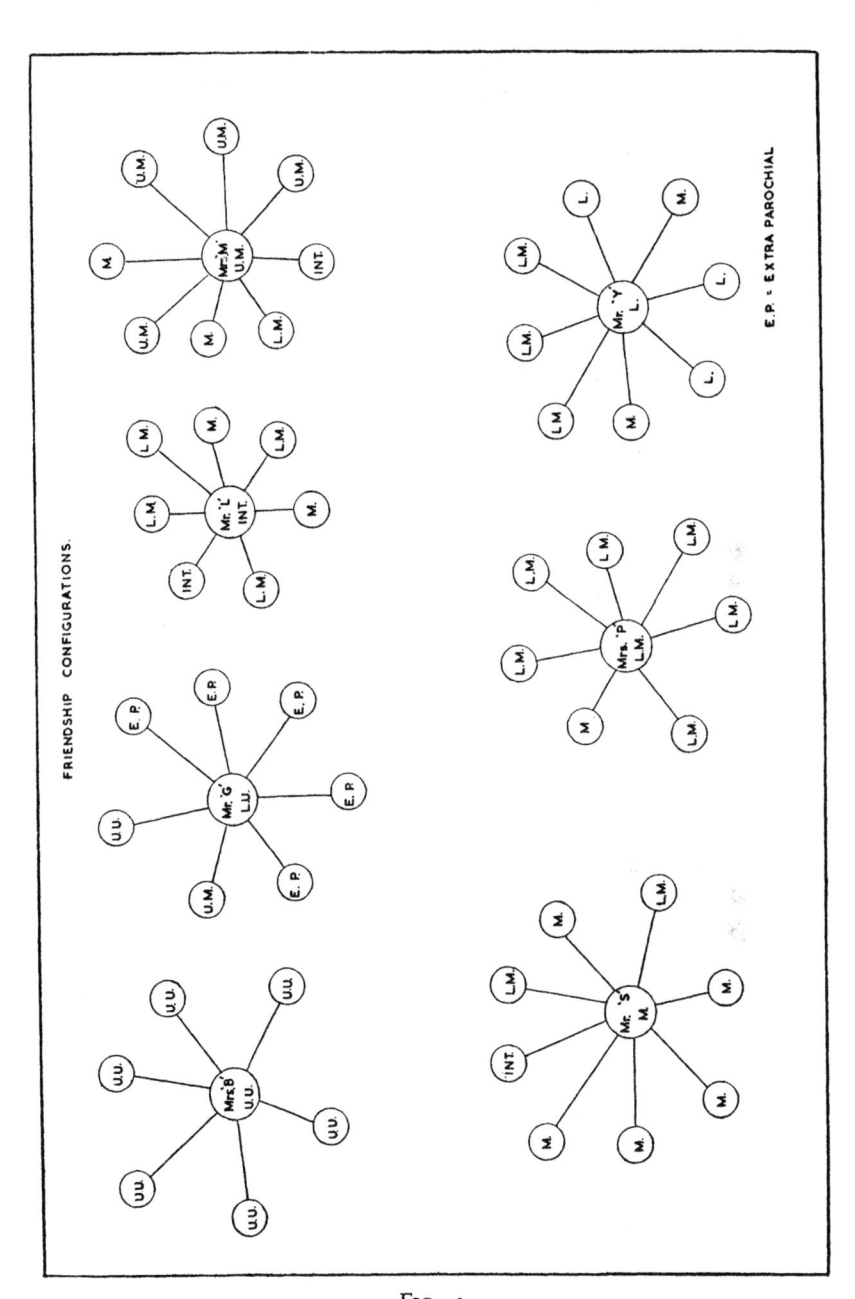

FIG. 5.

social scale. Mrs. 'M', for example, named the Intermediate and Upper-Medial members of her configuration as her 'really close friends', and did not mention the two from the Lower-Medial class. The latter, however, both named Mrs. 'M' as a 'close friend' and certainly they visited her very frequently. Mrs. 'M's conversation often included such remarks as, 'I'm dead against the class system, but working people in Gosforth won't look at you if you try to better yourself. Decent folk wouldn't stay five minutes in "Z"'s house (Lower class). It's a real padding-can (i.e. extremely squalid). I don't suppose you've met them yet, but you'll find there's an awful lot of common people, real common, in this place. They think you're a snob if you try to do some good.'

The people of Gosforth also apply rank judgments to events ranging from one end of the life cycle to the other. Discussing the baptism of a child of Lower class parents, a housewife commented, 'I wonder how many more they'll have. Yance ower people used to have big families, but now it's only them sort have kids every year.' Two of the marriages that occurred during the field-work evoked much comment because certain people were not invited to the ceremony. 'He's too good for the likes of us now,' said one householder. 'We were the same mak o' folk (sort of people) when we were lads, but he's got big ideas since then.' One of these marriages prompted several parishioners to repeat the story that the bride's father's brother was prevented from marrying another man's daughter because 'she was beneath him'.

Death too is invested with prestige. The social class of the pallbearers, the number and composition of the congregation at the burial service, the wording of the obituary in the local newspaper and the parish magazine—all reflect minutely the rank of the deceased. Persons of a particular social class are expected by others to be buried in a particular way, and failure to do so brings immediate comment. When a headstone was placed recently on the grave of a woman who had ranked high in the Upper-Upper class, its simplicity and relative smallness resulted in such remarks as, 'You'd hardly a' thought such posh folks would have such a laal thing as yon.'

This last example illustrates a further important point. The headstone was not considered suitable by the lower class, but was chosen as appropriate by members of the Upper-Upper class, that is, value judgments tend to vary according to position in the social scale. It was mentioned earlier that during interviews with the 'Upper Ten', questions were asked concerning the University I attended. Among the Lower-Upper class I was usually asked if I had a car, while the Lower-Medial and Lower classes were impressed by the fact that I did not 'work for a living' and was (presumably) paid for 'just messing around'. This variation of standards in turn provides an ideal pattern of behaviour for each class level. What is 'natural' and 'suitable' for the 'Upper Ten' is ostentatious and eccentric at another social level. That Mr. 'A' (U.U.) employs several gardeners, spent a considerable amount of money in constructing an artificial pond in front of his house, uses a shooting-stick and subscribes generously to many local organizations, is regarded by most people as perfectly 'natural'. And *mutatis mutandis* each class justifies this behaviour according to its own standards. By the same token, Mr. 'K's four cars, his numerous large gifts to local sports clubs, and his frequent alterations and additions to his house are adjudged to be 'showing off' or 'making sure everybody knows how classy he is'.

The fact that everyone is expected to act according to a prescribed code of social behaviour, dependent on individual rank, is of enormous importance as a controlling factor in everyday life. On occasions far too numerous to count, a person's actions in a specific situation were explained as having taken place because 'He (she) was afraid people would think he (she) was a snob'.

Miss 'D' (Upper-Upper) proposed at a Church meeting that the parish should be canvassed for volunteers to clean the Church in preparation for the Harvest Festival. Mrs. 'G' (U.U.) seconded the motion, which was duly passed, and Mrs. 'Q' (Lower-Medial) was nominated to find the volunteers. Eight villagers (all Lower-Medial) cleaned the Church in due course, while Miss 'B' and Miss 'E' (both Upper-Upper) decorated the pulpit. One of the cleaners commented afterwards, 'It's all very well for them class folks to say the Church needs cleaning, but they make damn sure they don't come and do it themselves. . . . They won't get me to do it another time, and I know that Mrs. "S" and Mrs. "R" (both Lower-Medial) only came because they thought people would talk if they didn't. That will be the day when I'm up there draping them flowers all over t'place and them two (i.e. Miss "B" and Miss "E") are scrubbing out.'

The role each woman played in this incident was largely determined by her social status. Miss 'D' and Mrs. 'G' are 'prominent Church workers', but the extent and nature of their efforts are limited to initiating and delegating tasks which are performed by people in lower social positions. Since they are firmly established in the uppermost social class, they are the least susceptible to criticism by others. On the other hand, the efficacy of 'what people will say' as a deterrent or stimulus to a particular course of action among people of inferior social grades ensures that Mrs. 'S' and Mrs. 'R' come forward as volunteers.[6]

Other examples of behaviour influenced by class considerations were to be seen whenever a number of people gathered together. For instance, during almost all the meetings I attended in the Public Hall, the front row of seats was left vacant for officials (who are mainly upper class) and other 'big nobs'. People from the other social classes prefer to stand at the back of the hall if necessary, even when there are still vacant seats when the meeting begins. These seats then remain empty throughout the evening. Again, in many of the village shops (but not all) members of the Upper-Upper class would be served immediately they entered, although there might be several other people in the shop already.

When a person fails to behave 'properly' and ignores the comments and criticisms of neighbours, then he or she ceases to be regarded as a living member of Gosforth society to all intents and purposes.[7] There were several people in the village, surrounded on all sides by neighbours, who had 'no friends or visitors'. One, a middle-aged woman who had lived in Gosforth all her life, said, 'There are cliques in Gosforth and if you don't belong to them you are ignored. I'd leave here to-morrow if I had the chance, but I have nowhere to go. If it wasn't for me cousin (living in an adjoining parish), you're the first one who's been in my house since my husband died' (i.e. eighteen months). These socially isolated people are all very anxious to leave the parish, a point of view that contrasts sharply with the opinion of the majority, who 'wouldn't live anywhere else'.

When the socially maladjusted person is a stranger the isolation is even more marked. The family with no kinship ties coming to live in the parish for the first time is soon assigned a position in the class system, and is thereafter expected to live in the same way as other families of equal rank. When this does not happen, the newcomers find themselves living in a social vacuum. There are three such families in the parish who have lived there two, five, and seven years respectively. The first of these is known by name to most people in Gosforth, but no one admitted to knowing the family personally or could think of anyone who did. The names of the other two families were known only to their immediate neighbours, and people living less than half a mile away from them stated that they had never heard of them. This was often demonstrably untrue, but it was undeniable that as a social fact their existence was, and would probably remain, unrecognized.

The position of a stranger who settles in the parish is very interesting when considered in the light of class distinction. How quickly his rank is determined is well illustrated by the sale of a house that took place early in 1951. There were two rival bidders at the sale. One, a native of the parish (Lower-medial) bid up to £3,100, only to be outbid finally at £3,200 by a complete stranger. (The local bidder was Mrs. 'T', referred to earlier. Her prestige and rank remained unchanged by this public revelation of her wealth.)

The stranger was universally referred to after the sale as a 'gentleman', that is he had already been assigned to the upper class. This ranking was apparently based on the fact that he was prosperously dressed, arrived in a large car, that he spoke in the accent normally associated with the 'Upper Ten' in Gosforth, and that he treated the whole affair with outward indifference—an attitude that contrasted markedly with the anxiety of the local bidder, and one which undoubtedly conformed with the local belief that the Upper-Upper class considers money matters as mundane and comparatively unimportant.

Members of the Upper-Upper class who were present at the sale said of the newcomer, 'He seems a decent sort of chap' and 'He looks as if he'll tidy the place up a bit and have a decent garden'. Otherwise they were characteristically non-committal in their assessments. Their caution probably arose from the fact that although the stranger was apparently Upper-Upper class he might, for one reason or another, be assessed eventually as a member of the Lower-Upper class. Upper-Upper people are very 'reserved' in their behaviour towards strangers, a trait which helps to preserve the exclusiveness of their class.

The only member of the Lower-Upper class at the sale said, 'Well *I* wouldn't have paid that much for a house like this, but I suppose he thinks he knows what he's doing. Anyway, if he can afford a car like that I don't suppose he's much worried about how much it cost him.' This is, of course, in keeping with the importance that many people in this class attach to wealth and may reflect a somewhat grudging admission of the stranger's social superiority.

The people from the other social classes 'provisionally' placed the newcomer in the 'Upper Ten' and their comments reflected the attitudes of their respective classes towards that grouping. A woman in the Upper-Medial class, for example, remarked, 'He seems a nice gentleman. I suppose he'll have everything marvellous when he comes.' One of the Lower class commented, 'We'll not see much of him I doubt. He'll be spending all his time with that bloody lot yonder' (a group of Upper-Upper people).

This particular offcomer differs however from the majority in being upper class. When the rank of a newcomer implies that his future acquaintances are likely to be widely distributed (i.e. Intermediate downwards) the process is very different. He is, and always will be, an 'offcomer' and as such is thought to be of lower status than any of the natives in the same class. There is a local saying which runs 'They've got to summer you and winter you and summer you and winter you, afore you mak friends in Gosforth.' Estimates of the time one is required to live in the parish before being 'accepted' vary from twenty to forty-five years. Furthermore, his exact rank will depend both on his own behaviour and on what details of his antecedents emerge as time passes. When it was discovered that a newcomer, who had been 'placed' in the Upper-Upper class, had risen from very humble origins and had attended an elementary school 'like t'rest on us', his class was 'amended' and he is now considered to be highly placed in the Lower-Upper group.

It will be clear from what has been written in this section that since the 'social perspective' varies from class to class (compare, for example, the respective attitudes of the 'Upper Ten' and the Lower class to a stranger) each class will have its own conception of the other classes and behave towards them accordingly. Since there are seven classes, even representative attitudes cannot be considered fully, let alone deviations from the norm; but some conception of the more important differences may be gained from the following 'class perspectives'.

(i) *Upper-Upper class:*

Upper-Upper class —	'Our social level.' 'Better class.'
Lower-Upper class —	'Social climbers.' 'Not quite our class.' 'He *tries* to behave like a gentleman, but . . .'
Intermediate	— 'Neither here nor there. More intelligent than the normal run of people around here.' 'Quite well educated and very handy when you have about a dozen village organizations to see to.'
Upper-Medial	— 'Social climbers in the village.'
Medial and Lower-Medial	— 'Villagers and farmers.' 'Decent lower class people.' 'The country people.'
Lower class	— 'The immoral element in the village.' 'The worst kind of countryman.' 'The worst of the lower orders.'

(ii) *Lower-Upper class:*

Upper-Upper	— 'The Upper Ten.' 'The people who have more breeding than sense.' 'They have no money, but because they talk like a B.B.C. announcer and their great-grandfather was a tuppeny-ha'penny baronet, they think they own the place.'
Lower-Upper	— 'Ambitious people.' 'Go-ahead people.'
Intermediate	— 'In between.'
Upper-Medial	— 'The village aristocracy. They try their best to get ahead, but everything is against them.'
Medial	— 'Farmers and small professionals.' 'Farmers and village tradesmen.'

THE SOCIAL CLASSES

(ii) *Lower-Upper class:—continued.*

Lower-Medial	— 'The village.'
Lower class	— 'Dirty people. I can't understand them. Some of them are quite well off, but you'd never think it to look at them.'

(iii) *Intermediate class:*

Upper-Upper	— 'The Nibs.' 'The usual well-off people you find in the countryside these days. Mostly retired people; very few of them are old established.'
Lower-Upper	— 'The money-maker class. They have ambitions of climbing, but they don't seem to have much luck.'
Intermediate	— 'We are in a class of our own.' 'Our position is not a very easy one to understand.'
Upper-Medial	— 'The kind of people who don't mix with their neighbours. Usually they are social climbers.'
Medial	— 'The majority of ordinary people with good jobs—including farmers, of course.'
Lower-Medial	— 'The average villager.'
Lower class	— 'An unfortunate minority. You can tell them by the way they live. Most of them are dirty.'

(iv) *Upper-Medial class:*

Upper-Upper	— 'The sort of people you can really look up to.' 'The proper gentry.' 'The better class people.'
Lower-Upper	— 'They are not Upper Ten but they like to think they are. They are not all that different from us, except for their money.'
Intermediate	— 'School teachers and that sort.' 'I think folks make far too much fuss about them.'
Upper-Medial	— 'People who keep themselves to themselves.' 'Decent people who try to get on.' 'The sort of people who try to improve themselves a bit.'
Medial	— 'Farmers and such.'
Lower-Medial	— 'Village people.' 'The ordinary working class people.'
Lower class	— 'People who don't try to lift themselves.' 'Dirty people who have no self-respect.'

(v) *Medial and Lower Medial:*

Upper-Upper	— 'People who are higher class than we are.'
Lower-Upper	— 'Folks like X who have plenty of money and plenty of cheek. They want to get on in t'world.'
Intermediate	— 'In between because of education.'
Upper-Medial	— 'Snobs.' 'Stuck-up folk.'
Medial and Lower-Medial	— 'Ordinary Gosfer' folk.'
Lower class	— 'Folk who don't care what they look like.'

THE SOCIAL CLASSES

(vi) *Lower class:*

Upper-Upper	— 'Them posh folks living in the big houses.' 'They won't acknowledge you and the way some of them behaves you'd think you was some mak o' animal.'
Lower-Upper	— 'The folk with brass who acts like they was big nobs.' 'Bloody snobs.'
Intermediate	— 'Don't know much about them. A lot o' bloody barrack room lawyers if tha ask me.'
Upper-Medial	— 'A lot o' ***** ***** ***** snobs.'
Medial and Lower-Medial	— 'Village folk like us, but some on 'em is very high and mighty.'
Lower class	— 'Decent folk.' 'Folks that like to do what they wants to.'

One further example may also be quoted which shows clearly how class concepts influence the outlook and behaviour of the different classes. The following is a verbatim excerpt from a conversation with a member of the Upper-Upper class.

'I think the class system is less defined since the War. I don't know exactly how you would recognize it, but I can't recall any movement in the village which ever had any success unless someone of the so-called higher class takes an interest, not even necessarily in an official post. The Dramatic Society is an exception, but that has "Y" who is a stranger and that's replaced class distinction there. . . . The upper class, by the way, strongly objects to doing these jobs (i.e. in village organizations) but they are pushed into it. Anyone stuffy is heavily criticized by the village folk. . . . . When "U" left the Home Guard during the War, "V" (Lower-Medial) became O.C. . . . "V" is a good chap, but always worked under someone in the old days. He was a sort of major-domo to the gentry, he never ran anything himself. Once he was appointed the fat was in the fire at once; *we* didn't mind, but the other fellows didn't like it a bit. They would have preferred someone of the upper class even if he was inefficient. He tried his best, but you can see what I mean. Another thing was that all the villagers, even the Sergeants, used to treat me with great civility—although I was only a private; and the G.O.C. often used to ring me up for a chat. Well that's the sort of thing I mean.'

Some mention must also be made of the concept of 'the old standards' in relation to the social classes. The people to whom 'the old standards' are ascribed are generally those whose families have lived in Gosforth for generations, even centuries. While they are not confined to one social level, they are to be found mainly in the Medial and Lower-Medial classes, and never in the Lower-Upper class. Being of the 'old standards' implies high rank within a class, but at the same time there is a strong suggestion that these families are in some way outside the normal working of the class system. People would often remark that 'Such and such a family isn't in the same class (as "A", "B" etc.) but they are the real old standards you know' or 'That mak o' folk is different from the rest of us'.

This differentiation is particularly marked in the matter of sexual ethics. It is, for example, firmly believed in Gosforth that 'immorality' is more prevalent at the bottom of the social scale than at the top, but this and other short-comings are not attributed to families which adhere to the 'old standards'. Four of the households known as the 'old standards' have illegitimate children. In three of these cases, people who had proved experts in local genealogies and who knew the parentage of 'merry-begots' in all other families were quite unable to account for these children at all. Two very reliable informants stated that in one case no-one in the parish knew of the existence of one child until it was brought to school. It was said that the family concerned were heavily fined for failing to register its birth. Certainly the investigation of the life of these families was very difficult. When, for example, people with 'the old standards' were asked for details of their children, they would often omit one child (or more) altogether, or give dates of birth that were transparently untrue or even biologically impossible.

The failure to account for these children by local 'experts' was usually explained as 'They're the real old standards are the ———'s. They've been intermarried nigh on as long as I can remember, and tha doesn't like to ask too much because there's been so much interbreeding. It's not that they are dummel-heads (i.e. mentally deficient) or anything like that—they're the old standards and their families is a lot different from ours.'

In the same way, life-long bachelorhood and marriage of

THE SOCIAL CLASSES

first cousins, both of which are more typical of families belonging to the 'old standards' than of others, are considered 'natural' to the former and very abnormal otherwise.

(To remain unmarried all one's life is thought to be an unfortunate state of affairs in Gosforth. For men, such a condition is believed to result frequently in a psychological state known locally as 'woman keen'. This is apparently an ambivalent attitude in which a man finds all women attractive, but is unable to approach them in any way. The resulting conflict is said to result eventually in his becoming 'as daft as a brush'. Several of the bachelors in the parish are alleged to be in this interesting condition—all, incidentally, from families of the 'old standards'.

Marriage of first cousins is believed to result in childlessness or in failure to produce male offspring. Examples are often quoted to support this belief, in spite of the fact that several families in Gosforth prove it untrue.)

The importance of the human desire for prestige and the variety of ways in which this desire may be expressed in different societies are widely stressed in anthropological literature. The part that the hope of gaining prestige, or the fear of losing it, plays in the social life of Gosforth is the subject of this section. For ease of treatment the parish is divided into 'the village' and 'the farms', and each will be dealt with in turn. The 'village' includes all those people who are not farmers or directly connected with farming. For example, a postman living at New Mill is included in the village, although he actually lives over a mile away from it. This distinction between 'villager' and 'farmer' is one in general use in Gosforth, and in very broad terms applies to rank and prestige. What is important for prestige purposes to the farmer is very often unimportant to the villager, and conversely the villager's efforts to gain prestige may seem futile to the farmer.

Life in the village is greatly influenced by two important facts. Firstly, that the people live close together, and secondly, in part as a result of this, that they see much more of each other and of strangers. Consequently there is ample scope for the development of devices to increase personal status, the maintenance of which occupies much of the villager's time and energy. As one villager remarked 'You can't blow your nose in Gosfer' without ivverybody knows about it; and half on 'em knows about it afore you does it.'

When a detached house was sold recently in the village, its prominent position prompted many housewives to comment that the provision of curtains for the windows would be very expensive, since all the sides of the house were visible from the main road. The type of curtain material to be found on the windows of most village houses varied directly in proportion to the general visibility of each window. The 'best' curtains were to be found where they could be most clearly seen, and were far superior to those on windows which were hidden from the public. Furthermore, it was common for that kind of material which has a design printed on one side only to be used in such a way that the design faced outwards. This use of the most 'fashionable' and most expensive material so that it can be seen to the best advantage is a typical device for gaining prestige.

Cheap 'lace' curtains were thought to be a symbol of very inferior social rank when used alone, and it is generally true to say that the social status of a household could be measured by the type of curtains it used. Significantly enough, the most costly and 'exclusive' materials adorned the windows of the houses of Lower-Upper class families.

The purchase of comparatively expensive curtain materials was stated to be 'cheaper in the long run' or because 'The old ones were wearing out, folks could see through them when the light was on'. Where paper blinds were used in addition, it was said that 'the room would look bare without something up'. Such statements are obviously rationalizations; the actual type of material and its mode of use resulted from either emulating the pattern set by neighbours of higher social status or from accepting the standards of magazines which purport to describe the way of life typical of the upper class in Britain.

The same desire for prestige is expressed in details of household furniture, personal attire, reading habits and innumerable other forms of personal display. In the later stages of the field-work it was possible to forecast with reasonable accuracy the type of furniture that would be found in the sitting-room, once the social class of the housewife had been assessed by other informants. Generally, among villagers below the upper class level, Victorian and Edwardian furniture is considered old fashioned, and has been replaced by the 'modern' type produced in vast quantities by mass-production methods. Antiques and the work of local craftsmen also carry little prestige and they are now extremely rare in these homes. The few examples that remain have been retained for reasons connected with kinship or family sentiment. The furniture in upper class homes is also modern normally, though it is more expensive and often hand-made. At this social level, however, 'period pieces', particularly those made by local craftsmen—for example court cupboards and long-case clocks— are held in high esteem, and as a rule the greater their antiquity the more do they enhance the prestige of their owners.

The community generally does not emulate the upper class in this respect because it lacks the wealth to buy antiques and the space in which to accommodate them, but this is not the main reason. The upper class is firmly established at the top of the social scale and therefore its status is only very slightly influenced—if at all— by the concept of 'bettering oneself'.[8] In the remainder of the village, however, to 'better oneself' is thought to be a highly desirable and praiseworthy thing, and since villagers have a high regard for urban culture they tend to copy it. It is significant in this connection that villagers attend the cinema more often, and read a far greater number of 'popular' magazines than do the farmers and gentry.[9]

The same is largely true of other forms of personal display. For example, clogs are very rapidly disappearing and are now to be found mainly on farms where they are still general for everyday use. In the village, clogs are rare and are certainly a sign of low class position. One housewife (Lower Medial) said defensively of her children, 'They wears clogs to school, but they takes them off the minute they get (home) and anyway it don't matter what they has on their feet; anybody can look at what they wears above (their clothes) any time.' Clogs are 'old fashioned', boots less so, and shoes are a token of modernity, and for this reason shoes are preferred by those who are anxious to 'better themselves'. All kinds of clothing are given a prestige value, to what extent may be seen from an informant's comment about a member of the Lower-Upper class—'He dresses ower posh to mak folks think he's a gentleman, but only that mak o' folk has to do that like.'

Among farmers the maintaining of prestige is a very different matter. The farmer is not surrounded by neighbours, sees few strangers and, as a member of a sharply defined occupational class, does not mix a great deal with people from other walks of life. For this reason farming families do not indulge in so much personal display as villagers. Clogs are not looked on as a sign of social inferiority and farm households buy far fewer clothes than do those in the village. Farmers' clothing is more often 'tailor made' and lasts for a surprising number of years. At important social gatherings the farmers and their families are often easily distinguishable by the outmoded style of their clothes, which in a few extreme cases may be as much as twenty years old. Farm furniture is not normally urban in type and many of the farms are furnished to-day almost exactly as they were thirty or more years ago, except perhaps for the addition of a bathroom during the last five years or so.

The farm family derives most of its prestige from the manner in which it farms the land. A farmer who plants his crops and maintains his livestock according to what are locally thought to be the best methods, and who keeps his machinery and outbuildings in good order, is assured of high prestige among his fellows. When farms were being visited, it was very noticeable that the informant (often the farmer's wife) would take pains to point out a new byre or some improvement in the barn, but would rarely mention any alteration to the dwelling house. A farmer is judged by the state of his farm rather than upon the state of his house.

Considerable time and money is spent on the care of 'dykes' (field boundaries) though retired farmers insist there has been a decline in standards since the old days, when 'farms were like gardens, the dykes were that tidy'. A dyke consists of either a thorn hedge planted on a bank of earth and stones, a thick hedgerow planted directly into the ground, or a stone wall. Even to-day a farm is judged largely by the condition of its dykes, and these seem to be much thicker and higher than is necessary for strictly utilitarian purposes. In many cases they are ten to fifteen feet high and three to four feet wide.

The history of the Barony of Coupland, of which Gosforth was a part in medieval times, is described by a modern historian as 'a howling wilderness of blanks'. Little can be said with certainty regarding the social life of the parish until comparatively recent times.

The available evidence suggests very strongly that Gosforth, although intermediate between the fells and the coastal lowlands, was little influenced by the way of life that obtained on the wild uplands to the east, where until the beginning of the seventeenth century 'Society consisted of mounted clans of farmer warriors at feud amongst themselves and at war with the Scots'. Land in the Gosforth area in the Middle Ages was held by the Priory of St. Bees [10] and by secular lords, some of whose families remained in possession for many generations.[11]

In those remote times society was composed of lords and tenants,[12] and so it remained until a class of yeomen arose who, as owners of land or employers of labour, occupied a position between them. Entries in the Parish Registers during the early seventeenth century reflect this tripartite division of society. Names of members of the upper class are accompanied by the terms 'generosus', 'armiger' or 'gentleman', and often by the prefix 'Mr.' Yeomen are so described in the Registers, while the remainder of the population are entered with such additions as 'nothus' (bastard), 'mendica', 'pauper', 'a poor widow', or more commonly with no accompanying description at all. Equally interesting are the entries found in the Burial Register for the period 1683-85. On 15th August 1683 'John Shearwen, son of Jo: Shearwen was buryed in linnen. His father paid a fine according to the late law for burying in Woolen.' Then follow thirteen burials 'in woolen', and then on 24th June 1685 'Isabella Copley of Gosforth, gentlewoman, was buried in linnen. A fine was paid by her Administrators according to the law for being buried in linnen.' John Sherwen was a yeoman farmer of some means, and Isabella Copley the wife of Robert Copley, 'gentleman'. The period to which the entries relate was one when burial in linen was subject to a fine, and such burials were possible only to prosperous families.[13]

In the eighteenth and nineteenth centuries the positions of these three classes relative to each other remained essentially the same as in the seventeenth century. The classes themselves fluctuated in size over this period, but the general division of the community into a small and wealthy upper class, a somewhat larger but less prosperous and less influential intermediate class, and a lower class embracing the greater part of the population, many of whom lived in utmost poverty, was unchanged.

Among the upper class the most important change came with the Industrial Revolution. The rise of the *nouveau riche* in the nineteenth century and their infiltration into the hitherto inviolate ranks of the upper class is too well known to require recapitulation here. In West Cumberland, people who had made immense fortunes from shipping, coal, and iron ore acquired country mansions and bought small estates and other holdings from yeomen whose families had farmed the land for centuries. In the adjoining parish of Irton, Mr. Thomas Brocklebank 'an opulent merchant and shipowner of Liverpool'[14] bought the mansion of Greenlands in the middle of the nineteenth century, and in less than fifty years he and his family had extended their holding to include much of that parish and part of Gosforth. Other wealthy people bought land in and around Gosforth with the result that from 1829 to 1889 the number of yeomen in the parish fell from thirty-three to eleven.[15] At the same time the upper class changed in membership to include these new arrivals, whose families were in time destined to replace their predecessors at the top of the social scale.

The decline of the statesmen continued into the present century and emphasized the distance between the upper class and the remainder of the population. In the eighteenth and nineteenth centuries these yeomen were prosperous farmers,[16] whose position and behaviour as a class were influenced by long residence in the area and close kinship ties which were the result of marriages with local families over the centuries. To most parishioners they undoubtedly linked the highest and the lowest classes: their prestige and wealth placed them socially nearer the upper class than the lower, while their affinities with the bulk of the people through marriage and tradition ensured the absence of that social isolation and exclusiveness that characterized the gentry.

The period from about 1850 to the outbreak of the first World War saw an improvement in the standard of living of the lower class, a struggle by the yeomen to maintain their status, and the gradual absorption of the new landowning class into the uppermost social level. The Parish Magazine, begun in 1887, provides abundant documentation of the social stratification of this period. The Churchwardens are invariably 'gentlemen' or the more influential statesmen. Subscription lists of every description are headed by large sums donated by members of the upper class. Burials of the occupants of the 'big houses' are the subject of long and detailed obituaries, while the rest of the population are dismissed in a single line.

The older residents of the parish to-day graphically describe the opulence of the country mansions, their large staffs, the impressiveness of the carriages with their uniformed footmen and buglers, and the behaviour the owners of these houses expected and demanded of their social inferiors. One villager remarked, 'When I was a laal lad like, ivverybody had to do their honours to Miss Senhouse and that mak o' folk. If tha didn't, then father would soon know about it likely, and *he* made sure it didn't happen ower much. He used to play Hamlet (havoc) about it many a time.' Another stated, 'If you offended the gentry they got their own back on you in lots of ways', and described how a villager with a very large family, who had displeased his upper class employer, had been dismissed immediately and evicted from his cottage. He was forced to live for several months thereafter on 'haver-meal poddish' (oat-meal porridge) in a disused barn until he could obtain fresh employment, because 'nobody would tak him on after that'. (This incident occurred when the villager's cottage had been extensively repaired by his landlord, a man who had a considerable local reputation for improving the lot of his tenants. When asked by his employer what he thought of the repairs, the tenant is said to have replied, 'It's nobbut an alteration without an improvement.')

For centuries then, the inhabitants of the parish had been divided into three classes, in such a way that the members of the upper class, in virtue of their great wealth, their ability to take drastic action, and the ostentation of their way of life, were at an immense social distance from those immediately below them in rank. Within the upper class the newcomers established themselves very rapidly. They were anxious to identify themselves as quickly as possible with the old-established gentry, and towards this end they assimilated as much 'local colour' as possible. This took the form of surrounding themselves with all the visible tokens of local tradition. Thus court cupboards, clocks and the like became popular in upper class homes, a state of affairs that has continued to the present day, hence the furnishing of many of the homes of the 'Upper Ten'.

Such a long-established conception of social classes has not been submerged by the events of the last three decades. In Gosforth, as in many other parts of England, the last thirty years have been marked by a decline in the importance of the large country house and estate as a territorial and social unit. In 1921 the biggest landowner in the area attempted to sell his estate, without success. In that year there were seven large houses in Gosforth occupied by members of the upper class, each employing a large staff of domestic servants, gamekeepers and estate workers. To-day there are few large estates in the district; two of the Gosforth mansions are empty, one has become a preparatory school, another has been divided into flats, and only one of the remaining three is occupied by a landowner employing full-time labour.

In England as a whole this change has been accompanied by the growth of a belief in equality, but in Gosforth there seems to have been no marked change of attitude. The Upper-Upper class is still placed at an immense social distance from the remainder of the community, despite the fact that the gap between them has greatly decreased. The persistence of the old way of life is especially evident in local attitudes to domestic service. A large percentage of the adults in the village have been employed as servants in the 'big houses' at one time or another, but there is no stigma attached to such work. On the contrary, it is considered a social asset. Many informants spoke at some length of 'the old days' and of their life as servants in the mansions of the district. A typical comment in this context was 'They were proper ladies and gentlemen who were very grateful to you for what you did. They were people you could look up to, and it was a pleasure to work for them.'

Traditional values have not, however, remained unchanged. As we have seen, standards derived from the 'new' urban way of life have been adopted, particularly in the sphere of material culture. In addition there has been a growth of social mobility and the rise of the Lower-Upper and Upper-Medial classes—groups that were practically non-existent fifty years ago.

In addition to the vertical division of the population into social classes, there is a geographical division of considerable historical interest. This is the splitting of the village into two parts, known respectively as 'Gosforth' or 'the village' and 'Wellington'. This boundary has no correlation with the class system, there being representatives of all classes in both parts. Wellington is firmly believed to be socially inferior to the village, and I often heard such remarks as 'Village folk look down on Wellington folk' and 'They (the villagers) looks down on us because we don't dress up the same and sweep the steps in t'morning'. It is believed in the village and on farms that the inhabitants of Wellington, taken as a group, are more immoral, more intemperate, live in more squalid conditions, and are generally less respectable than the remainder of the parish. In turn the Wellingtonians regard other parishioners, taken as a group, as snobbish and comparatively unfriendly.

This division is thought locally to have arisen recently as a result of the fact that Wellington contained two common lodging houses until about thirty years ago. These lodging houses catered for tramps, beggars and other undesirables, and such was their behaviour that Wellington became known as the 'rough end' of the parish, a reputation it has failed to live down. This belief is supported by a large fund of stories about these lodging-houses and their custodians, one of whom, it is said, kept order by using a poker to good effect, or, if this failed, by depositing any disturber of the peace into the cold waters of the Bleng, which ran close by.

This explanation does not, however, account for the *establishment* of both these houses in Wellington in the first place, and it seems likely that this part of the parish must have been thought of as a socially inferior place to live *before* the lodging houses were set up. Other evidence suggests that this territorial dichotomy is far older than half a century or so. Before Wellington took its name from the Wellington Inn in the early part of the nineteenth century, it was known as 'Gosforth Bottom', a designation that owes nothing to its height relative to the remainder of the village. The terms 'Top' and 'Bottom', 'Upper' and 'Lower', 'Great' and 'Little' which are so common in place-names require further investigation on a comparative basis. They occur in many parts of the world, and preliminary studies suggest that they bear witness to an ancient twofold division of communities both socially and territorially.[17]

CHAPTER VI

FORMAL AND INFORMAL ASSOCIATIONS

GOSFORTH is known for miles around as a parish 'where there is always something on', and certainly in comparison with its neighbours it has a very large number of village organizations. There are in all thirty-one of these, varying greatly in size and importance and exhibiting several types of internal structure and membership. Some, such as the Women's Institute, are confined to one sex; others such as the Mothers' Union and the British Legion, have special qualifications for membership in addition to that of sex, while several are open to all who wish to join. Similarly, their internal structure may vary from the elaborate system of officials and committees found in the Agricultural Society to the almost informal character of the Men's Football Club. (For a list of organizations see Appendix VII.)

From what has been written in the previous chapter on class distinction, it is to be expected that village organizations—which imply meetings of comparatively large numbers of people—will reflect the class system to a high degree. As we shall see, they are in fact exceptionally important as determinants of class position, as a means of maintaining individual prestige, and in the opportunities they offer for social advancement.

Unlike many larger communities, Gosforth has no organizations which are confined in their membership to one social class, and there are only two which are limited in their range to no more than three social classes,[1] (see Fig. 6). Alternatively there are only two associations which have members in all classes—the Wrestling Academy and the Church. Most of the organizations range over four to six classes, the actual composition of any one organization depending on the prestige value of its central interest to any class. The Football Club, for example, draws its members entirely from the lower classes, since football is a relatively unfamiliar and unpopular game to the upper class. The few members of the upper class who are young enough to play such games belong to a Rugby Union club in a nearby town, because this game has a much higher prestige value to them than Association Football. In the same way the School Outing Committee is drawn from the lower classes because it is beneath the dignity of the upper class to join in organized pleasure trips of this kind.

Members of the two widely separated classes, the Lower-Upper and the Lower class, belong to few village associations (see Fig. 6). More than three-quarters of the Lower-Upper class belong to no organization at all (i.e. in the parish) and only three of its members belong to more than one organization. In the Lower class only three adults belong to any of the associations shown in Fig. 6.[2]

This lack of participation arises from very different causes in each of these classes respectively. The Lower-Upper class contains several people like Mr. 'F', whose interests are centred outside the parish. Moreover it seems very probable that Lower-Upper class people try to avoid joining associations in which they might find themselves in an inferior position to, say, a member of the Lower-Medial class, with little hope of improving their status. Again, in those organizations with officials of the Upper-Upper class, a man from the Lower-Upper class and someone from the Lower class would be of equal rank as ordinary members. This explains the statement of the Lower-Upper class informant who said, 'I've never been "organized" yet and never will be. Why should I join anything in the village when every Tom and Mary behave like a Jack-in-Office. Half these people think that because they belong to this Committee or that Committee they can boss everyone about—but not me.'

Members of the Lower-Upper class attempting to rise from their subordinate position in the upper class, by emulating those at the top of the social scale, are aware that the 'Upper Ten' are firmly established in all those official posts which have high prestige and that they cannot hope to compete with them for these public offices. For this reason they do not normally join associations and content themselves with expressing such views as 'The Women's Institute is only an excuse for gossip' or 'Our lives are

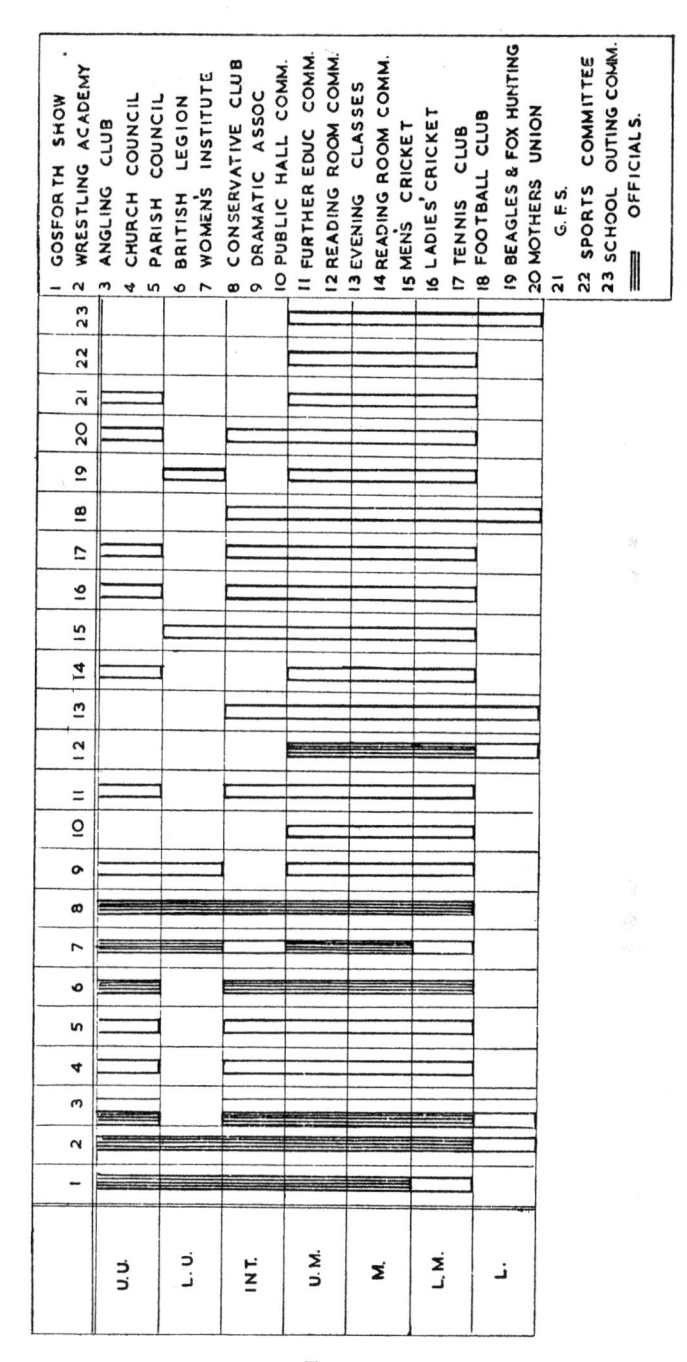

Fig. 6.

regimented enough as it is, without having to go to the Public Hall twice a week'.

The Lower class, situated at the bottom of the social scale, has no need of such care about its class position. Only two people from this lowest social level sit on committees. This is largely because members of a class so low in prestige are not considered suitable for election by the remainder of the community, and because the Lower class indicates by its behaviour that it cannot reconcile its own way of life with the standards which Gosforth requires from 'one of them flaming big-wigs that runs the village'.[3]

The absence of Lower-class people from membership of organizations seems to be less a matter of class than of interests. It is a prevalent attitude among this class to regard associations as 'something for them posh folk to do, not for folk like us', but this does not prevent some Lower class people from joining certain associations, even those with upper class members. This attitude is therefore probably a rationalization by which the inferior person denies interest in what he cannot possibly achieve. In general, Lower class interests are directed towards horse-racing, hound-trailing, Rugby League matches and visiting public houses.

With the exceptions already mentioned, status within the village organizations tends to reflect the status system within the community generally. The position of President is confined to the Upper-Upper class, except for the Presidency of the Dramatic Society, an association that has not attracted the active interest of the 'Upper Ten'. The posts of Chairman, Vice-Chairman and Vice-President are distributed in such a way that the upper class, who form a little over 6 per cent of the total population, occupy more than half these positions. The Upper-Upper class alone, that is about 3 per cent of the population, occupy just under half of them. Lesser official positions are filled from the lower classes (see Fig. 7). As regards ordinary membership of the associations, the status groups are represented roughly according to their strength in the community generally. For example, upper class people in this category are rare, Intermediate and Medial people less rare, and so forth.

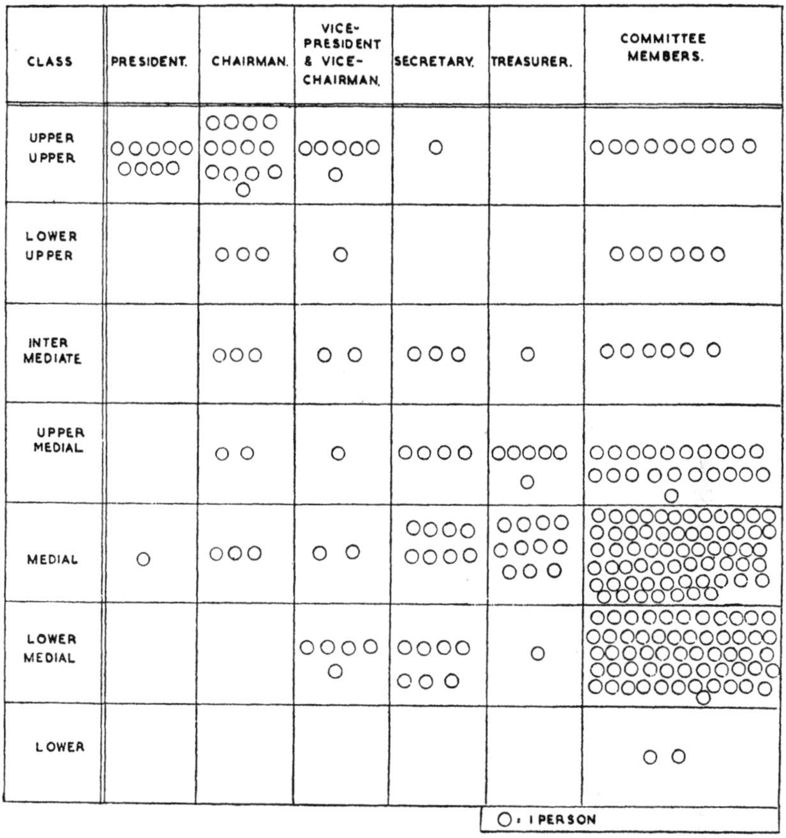

FORMAL AND INFORMAL ASSOCIATIONS

CLASS	PRESIDENT.	CHAIRMAN.	VICE-PRESIDENT & VICE-CHAIRMAN.	SECRETARY.	TREASURER.	COMMITTEE MEMBERS.
UPPER UPPER	ooooo oooo	oooo oooo oooo o	ooooo o	o		oooooo oo o
LOWER UPPER		ooo	o			oooooo
INTER MEDIATE		ooo	o o	ooo	o	ooooo o
UPPER MEDIAL		o o	o	oooo	ooooo o	oooooooooo ooo oo ooooo o
MEDIAL	o	ooo	o o	oooo oooo	oooo oooo oo o	(many o's)
LOWER MEDIAL			oooo o	oooo ooo	o	(many o's)
LOWER						o o

O : 1 PERSON

FIG. 7.

The following examples show schematically the structure of two actual associations.[4] The order of officials is given exactly as in the Statement of Accounts of each of them.

The Wrestling Academy.

Position.	Social Class.	
President	Upper-Upper	
Vice-	Upper-Upper	5
Presidents	Lower-Upper	1
	Intermediate	2
	Medial	2
Chairman	Lower-Upper	

The British Legion.

Position.	Social Class.	
President	Upper-Upper	
Vice-	Upper-Upper	1
Presidents	Intermediate	1
Chairman	Upper-Upper	

FORMAL AND INFORMAL ASSOCIATIONS

The Wrestling Academy.		The British Legion.	
Position.	Social Class.	Position.	Social Class.
Treasurer	Medial	Treasurer	Intermediate
Secretary	Medial	Secretary	Lower-Medial
		Assistant-Secretaries	Upper-Medial 2
			Medial 1
Committee	Upper-Medial 1	Committee	Medial 3
	Medial 9		Lower-Medial 8
	Lower-Medial 8		
Other members	Upper-Upper Nil	Other members	Upper-Upper Nil
	Lower-Upper Nil		Lower-Upper Nil
	Intermediate 1		Intermediate Nil
	Upper-Medial 6		Upper-Medial 2
	Medial and Lower-Medial 84		Medial and Lower-Medial 92
	Lower 2		Lower Nil

This pattern emerges in all the associations, although the details of course depend on the class range of each one.

The similarity between the structure of the class system and of the associations illustrates how firmly the former is established in Gosforth. Offices are given to people with high status and this enhances and confirms their status. Also, the giving of offices to people of high status enhances the prestige—and therefore the attraction—of offices. There were several people in Gosforth who reeled off a formidable list of appointments when asked to describe the part they played in village life, but who never in fact attended a single committee meeting while I was there. Furthermore, it follows that any new organization will be modelled on the class pattern if it is to flourish, and also that any vacancy on a committee or in an official appointment is limited in practice, if not in theory, to a small section of the population. One Upper-Upper informant remarked, 'I can't recall any movement in the village that ever had any success unless someone of the so-called higher class takes an interest.'

As a result, many of the associations tend to have the same officials and committee members. 'S', for example, is the Chairman of the Angling Club, of the Services Committee of the British Legion, and of the Further Education Committee. He is Vice-Chairman of the Parish Council and Vice-President of the Agricultural Society, the Wrestling Academy and the Dramatic Society. He is also a member of the committee of the Conservative and Unionist Association. Mr. 'W' is Chairman of the Dramatic Society and of the Evening Classes Students' Committee. He is Vice-President of the British Legion and of the Wrestling Academy. He is Secretary of the Further Education Committee, the School Outing Committee and of the Angling Club, and also Treasurer of the latter. He sits on the committee of the Agricultural Society and is a Parish Councillor and a Church Councillor.

Some women also take a much more active part in the associations than others. For example, Mrs. 'P' is Secretary of the Dramatic Society and a member of the Women's Institute Committee, the Agricultural Society Committee, the Conservative and Unionist Association Committee, the Public Hall Committee, the Playing Field Committee and the Further Education Committee.

When the Secretary of the Women's Institute resigned in the summer of 1951, her place was taken by a young lady of the Upper-Upper class who was one of the youngest members of that association. Now Gosforth is no different from other parts of England in its belief that the older and more experienced a person is, the more suitable that person will be to fill a position of responsibility. Despite this belief and also despite the fact that the proposed secretary had returned only recently to the parish after a prolonged absence, her election was not contested. Characteristically, this was the subject of much comment in the parish. One housewife, who was a member of the Committee of the Women's Institute, remarked, 'When I came back to Gosfer' the "W.I." was all married women. Everything was very cosy. Now all these young girls have come in with their new ideas and spoiled it. I don't like these lasses of school-leaving age getting all the jobs, it's not right.' A farmer's wife said, 'Older women are leaving t' W.I. because these young folks laiking (playing) about have made a proper mess of things. There's twenty folks have left already and there'll be another twenty likely if they carry on like this.'

Remarks like this were very common, but none offered an explanation for Miss 'A's election—a result of the divergence between the ideal conception of the association and the socially modified reality.[5]

One of the older parishioners, though offering no explanation for this particular election, remarked that 'it will be a gay good thing for t'W.I.' because the new Secretary's father was a wealthy landowner and very influential. Underlying this statement is the fact that a small minority are able to exert considerable influence on the affairs of the parish, since the same people sit on nearly all the committees of village organizations. Since they are mainly Upper-Upper class people this influence is naturally in accordance with Upper-Upper class standards. And since many of the matters that are dealt with by the various committees affect only the people in the lower classes, then the decisions that are made are highly coloured by the ideas which the upper class holds concerning what is best for other people. The Parish Council, for example, is responsible for the allocation of houses built by the Local Authority, but members of the upper class do not live in Council houses. The Playing Field Committee decides what use shall be made of the playing field (which was donated by an Upper-Upper Parish Councillor) although the upper class only uses its facilities on rare occasions. The Upper-Upper class, conditioned by a public school education to believe that physical recreation is very important in individual well-being, regards the provision of a playing field as almost essential. It has the means to provide one and the leisure to administer its use, and so the parish as a whole benefits.

One other association deserves mention here. This is the Trustees of the Gosforth Charities. The regulations of one of these Charities [6] provides that the yearly income shall be used for the 'benefit of the poor of the ancient parish of Gosforth generally, or of such deserving or necessitous persons resident therein, as the Trustees select for this purpose, and *in such a way as they consider most advantageous to the recipients, and most conducive to provident habits*' (italics mine).

For almost a hundred years the Trustees have met annually to allocate the money from these charities, although National Insurance has greatly reduced the need for it in the last few years. The Trustees are appointed every five years by the Parish Council. They are, with one exception, all members of the upper class. It is clear from the wording of the regulations that it is assumed that certain people are subordinate to others and that those in the superordinate position have the ability to decide what is appropriate behaviour on the part of the rest of the community. Grants are still made in 'deserving cases', and I could find no one who was critical of the Charities, and no case of anyone refusing a grant.

The influence of village organizations is not however confined to within the parish boundary. The Football Team plays matches all over West Cumberland, the Wrestling Academy entertains teams from as far away as Gilsland,[7] and the Women's Institute has speakers drawn from several strata of society and from all parts of the country. Also many of the organizations are local branches of national associations and send representatives to County or regional bodies which meet in places as far apart as Carlisle and London. The effect of this is to widen the social horizon of many of the inhabitants, who would otherwise travel no further than the nearest town and meet few people other than those living in the immediate neighbourhood. This assists considerably in the breaking down of parochial isolation and enlarges the individual's knowledge of the world, processes that are part of the contemporary major trend of reducing all differentiated local societies and their several ways of life to a nationally uniform whole.

One of the most flourishing associations in Gosforth is the Wrestling Academy. This was re-established in 1946 after a lapse of over twenty years, although out-door wrestling on informal lines had continued during the interim period. As a branch of the Cumberland and Westmorland Wrestling Association, the Gosforth Academy is run according to a written code of procedure and matches are played in much the same way as in other 'organized' sports. The Academy has classes for the training of would-be wrestlers, practice periods for those already proficient, and periodic matches during which the parish team competes against other Academies in the Association.

The skills of wrestling in the 'Cumberland and Westmorland style' are only very briefly described in print, and are transmitted from one generation of wrestlers to another by verbal instruction and practical demonstration.[8] It is a sport with a specialized vocabulary of its own, and accounts of wrestling matches in the local newspaper mean little to the layman. At present the parish team of wrestlers, like others in the Association, is composed almost entirely of farmers' sons and farm labourers, but keen interest in wrestling is shown by people of both sexes from all occupational and social levels. Proficiency in wrestling brings very high prestige in Gosforth, much more so than skill in such games as football and cricket. On numerous occasions people would single out a young man and say, 'Tha knows that lad likely. He's a gay fine "russler" is yon', and then proceed to describe his skill and triumphs in considerable detail.

The achievement of high prestige by winning at wrestling dates back at least to the end of the eighteenth century in Cumberland. At that time the winner of an important match almost invariably appeared in Church the following Sunday, wearing his 'belt', and the Sunday after at a neighbouring Church. It is said that matrimony often followed the winning of a prize.[9]

However, wrestling is much more than a mere contest, whether it be under the supervision of two umpires and a referee at an 'official' match, or just a chance encounter between two children at play. In *every* wrestling match there is a prescribed and unvarying sequence of actions which justifies the use of the term 'ritual' to describe it. Immediately before the match the two wrestlers stand on the mat, chatting to their friends among the spectators. When the signal to begin is given, the contestants become very solemn in demeanour and shake hands very formally. They then take up their initial positions in complete silence and with circular arm movements that are stereotyped and seemingly in no way necessary to the progress of the match.[10] When the two men are in position they remain completely immobile for a few seconds and then the match begins. If it lasts for one round only, the winning fall is followed by another formal hand-shake, which signifies the end of the match and the fact that the contestants may resume normal behaviour once again. If the match lasts for more than one round the contestants shake hands at the beginning of each round and at the end of the contest. When—and this occurs frequently—a round has to be recontested, the two wrestlers remain on the mat, sitting well apart from each other in complete silence, and apparently totally unaware of each other's existence or of the spectators if there are any.[11] The solemnity of the occasion is increased if a referee is present, since he remains completely silent throughout the match and gives any decisions by a series of signs with the hand.

The ritualistic element in local wrestling, perpetuated by oral instruction, is sufficiently marked to suggest that it has strong affinities with the ritual contests which are so prominent in the history of so many societies. In its stereotyped movements Gosforth wrestling is similar to the stylized wrestling of French West Africa, the contests held by the Jats and Pathans of India and the highly ritualized 'sumo' and 'ju-jitsu' of Japan. Until recently, wrestling bouts were a feature of the celebration of Mid-summer Day, New Year's Day, Whit Saturday and Easter Monday in Cumberland. Wrestling was also an accepted part of the festivities which followed a wedding, to which the people of the district were usually invited by the insertion of a notice in the local newspapers listing the wrestlers who would be taking part.[12] The celebration of the Jubilee of Queen Victoria in Gosforth was marked by a series of wrestling contests that lasted the whole day.[13] The relation of wrestling to holidays or to events of a religious or quasi-religious nature suggests that it began as a ritual like many other games.

Although wrestling is very popular in Gosforth at the present time—the Public Hall is very crowded indeed during most of the Academy matches—most of the parishioners say that it has declined a great deal during the last thirty years or so.[14] This is certainly true of another sport, that of cock-fighting. This sport, which retained its popularity in Northern England long after it had died out in the Midlands and South of England, was firmly established in the parish at the time of the outbreak of the second World War in 1939. Illegal since 1849, cock-fighting entailed a battle of wits with the local policeman, and numerous anecdotes are told in Gosforth of narrow escapes from arrest and of the many devices employed to ensure secrecy. In the late 'thirties 'mains' were held at farms situated less than a mile from the village, and cocks were brought to these from as far away as Millom and Wigton.

Since 1939 'cocking' has lost its character of an 'open secret' and superficially has died out completely. It still continues however, and probably has adherents only slightly less in number than in pre-war days. Gosforthians were exceptionally suspicious of any enquiries about this sport and the only result of months of circumspect questioning was the admission that cock-fighting was still carried on in Eskdale, or around Wigton or Millom—anywhere in fact except in the immediate neighbourhood. Only when the field-work was in the final stage were certain people prepared to discuss this sport in a local context, and then only in a highly indirect and impersonal manner. This is, indeed, a very good example of the type of information which may more readily be collected by a student studying his own area.

From these conversations it appears that cock-fighting rarely, if ever, takes place within the parish boundary at present, but does occur in adjoining and neighbouring parishes, and that men from Gosforth participate, either by preparing the animals for the actual contest, or as owners or interested spectators. Mains are held in barns or other outbuildings, the floors of which are covered with turf for the purpose, or, more commonly, in the open. The former practice of surrounding the 'pit'—a circular piece of grass six to a dozen yards in diameter—by a narrow trench has been discontinued now that the police are mechanized and their activities correspondingly wider in range. Like wrestling, 'cocking' has a specialized vocabulary, a characteristic that tends to intensify its secrecy. Methods of rearing and preparing the birds for contest are closely guarded secrets, even among participants. Such methods are nearly always family property, handed down from father to son by word of mouth. For example, one man in

Gosforth has inherited the recipe for 'cock-loaf', the food on which game-cocks are bred. Despite repeated assurances that I would not pass the information on, he flatly refused to divulge the ingredients of the recipe, but said I would be 'very surprised' if I were told, so presumably they are not normally associated with the feeding of animals.[15]

Usually several cocks are owned by one man, who 'walks' (distributes) them out to widely dispersed and remote farms. The birds are then put into pens and fed until the opening of the season, when they are collected in turn and taken at night to the mains, held in isolated spots during the hours of darkness. One man may own as many as twenty to thirty game-cocks, and to ensure that they are not all 'walked' so as to be ready at the same time, breeding sites are carefully chosen on the principle 'the nearer the sea, the earlier the birds'. Those cocks bred in the coastal lowland are then ready for contest first and those bred in the remote fells last. Farmers who 'walk a bird' are nearly always participants in the sport and are apparently well-paid for their services, since game-cocks are notoriously difficult to conceal. When the birds are adjudged ready for the main, they are prepared for contest by a 'clipper' who fits them with spurs. Spurs are made by a blacksmith and the leather straps used to fasten them on the cock by a shoemaker or saddler. A spur consists of a roughly semicircular band of steel about one-eighth of an inch in diameter, with a recess that fits over the trimmed natural spur of the cock, and with slots on either side for the retaining straps: from this band projects a steel prong one and a half to two inches in length and strongly resembling the curved surgical needles found in hospitals. The craftsmanship involved is of a very high order.

Cock-fighting is a seasonal sport lasting from Shrove Tuesday until Whitsun, and this may in part account for the great secrecy now surrounding this sport, since the police are thought to be especially watchful during this time. In sharp contrast to wrestling, success in 'cocking' does not result in the achievement of widely recognized high prestige, since participants are, of course, very careful to conceal their activities from the public. Its persistence in the face of numerous hostile influences cannot be explained entirely as due to the high prestige that can be gained within the limited participating group. It is pursued for its own sake, and its adherents described it as 'very humane', 'a bonny sport', 'finest sight in t'world tha knows is two birds ready to fight'. It was often said that many people would 'rather that than go to work'.

The numerous stories that were told of mains, and the preparations for them, invariably emphasized the interest of the narrators in the sport itself. But it was also clear that the flouting of external authority brought added satisfaction. Many mains were memorable not so much for the actual contest, but rather for the elaborate precautions or adventures that came before it. False rendezvous, particularly ingenious methods of siting a main, 'red herrings' in the form of driving cars at great speed through the night along winding lanes to innocent destinations—all these are prominent in informants' accounts. The discomfiture of a policeman who follows a false trail is remembered long after the contest that took place the same night.

Cock-fighting has persisted then largely because it is a traditional sport handed down within the family, deriving a high value from its mode of transmission. Its appeal is undoubtedly strengthened by the fact that it is done surreptitiously in defiance of laws to which the local community has never given its assent.[16]

Other blood sports popular in Gosforth are fox hunting and beagling. Both are organized on regional lines, the local associations being the Eskdale and Ennerdale Foxhounds and the West Cumberland Beagles. They are seasonal sports lasting from November to April and October to March respectively. Both sports are organized in the same way as elsewhere in England, for example each 'pack' has a Master, a Huntsman and 'whippers in', but unlike fox hunting in the Midlands, in Cumberland the hounds are followed on foot. The Master of the Beagles lives in Gosforth and a puppy show is held in the parish every September. Like cock-fighting, these two sports are believed by adherents to be 'humane' and were described in such terms as 'one of the least cruel and best sports there is'. One farmer's wife said of her husband 'He would not shoot a fox, even if it was killing all me hens', a statement that epitomizes the attitude of followers of these sports. Generally, however, beagling and fox-hunting are not very popular in Gosforth, and most people are either apathetic or, more commonly, very hostile towards them. The consensus of opinion is represented by the blacksmith, who has repeatedly refused requests to make a 'click-hook', a steel instrument very similar to a fisherman's gaff, which is used to drag out a fox that has gone to earth.

Other sports which are organized on a regional basis and which have a varying number of followers in the parish are hound-trailing, both types of Rugby, Association football and cricket. These are of interest to people of both sexes and many travel twenty miles or more at frequent intervals to watch their favourite sport. Discussion of the merits of a particular team, individual player, or some other topic connected with these sports form a large part of casual conversation in Gosforth, and the 'Sports Page' of the local newspaper is very widely and carefully read.

In addition, many of the inhabitants spend part of their time in local public houses. Thirty-two per cent of the male population between the ages of twenty and eighty visited public houses at fairly regular intervals: women went only at rare intervals, for example at Christmas.[17] It is true that women are seen in the 'pubs' fairly often, particularly on Friday night—when there is normally a dance in the Public Hall, but they do not live in Gosforth. It was very common to hear such remarks as 'Gosfer' isn't like Barrow or them places, tha knows. I've seen a man and wife gangin in regular for a drink down there, but there's nowt like that here. Yance ower, and not long since either, it were a terrible thing for a lass to go into t'pub or smoke in t'street; aye man, folk thowt it were a sin tha went straight till Hell for. Things is different now likely, but most folk don't like lasses in pubs, and they don't go.' At Christmas, or on other festive occasions, women living in the parish may visit public houses without causing much comment. Nevertheless, almost all the housewives questioned on this subject said they went outside the parish if they ever contemplated such a visit.

(This does not mean that 'drinking' is an exclusively male pastime. Many households, especially those outside the village, buy crates of beer for domestic consumption and the housewife often drinks some of this herself. Women therefore avoid public houses for 'social' rather than 'moral' reasons.)

There are five public houses in the parish, but one of these, the Boonwood Hotel, is a roadside inn that caters mainly for travellers and attracts very few local people, since it is located some distance away from the village, at the top of a long and formidably steep hill. The remaining four, the Wheatsheaf, the Lion and Lamb, the Globe Hotel and the Horse and Groom are all in the village, and each is locally thought to have characteristics of its own. The Wheatsheaf is a place favoured by the 'old standards' and has a reputation for fine singing; it is also the 'young lads' pub' (see Fig. 8). The Lion and Lamb is a 'place for a quiet drink' and is 'as clean as steel'. No games or singing are allowed there, and this is known as 't'old folks' pub'. At the Globe, darts, cards and dominoes are played every night, the atmosphere is described as 'free and easy', and this hotel attracts most of the strangers and visitors to the parish. At the Horse and Groom, or 'Kellbank' as it is invariably known, there is no singing and no games are played. It has the reputation of being the 'farmers' pub' and shares with the Wheatsheaf the distinction of being a favourite among the 'old standards'.[18]

Regular visitors to these public houses may be regarded as members of informal associations based on similarity of age and interests, and these associations exhibit considerable internal cohesion. The Wheatsheaf is patronized by young adults and bachelors in the main, the Globe by young and middle-aged married men, 'Kellbank' entirely by married men, predominantly of middle age, and the Lion and Lamb by the older men. In this respect each public house is the centre of an informal association which is also an age-group, and membership of which is influenced to some degree by marital status. As in the age-groups of other societies, the individual progresses from one group to the rest as he grows older, the exact nature of the progression depending on whether or not he marries. The young bachelor in Gosforth, if he wishes to become a 'regular' at a public house, will invariably go to the Wheatsheaf. If he remain a bachelor he will

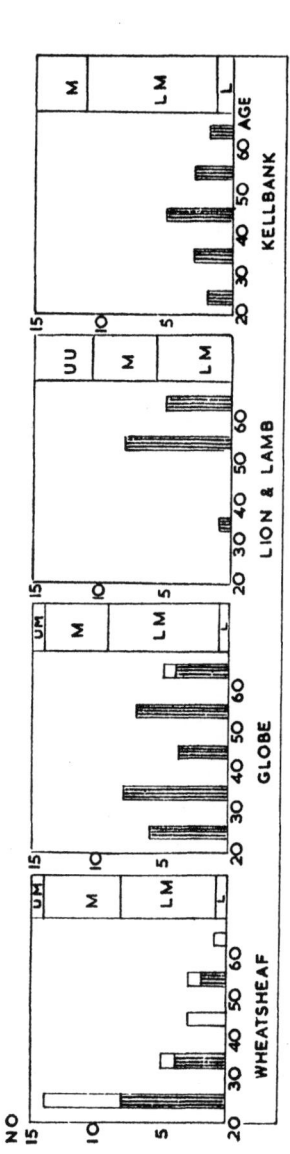

FIG. 8.—AGE, MARITAL STATUS AND SOCIAL CLASS OF PERSONS ATTENDING PUBLIC HOUSES.

stay in this group until he is too old to attend any more. If he should marry then he will either join the young married men in the Globe or Kellbank—which, will depend on whether or not he works on a farm—or remain, at least for a time, with the friends he has made in the Wheatsheaf.

This simple progression is to some extent complicated by factors of interest and social class. As we have seen, a change in status from bachelor to married man implies a choice between the Globe and Kellbank. The latter is very much a 'country pub' and it is not only a place 'where tha can buy a stitch o' taties or a cow any night o' t'week', but also a stronghold of the 'old standards'. Correspondingly, the Globe is attractive to those people who are 'modern' in outlook, a fact reflected in the number of strangers to be seen there every night. The Lion and Lamb is the centre of an informal group based on age and social class. Although its members are much older on the average than are the members of the other three groups, only rarely does anyone 'progress' from either of the other three to this 'old folks' pub'. This is because its 'atmosphere' is determined by the presence of Upper-Upper class men and of others who stand high in the Medial class, for example the Bank Manager, and therefore it does not attract people from the other social classes.

Attendance at public houses has declined greatly in recent years. Fig. 8 shows *total* attendance only and conceals the fact that Kellbank is often completely empty during week-nights and that only the Globe is well patronized throughout the week, a distinction it owes largely to 'casual trade' from outside the parish. There was a consensus of opinion that attendance at public houses and drunkenness were very much more prevalent twenty years ago than they are to-day. Formerly it was not uncommon for men to spend a period of days in a public house, and in this connection we may note that in 1857 there were nine inns in Gosforth, a figure that remained constant for thirty years.[19] In the days when a public house stood opposite the Church, it was the practice for male church-goers to walk directly from the service into the inn, a custom that so annoyed the Rector of that time that he bought it and had it demolished.[20]

The decline in the attendance at public houses is thought in the parish to have resulted from the great increase in the price of beer and spirits, and from an adverse change of 'atmosphere' which was said to be the fault of the publican. It is probable however that this change is related to the national decline in the popularity of excessive drinking,[21] and to the spread of urban standards which delimit hours of work and leisure with far greater precision than was typical of the local way of life forty or fifty years ago. Nowadays to sit in a public house for a day or more at will is likely to entail far greater material loss than it did in the 'good old days'.

CHAPTER VII

NEIGHBOURS

THE influence of the class system and of kinship upon the life of the people of Gosforth has already been discussed. Equally important as a basic factor in the social structure is physical proximity. Like blood relationship, proximity of residence is a pre-requisite but not a determinant of the degree of social intercourse. If it were a determinant, Whitehaven, with its closely packed rows of houses, would possess a much more developed and highly interwoven community life than Gosforth, whereas in fact the reverse is the case.

That Gosforth is in many ways an 'intermediate' parish has already been noted, and this intermediate position is also characteristic of its settlement pattern. With many dispersed dwellings and a large village, Gosforth falls midway between the upland parish with its one small hamlet and numerous scattered farms, and the industrial parish of the coastal coalfield, where the bulk of the population is concentrated into small towns, with few scattered farms and cottages. Although the parish consists of a single community, the pattern of social relationships which obtains in the village is different in many respects from that of the isolated farmsteads. For this reason the two sections of the community will be discussed separately.

The village consists of rows of houses situated a short distance from each other with occasional detached dwellings in between. As one progresses from the Square towards the blacksmith's shop in Wellington the distance between the rows increases, culminating eventually in a group of detached houses scattered within a short distance of each other. This change has some influence on social life inasmuch as in Wellington the grouping of 'neighbours', that is of people who associate more with each other in matters of everyday life than they do with other people, tends to be more compact geographically than it does in the remainder of the village. If each household were represented by a dot on the map of the parish, and the homes of neighbours joined, then Wellington would appear as a number of separate patches, each composed of several dots, and connected by a few links between them. That part of the village around the Square would appear as a haphazard patchwork of single dots and small groups of two or three, joined by numerous links criss-crossing in all directions. More important is the inordinate length of the village in comparison with its width. People tend to find their neighbours from among those around them, so that taken as a whole, the village is made up of a series of interconnected groups, with an occasional link between widely separated households—which may be the result of a childhood friendship or an interest closely shared.

The exact determination of a person's neighbours is extremely difficult as a rule, because neighbourliness is not easily defined. For example, neighbours borrow and lend things amongst themselves, varying from a spoonful of sugar to a car or a suit of clothes. However, the borrowing and lending of an article is no index of neighbourly feelings *per se*. Much depends on the nature of the article, because there are some things that one may borrow from almost anybody. A housewife may borrow a pint of milk from the woman next door without cultivating her friendship—indeed she may well consider her a most undesirable person to have as a neighbour. Similarly, people who own equipment which is scarce in the district or who are distinguished by unusual skills are visited by many who would otherwise never enter the house. In this category are the village schoolmaster, who is in constant demand for help in the completion of forms and documents too difficult for the average villager, the blacksmith who lends assorted pieces of equipment to almost everyone who asks, and the village housewife who possesses a secret cure for ear-ache.

'Good turns' among neighbours who are also close friends take so many forms that only a few can be mentioned here. These range from taking care of a young baby while its parents visit friends, or helping an aged widower to tend his garden, to assisting in the care of the sick or distributing the evening newspapers after the shop has closed. In contrast to many other societies, help of this kind does not place the recipient under a rigid obligation to return the favour.[1] The schoolmaster and the blacksmith lend far more of their services than they can ever hope to be repaid. Nevertheless there is a somewhat indefinite code of conduct which demands that a favour be repaid in some way or other. People who had failed to comply with this code were very heavily criticized, and in the rare instances of the flagrant abuse of the kindness of others the offender suffered a considerable loss of prestige. For example, the same disparaging tale about a villager who had failed to repay an obligation to two farmers was heard between twenty-five to thirty times during the field-work, usually accompanied by such remarks as, 'Tha doesn't want going till his spot (i.e. his house), maister, he's a gay bad one.'

The pervasiveness of neighbourliness is best illustrated in crisis situations. One woman, for example, said that ordinarily very few neighbours visited her, but that when her husband fell ill, 'half the village' called with offers of help and gifts of food and books—'Folks who hardly ever speak to me went out of their way to be good.' Another told the story of a woman living nearby, whose constant borrowing of small quantities of food precipitated a quarrel which severed all contact between them. She continued, 'When our lad got very poorly she came into t'kitchen with tears all down her face, she was that upset, and all the time he was in t'hospital she came to have a crack with me to cheer me up, and she brought eggs and suchlike for him.' When the boy recovered, the relationship between the two women reverted to something akin to an armed truce.

A death in the village brings similar manifestations of neighbourly feelings. In addition to the host of relatives who are normally present, representatives of households scattered throughout the length of the village attend the funeral, while the wives of neighbours are busy in the Public Hall or one of the local hotels preparing food for the mourners. The failure of a neighbour to attend a funeral for an insufficient reason, or of a household to send a wreath of flowers, is always the subject of much comment, for the obligation which results from the death of a neighbour is felt to be greater than any other. Further evidence of the strength of neighbourly emotions, and the way in which neighbour groups overlap is also evident at baptisms and marriages, and at such events as the welcoming of a villager from abroad after a long absence.

Neighbour groups in the village resemble groups based on blood relationships in that they function as a control over personal behaviour. The villager knows full well that to offend Mrs. X will result in what may be called a 'chain reaction' among her neighbours, who will be much less affable for some time to come. The neighbour group is, however, much less definite in extent, and the emotional bonds which unite it are weaker than those of the kin group, and the intensity of the reaction is correspondingly less. The kin group is capable of united action in times of crisis, the neighbour group is not.

Although the villager regards only a minority of families as his neighbours, he is closely linked by ties of friendship and familiarity to most people in the village, and feels that he is at least to some degree responsible for the welfare of its inhabitants. This feeling was clearly expressed during the last war by the founding of a branch of the Red Cross and a Comforts Fund for men and women serving in the Armed Forces, both of which met with a general response which would surprise most town-dwellers. A more lasting expression of neighbourliness is the 'Old Folks' Treat', held in January every year, at which the older inhabitants are given a sumptuous meal, followed by dancing and entertainments.[2] Although care of the aged is regarded as the responsibility of the family or kin-group, this annual event expresses the community's concern about those who are least able to fend for themselves.

Neighbours usually enter each other's houses without knocking, more often than not through the back door leading into the kitchen. This door is usually open during the day and seldom locked at night, an unconscious expression of trust in the other members of the community. The younger children of neighbours wander in and out of each other's houses, often eating with several families in the course of a week. Patterns of co-operation are constantly being established and others are maintained from one generation to another. One woman, for example, collects meat for several families each week. Another brings whatever small articles are required by the same families from Whitehaven every Thursday. A third member of this group escorts the smaller children to the village school. There is no conscious evaluation of these actions, and many similar arrangements were said to have been inherited from 'me father's time' or 'when me mother was alive'.

The relatively high degree of physical proximity in the village makes the neighbour relationship there more intensive than that characteristic of farms. A village housewife may visit half a dozen or more of her neighbours in one day and a correspondingly large number of people may call at her house. Where houses occur in rows, it is usual (but by no means invariable) for a household to count among its neighbours the families living in one or both of the adjoining houses. Where this is so neighbourliness tends to reach its greatest development. People see a great deal of each other throughout the day, and little happens in one house which is not known to the occupants of the others. During a visit to one of a row of houses, a housewife remarked that her son was late in returning from school. Within the next twenty minutes, four housewives from the adjoining houses came to enquire and comment on this unusual event.

Most of the dispersed dwellings which surround the village are farms, though there are a few cottages and houses not in this category.

The dispersal of habitations exercises some influence on neighbourliness between farmers. The numerous face-to-face contacts which are typical of village neighbours, for example, are obviously absent, but there is no simple correlation between the degree of physical proximity and the strength of the bonds which unite neighbours. Many of the more important aspects of neighbourliness, among them mutual aid in day-to-day activities and behaviour in crisis situations, are more highly developed among farmers than among villagers.

Most farmers borrow and lend equipment and machinery (see Fig. 9). The few farmers who do not need to borrow any equipment at all and who refuse to lend it to others, occupy

FIG. 9.

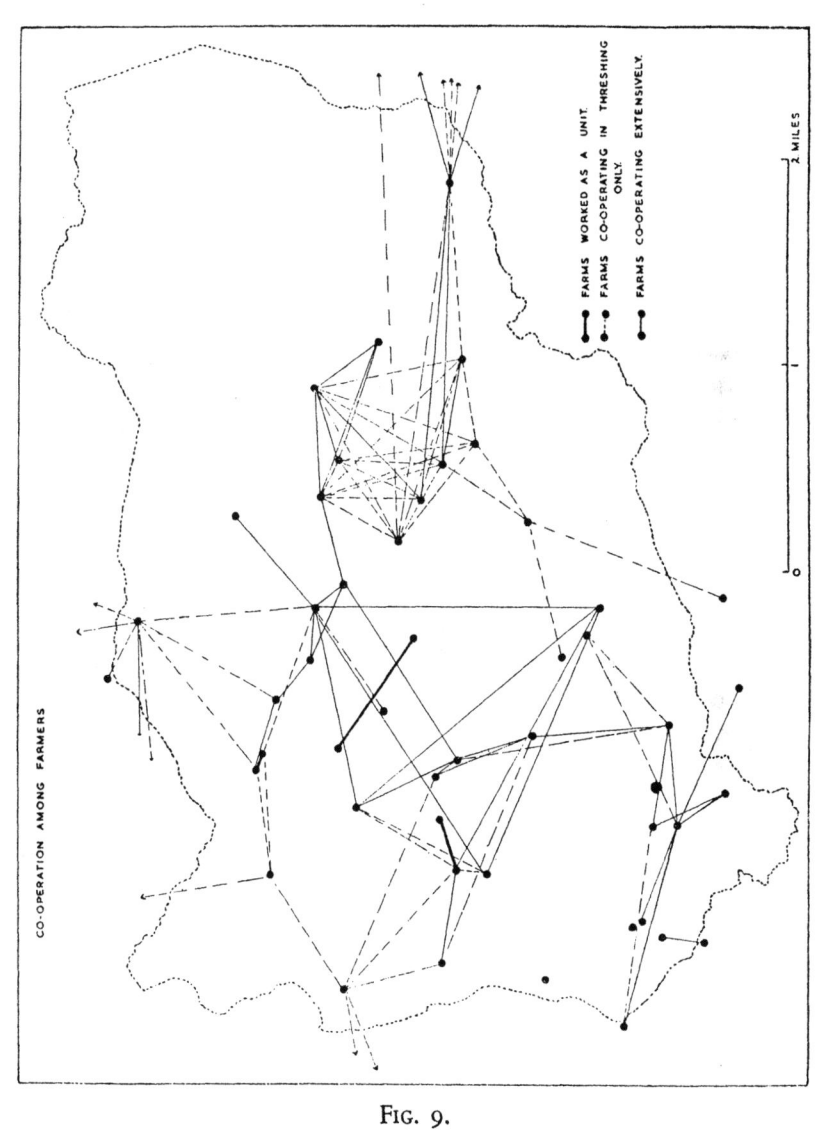

positions of low prestige, and are described variously as 'cunning laal joker', 'gay queer' and 'a poor mak o' farmer'. The refusal of these men to enter into friendly relations with others brings reprisals in many forms. They are criticized and derided for deficiences which are overlooked in others. Stories, many of them untrue, are told of their elementary mistakes in farm practice. They are accused of buying stock and machinery on hire purchase, of allowing their dykes to fall to ruin, or of allowing sheep in winterage to stray off their land—all of which are considered to be particularly offensive charges by farmers in Gosforth. If animals belonging to these farmers stray on to the roads there is no certainty that a passing farmer will place them safely in a nearby field, an action almost instinctive in normal circumstances. Retaliatory action of this kind, though often negative in character, is a threat sufficiently powerful to make several farmers lend machinery to others, often against their will. For example one farmer complained that about three weeks before I visited his farm he had more equipment out on loan than he had left on the holding. He said of his 'neighbours' that 'They comes first to borrow a swatcher (bill-hook), then they wants a lend o' tractor for half an hour; then it's a manure drill. I doubt next they'll be asking me to go ower to their spot because their animals wants milked.'[3]

Among the majority of farmers, however, borrowing and lending machinery was normal, and an excuse for a friendly chat on a variety of subjects. A farmer wishing to borrow a turnip drill will discuss almost anything except turnip drills for half an hour or so before mentioning the purpose of his visit. This is particularly the case when a journey outside the bounds of the normal co-operative group is necessary, and a farmer making a trip of this kind usually finds his family awaiting his return for news of events in the part of the parish he has visited. Some farmers stated that to borrow a neighbour's equipment in his absence was not uncommon, and that 'as long as tha knows he won't be wanting it' this would not cause offence. This practice was justified by saying that one's neighbours would know exactly who had taken the piece of equipment, and that they could be sure it would be returned in good condition.

Returning articles borrowed is not, however, always as prompt as this last point would suggest. The ethic of borrowing varies considerably with the thing borrowed. Major equipment is normally returned as soon as the need for it is ended, and if its use is required for more than one day it is considered polite to ask permission to retain it overnight, unless this has been previously arranged. Horses are only rarely borrowed, and on the few occasions when this occurred during the field-work one of the owner's sons accompanied it and brought it back at night. In this case the borrower is under a rigid obligation to feed the horse and the farmer's son, a custom that applies to all occasions when help takes the form of services by individuals. Tractors are borrowed more frequently than horses, and usually in this event also its owner sends someone to drive it. Smaller articles of farm equipment, such as scythes, harness, wheel-barrows, etc. are not usually returned quickly, unless the owner so specifies. Often they may be kept for weeks or even months, and more often than not they are ultimately collected by the owner, who makes use of the occasion to talk over recent happenings in the parish.

As in the village, there is no principle of exact repayment involved in mutual aid. Many of the more prosperous farmers lend equipment continuously and borrow nothing in return. In each neighbour group there is usually sufficient equipment scattered among the farms to meet all the normal requirements of the farming year. For this reason a farmer hesitates before buying a particular piece of machinery he knows to be available on a neighbouring holding, although in recent years the fact that capital expenditure in purchasing equipment reduces Income Tax has encouraged many farmers to buy very large quantities of farm machinery.

A more striking aspect of co-operation among farmer neighbours is the 'boon day'. 'Boons' or 'benes' are a custom of considerable antiquity in England which have persisted to a greater degree in the North than elsewhere.[4] Until about 1939, when the introduction of the tractor increased the amount of work that could be done by one man, 'boon ploughings' were always held in the lowlands when farms were taken over by new tenants. A farmer described such an event in these terms: 'T'old tenant who would be leaving on twenty-fifth o' March wouldn't bother to plough his land and the new man would be left to do it. He wouldn't have ower much time and ivverybody with a horse would go along and get it done in a day. If he was an offcomer then t'farmer on t'next spot would go around ivverybody telling them about it; sometimes he would tak the offcomer with him. All t'farmers came whether they liked it or not. Ivverybody who came was given a piece to plough, and they was fed through the day. I've seen as many as fifty-six pair o' horses at yan spot on yan day.'

Another important boon day was 'sheep clippin'. Before the reduction in the flocks of 'heaf-gangin' sheep during the depression years, 'clippin day' was an annual event of great importance on several farms, and gatherings of eighty or a hundred people were not unknown. To a lesser extent boon days were also held for sheep dipping and during the two harvests.

Boon ploughings have died out almost completely in recent years, and survive only on a few of the more remote 'horse' farms. When a change of tenancy occurs nowadays, the former tenant's neighbours usually call with offers of assistance during the first day or so, and normally this results in the newcomer inheriting his predecessor's position in the neighbour group. However, since there is very frequently at least one tractor in the group, ploughing no longer requires a large gathering of farmers. If there is no tractor the new tenant usually employs a contractor to do the ploughing for him. Only one farmer still holds a clipping day, and this, as we have noted earlier, is largely a family affair. The other three farms which have flocks of fell sheep co-operate amongst themselves for shearing, spreading the work over several days. One result of this decline in the popularity of the clipping day is that sheep shearing is rapidly becoming a forgotten art in Gosforth.[5] The harvests too are no longer occasions for boon days, and the 'kurn suppers' or 'harvest homes' which marked their end, and which farmers in the district still look back on as some of the most enjoyable events of the farming year, vanished soon after the outbreak of the last war.[6]

The one remaining boon day is threshing day. Several farmers have installed threshing machines, but on the majority of holdings the arrival of the tractor and steam thresher marks the beginning of one of the busiest days in the yearly round of work.[7] Arrangements are usually made with the contractor some weeks in advance and the farmer calls on his relatives and neighbours, including several with whom he does not co-operate except for threshing, to inform them of the date and to ask them to 'help out'. It is considered most inappropriate for anyone but the occupier himself to make this round of calls, although the farmers invited to the threshing may send sons or labourers instead of attending themselves without incurring any displeasure. Generally however, it is the farmer himself who attends the threshing and he is glad of the opportunity to meet a large number of his friends in an atmosphere of boisterous good will. The work is accompanied by good-natured chaffing and endless stories, most of which would be thought indecent or at least vulgar in polite society. In the farm kitchen the occupier's wife, assisted by her daughters and possibly one or two friends, is busy preparing food for the 'men folk'. Conspicuous consumption of food was characteristic of all boon days in the past, and threshing days are no exception.[8] The amount and quality of the food is extremely important as a measure of the farmer's good name. With so many neighbours present no expense must be spared. The best ham has been stored away for this event and it is not unusual for farmers' wives to remark after the threshing day that 'We have to scrat along as best we can for many a week'. The best china and cutlery are used and tea or coffee is available throughout the day.[9]

The number of neighbours present at a threshing varies from fifteen to twenty-five and the same people tend to come every year. When a change of tenancy occurs, the new occupier is expected to fill his predecessor's place, and a farmer sees nothing unusual in inviting a stranger from a farm a mile away, even though he may not call on people much nearer his home whom he has known all his life. A characteristic explanation of this practice was that of the farmer who said, 'Folks have been coming to our threshings from that spot yonder all me life and in me father's time afore me, and I'll not be starting to change it now.'

This custom is so firmly established that nearly all the farmers who have installed threshing machines continue to attend their neighbours' threshings, as their fathers did before them. A man from another district who had recently bought a farm in the parish mentioned his surprise when he found that seven of the farmers who attended his threshing day had threshing machines of their own, and did not need the help of neighbours on their own farms.

Since the number of farmers co-operating varies with the task in hand from twenty or more during threshing to two or three during the hay or corn harvests, it will be apparent that the farmer's concept of a neighbour is an elastic one. However, most farmers describe as their neighbours those people with whom they co-operate from day to day. And their relationship with them—as distinct from those people with whom contact is largely confined to threshing days and sporadic visits—is very similar to that typical of the neighbour group in the village.

Unlike the women of the village, however, a farmer's wife and daughters tend to have little social intercourse with the women folk of neighbouring farms. The farmer and his sons visit their neighbours frequently, walking into the kitchen without knocking when the day's work is over, or whenever they happen to be near. His wife and daughters call on their friends at neighbouring farms only when they have a special reason for doing so, and often a farmer's wife will leave her home no more than once a week—perhaps to go to Whitehaven on market day, or for a periodic visit to relatives. A farmer's wife who had been living in the parish for eight months said that she had never seen the wives of two farmers who lived in farmsteads less than a quarter of a mile away, while her husband was on very friendly terms with both of them.[10] This difference between the sexes seems to result largely from the inferior status of women in many farm families. The patriarchal organization found on so many farms permits the farmer and his sons to leave home every night without question: the farmer's wife, who is too busy for social calls during the greater part of the day, would not think of asking her husband to take care of the house and the younger children while she went out in the evening, except in such circumstances as a neighbour's illness.[11]

NEIGHBOURS

Loyalty to one's neighbours is emphasized during crisis situations on farms no less than in the village, and is expressed very clearly at farmers' funerals. These are often more impressive than most of the funerals in the village, since the farmer's contacts extend over a much wider area than those of the average villager. The funeral of one farmer in 1950 was attended by friends from farms thirty miles away from Gosforth. A farmer will go to a great deal of trouble to help a neighbour who is ill, and I heard numerous accounts of such good deeds. For example, when the tenant of the holding which carries the largest flock of sheep in the parish fell ill, a farmer living nearly ten miles away called with an offer to bring the sheep down from the fells, one of the most trying tasks of the farming year. Other farmers 'were in t'yard every five minutes to ask if anything wanted doing'. The invalid's wife, who has lived in the parish all of her thirty-seven years, remarked (significantly enough) that this farmer was a complete stranger to her.

This feeling of neighbourliness, although it extends far beyond the confines of the farmer's neighbour group, is not universal. During the field-work it was impossible to tell from one day to another what kind of reception I was likely to receive at different farms. At many the hospitality was so lavish as to be almost embarrassing. At others, situated possibly several miles from the village (the only place where a meal could be obtained) the conversation would be terminated on some pretext or other so that the family might eat alone. It was my impression that shyness, rather than hostility or impoliteness, caused many farmers to send strangers away without offering even a cup of tea. Certainly at some farms where the farmer and his wife were most ready to answer questions, I felt that they were most anxious to ask me to join them at dinner, but were afraid to do so in case the standard of the meal should seem to me to be inferior.

Neighbourliness and a strong distrust of strangers coexist in Gosforth and probably the conflict between them has much to do with the reception a stranger receives. At some houses this distrust was very obvious, and it is significant that several people who had been openly hostile when first interviewed apologized very profusely and became extremely hospitable when they discovered that their friends and neighbours had accepted my explanation for visiting them and 'asking all them damn questions'.

One of the first lessons learnt during the field-work was that one should never offer money in return for, say, the dozen eggs which were often a part of the farewells that ended an interview. Clearly such an offer was only excusable because of an ignorance of local custom. From someone living in the district it would be almost an unpardonable insult. However, when it was discovered that the photographing of farm-houses and the recording of pedigrees from the Parish Registers were part of the investigation, it became common for farmers to make it clear that a photograph or pedigree would be very acceptable and that this was appropriate repayment for the dozen eggs. Since the periphrasis typical of much of rural Wales and Ireland is virtually absent from Gosforth, these requests were usually put in such terms as 'If tha's got a spare photo, maister, it would be very welcome, and here's *another* bit o' sausage for breakfast.' On another occasion the printing of a sign to show that potatoes were for sale was repaid a few days later by a large paper bag full of them. These examples are characteristic of all the exchanges that take place between neighbours. Payment in money for the loan of a piece of farm equipment or the assistance of a farmer's son for a day is completely alien to the district. When a neighbour's services cannot be repaid by some form of assistance, a basket of eggs, a bag of meal, or a piece of ham may be sent a few days later. More often, however, the obligation is thought of as existing until the chance for repayment by some form of help on the farmstead occurs in the future.

The dispersal of farms results in a lack of the sense of unity which is characteristic of the village, but the farmer's friendships are by no means limited to his own neighbour group and the contacts made annually at threshing days. The meeting of farmers living some distance away from each other is marked by a discussion of the events which have happened in the locality since they last met, and often ends by one inviting the other to his home for a 'crack'. Moreover the introduction of the motor car in recent years has greatly extended the range and frequency of the farmer's social contacts. In particular the period from late September until about the end of November, when the pace of agricultural activity is relatively slow, is the most popular time for visits beyond the immediate locality of the farm. This coincides with the holding of most of the annual Agricultural Shows in West Cumberland, which function (*inter alia*) as a meeting place for all the farmers in the area.

The attachments formed between the farms of a neighbour group, and to a lesser extent with other farms beyond its limits, enable the individual farm family to live in an atmosphere of communal life which is only slightly less developed than that characteristic of the village. This reduces the isolation imposed by the physical environment to a minimum. Furthermore, the popularity of the motor car among farmers and of the motor cycle among their sons suggests that farming families are no longer content to live a restricted social life. This extension of the social horizon also has its effect on the female members of the farm family, who are gradually extending their friendships beyond the traditional limits of the kin group.

Farmers' daughters were frequently seen at dances and wrestling matches, and in recent years there has been an increase in attendance of farmers' wives, especially the younger ones, at village whist-drives and the Women's Institute. The fact that farmers' wives and daughters meet many townspeople at these village gatherings has made them somewhat dissatisfied with their traditional roles and introduced elements of conflict into the patriarchally organized farm family.

Many of the older farmers criticized this 'gadding about' at great length. They drew very unfavourable comparisons between the modern farmer's daughter 'who thinks about nowt except dances and Young Farmers' Meetings and such like' and the daughters of farmers 'in t'old days', who were apparently models of obedience and who 'would mak a good lass for any man'.

The concensus of opinion in the parish is that neighbourliness has declined considerably in recent years. Such remarks as the following were very frequent indeed: 'Gosfer' is full o' offcomers now. Yance ower ivverybody was friendly wid ivverybody else in t'parish, and tha couldn't walk from t'Church to t'Square without have a crack wid a whole lock o' folks on t' road. Now tha can walk up and down t'village all day without speaking to any folk at all.' If informants are to be believed, the village in particular was formerly characterized by a very high development of neighbourliness. How much truth there is in this, and how much may be attributed to the well-known habit of representing the past as a Golden Age in comparison with the present, is difficult to judge. It is however true that Gosforth fifty years ago was a much more homogeneous community than it is to-day, and social practices based on neighbourliness, such as 'kurn suppers', 'Old Folks' Treats', 'Tatie Pot Suppers', were much more important than they are at present. Furthermore, accounts of marriages, funerals, etc. suggest that neighbours were much more closely linked than they are nowadays, and from the total evidence it seems reasonable to suppose that neighbourliness has in fact declined a great deal in the past twenty to thirty years.

This decline may be attributed to the influx of 'offcomers', each with a different social background, the increasing acceptance of urban culture, which places a premium on individual mobility and implies a more atomistic conception of society, and to a lesser degree to the introduction of a pseudo-materialistic philosophy, by which actions are judged by ultimate profit. Many of the villagers and some of the farmers tend more and more to think of money as synonymous with happiness, an attitude severely criticized by the older inhabitants. One farmer summed this up by remarking of a neighbour, 'The man that farmed in that spot yonder in t'old days was a queer laal customer, but he was a good neighbour. He used to chunter (grumble) away when tha asked him for summat, but he always gave it in t'end, and he wouldn't have done that unless he thowt it was right likely. This feller there now would stop t'birds flying ower his spot if he could, because they don't pay rent ivvery Martinmas. Tha can't ivver borrow a swatcher from that spot now without him running ower ivvery five minutes to ask for the damn thing back. I doubt he'll be hiring out his tackle by t'hour afore long.'

CHAPTER VIII

COMMUNITY

THE dichotomy of village and dispersed farms is a relatively recent feature of the social life of the parish. There was no village in the old days.

Little is known in detail of the location of dwellings in medieval Gosforth. Most of the places mentioned in early documents cannot be identified to-day, and the few names that survive refer mostly to natural features where no dwelling is known to have existed. Fortunately, however, such documents as the Chartulary of St. Bees contain extremely detailed descriptions of the location of places relative to each other, and include many references to dwellings, so that it is possible to make some generalizations concerning the settlement pattern in Gosforth in medieval times (see Appendix VIII, Part I).

It is, for example, fairly certain that most of the dwellings were scattered, and although small hamlets may well have existed,[1] there is no evidence at all of a large nucleated settlement around the church, similar to those typical of the 'champion' country. Nearly all the dwelling sites which can be identified have remained inhabited up to the present day, while place-names suggest that other places mentioned in medieval documents were in fact inhabited long before the date of any existing records.[2]

Whatever uncertainty there may be about the settlement pattern of the parish in the thirteenth and fourteenth centuries, there is no doubt that the dispersed habitat prevailed when the Parish Registers began in the latter half of the sixteenth century. In particular, the two plague years 1596–97, when over 150 people were buried, furnish a very valuable record of the location of dwellings. The distribution of place-names entered in the Registers from the date they begin until the first decade of the seventeenth century is given on a map (Fig. 10) which shows all the sites known to be inhabited at that time. This clearly illustrates the primacy of the isolated homestead and the comparatively weak development of nucleation. Several hamlets existed, for example at Sevenhoues, Pyel, Howesbarrowe and Benbank, but there is no significant concentration of houses in any one place.[3] The period from 1600 to 1800 was marked by an increase in the number of inhabited sites, and from a comparison of the maps of the parish in those two years (Figs. 10 and 11) it is clear that the dispersed habitat remained predominant. The village had, by the time of the later map, begun to assume its present proportions, but its growth was more than counter-balanced by the numerous isolated dwellings which had sprung up elsewhere. The number of hamlets remained more or less constant.[4]

From 1810 until well into the second half of the nineteenth century there was no significant change in the general pattern. Then from about 1870 until the end of the century there was considerable building in the village, while in the surrounding countryside, homes inhabited for centuries were allowed to fall into ruins. As a result, by 1900, for the first time in the history of the parish, the number of people living in the village exceeded that of those living in dispersed farms and cottages. The hamlet declined during this period until eventually Hall Senna was the only one remaining. The first half of this century has been characterized by a further growth of the village while the countryside has remained almost unchanged.

These changes in the settlement pattern are reflected in the history of the territorial and administrative units of the parish. Unfortunately this aspect of parish history is not very well documented and the small amount of evidence available is so conflicting that little can be said of the different subdivisions of the parish until comparatively recent times (see Appendix VIII, Part II).

The first mention of parochial officials in local documents occurs at the beginning of the seventeenth century. Churchwardens represented the inhabitants of the scattered dwellings of each township after 1600 and, in virtue of their close relationship to the incumbent, played an important part in the administrative life of the parish. During the period from about 1600 until roughly the end of the last century the township was the division of the

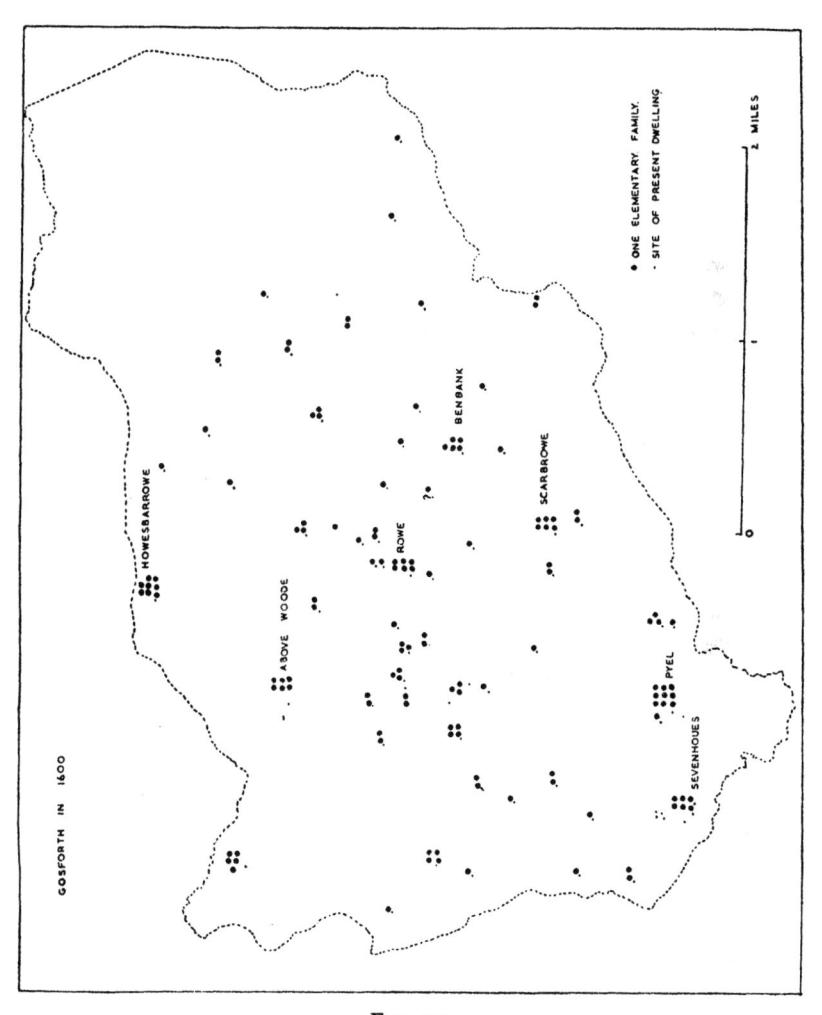

FIG. 10.

parish used in nearly all matters of civil and ecclesiastical government.

From the beginning of the seventeenth century until about the last two decades of the eighteenth century the township system in Gosforth implicitly recognized the predominance of the dispersed type of settlement. During this time the group of dwellings around the Church was included in Boonwood township (see Fig. 12). By 1780, however, what was to become the village had grown to sufficient importance to be considered worthy of a division of its own. In a document of that year we find the township of Gosforth first mentioned in addition to those already in existence. The formation of the new unit did not apparently affect the boundaries of the pre-existing townships. The growth of the village during the nineteenth century enhanced the importance of the new township and established it so firmly as a territorial division of the parish that it became the custom to appoint a churchwarden to represent it. In order to keep the total number of these officials the same, representatives from the much older divisions of Seascale and Boonwood were chosen in alternate years.[5]

The growth of the village did not result in a severe disruption of the countryside, with its isolated farmsteads and cottages, as a well integrated whole.[6] By 1860–70, the village was becoming increasingly important in size and population. The surrounding countryside, with its own tradesmen and craftsmen, seems to have remained largely independent of it. In the township of Boonwood, for example, there were two blacksmiths, two millers, two innkeepers, as hoemaker, and a dyer; in the other townships there were blacksmiths, basket-makers, tailors, and stone-masons living in widely separated localities. Many of these continued to live in the countryside within living memory, and only in the last twenty or thirty years have all craftsmen been concentrated in the village.

The social structure of the parish has adjusted itself gradually to the new conditions and there is now a very high degree of integration between 'Gosforth' and the remainder of the parish. Still, the recent ascendancy of the village in economic matters has

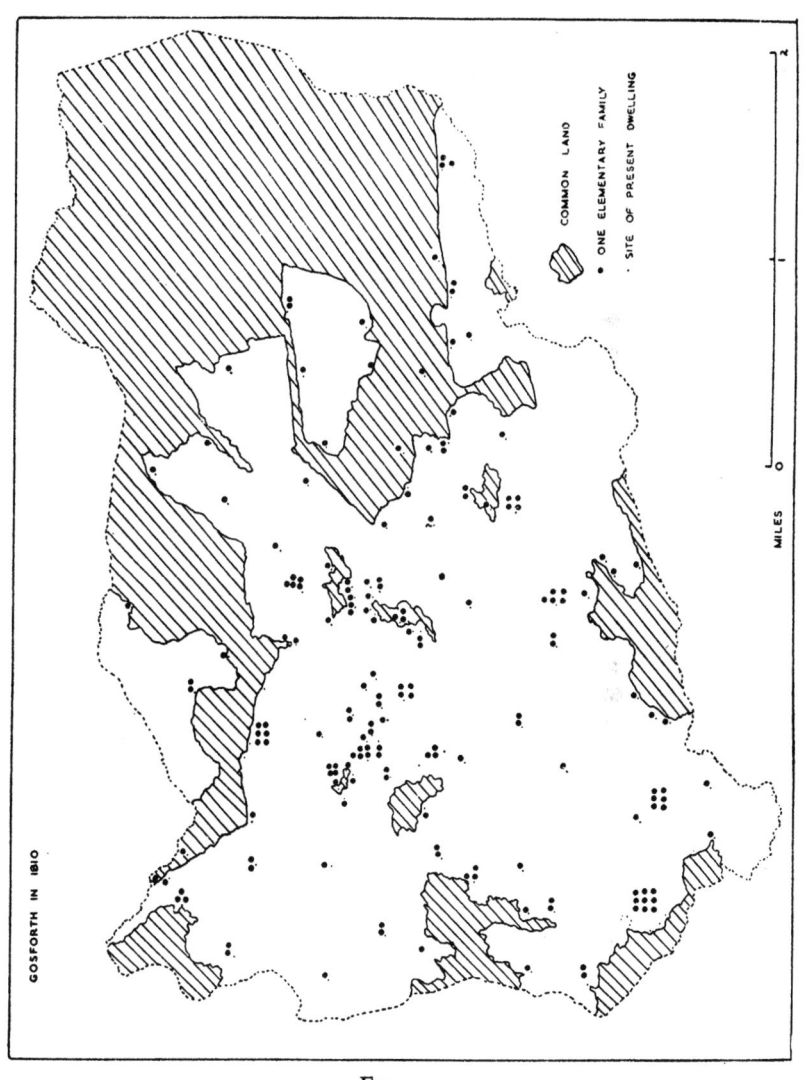

FIG. 11.

as yet had little effect on many of the old-established patterns of social relationships, although its influence will probably be increasingly felt as the proportion of villagers who were born on farms or in isolated cottages decreases. Important in this context is the fact that almost all the children in the parish now attend the village school, where emphasis tends to be laid on technological progress. Until about the middle of the last century there was an 'academy' in Boonwood, while for several decades after its establishment the village school seems to have had little influence on the attitude of the pupils towards urban culture.

The rapid rise of the village in size and influence after 1860 was accompanied by a decline in the part played by the townships in the life of the parish. By the end of the last century, the practice of electing churchwardens for each township had died out completely. Many of the present inhabitants of the parish were unaware that townships had ever existed.

The countryside, however, is not thought of as a completely homogeneous unit surrounding the village. Although there is a general distinction between 't'farmer' and 't'villager', a dichotomy also exists between upland and lowland farmers which is very apparent in their conversation. Those in the lowland think of the fell farmers as a group whose methods of farming are a form of esoteric lore which can only be learnt by being born and bred 'up on t'parks'. Numerous stories are told of their skill in handling Herdwick sheep which reflect this viewpoint. There is a general belief that to be a successful fell farmer one must be born with an 'eye for sheep', and it was common to hear tales of men blessed with this gift who could pick out one of their animals from hundreds of others at a glance. In addition, those from the lowland consider upland farmers as 'old-fashioned', 'secretive', and 'clannish'. There is a lowland saying which runs, 'When money goes up yon road (i.e. to the fells) it nivver comes down again.'

The hill farmers, on the other hand, criticize those 'in t'hollow' for their ignorance of sheep farming, and point out with considerable justification that a high degree of mechanization is impossible and unnecessary in the upland. The frequent disputes which

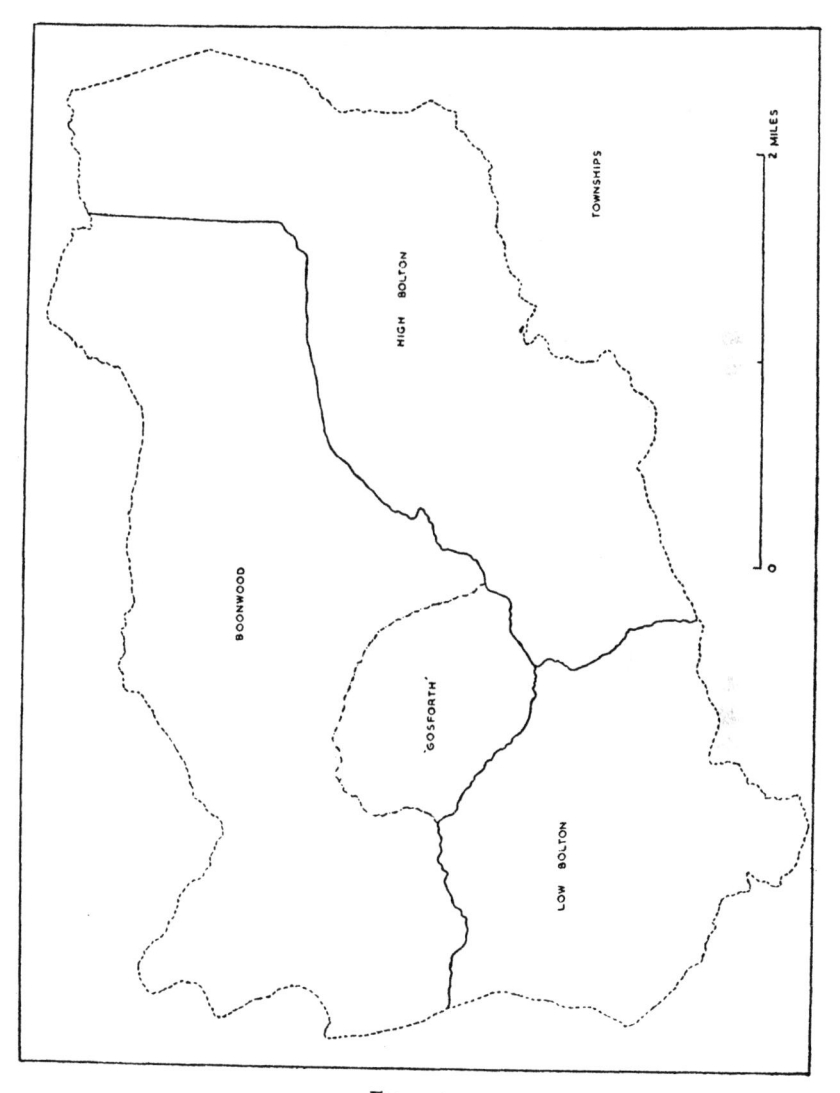

FIG. 12.

occur between lowland farmers over sheep in winterage which stray on to each other's land are used by the fell farmers to accuse the former of intolerance.[7] Again, the fact that farmers accepting sheep for agistment insist on knowing exactly how many animals there are conflicts with the upland belief that it is very unlucky to count the flock.[8] The lowland farmers' heavy expenditure on machinery is the basis for charges of undue extravagance and 'text-book farming', and their recent acquisition of motor cars results in accusations of laziness.[9]

This dichotomy, however, is in many ways a convention, used particularly when talking to strangers. The fell farmers, for example, admitted after I had visited them several times that the lowland farmers were justified in their concern over straying sheep because of the need to protect growing crops, which is largely absent on the fells. Alternatively many lowland farmers went so far as to describe those on the upland as much more hospitable than they were themselves. More important, the dividing line between upland and lowland is completely ignored in all aspects of mutual aid, and several neighbour-groups include both sheep farmers and dairy farmers.

Farmers, in fact, form a closely knit group, and the distinction between lowland and upland is no more important than the distinction between farmers and villagers. These divisions add interest and colour to local life. People try to score points at one another's expense, but they do not take their disapproval seriously. It is a kind of play which makes it easier for the different groups to get on with one another. Therefore, in spite of these divisions—if not indeed *because of them*—Gosforth is a social unit as well as an administrative unit.

The integration of the village and the farmsteads has been a gradual process characterized by uneventfulness rather than spectacular conflicts. The absence of litigation and of disputes or feuds between villager and farmer is itself an indication of this. As a positive factor may be cited the means by which facts and ideas are transmitted throughout the community. Before the village rose to its present position, items of local news were diffused through the parish by the peripatetic 'sewing women', tailors, etc., travelling from one house to another, and from mouth to mouth at formal and informal meetings.

The change in the settlement pattern and the centralization of economic and educational agencies in the village disrupted the system of transmitting information about local affairs only slightly because the network of neighbours and kindred remained essentially unaltered. Parochial matters are still passed on from neighbour to neighbour, brother to brother, and uncle to nephew, and the occupiers of out-of-the-way farmsteads are as well informed of recent events in the locality as the villagers living around the Square.

Innovations which accompanied the growth of the village were adapted to suit this traditional pattern. The concentration of the travelling tailors and sewing women in the village, along with the blacksmiths, shoemakers, masons, and other craftsmen formerly scattered throughout the parish, did not affect their role as agents for transmitting news. The smithy is known locally as 't'gossip shop' and in common with the shoemaker, the joiner, and all other tradesmen, the blacksmith performs the function of a 'clearing house' for parish gossip and distribution centre for messages between households situated far apart. Similarly the postmen, the newspaper woman and the milkman do not merely deliver the letters, papers, and milk. At each house they visit there is an interchange of pleasantries and items of local news. When an event of an unusual nature occurs a postman will take two and a half to three hours to complete a round that would occupy his counterpart in a large town thirty to forty-five minutes at most.

In the same way, village associations like the Women's Institute and the Wrestling Academy, which have to some extent replaced the informal meetings that once took place in scattered homesteads, are the vehicle for the interchange of views on subjects ranging from the sale of a house in the village to the price of pig-meal.

During the first half of the nineteenth century it was the custom in much of rural Cumberland for neighbours to congregate at each other's homes on different evenings, to pass the time in knitting, spinning, singing, vying with each other in the telling of 'tall' stories, etc.[10] Although these gatherings were informal they differed in many respects from those typical of farm neighbour groups to-day. The 'forthneet' of the last century moved from one house to another in approximate rotation, and seldom included less than half a dozen people. In present day Gosforth it is rare to find more than two farmers in a neighbour's house of an evening, and, as far as I have been able to determine, the sequence of such meetings is largely fortuitous. Moreover the 'forthneet' was essentially an interest group, and it is in this sense that it has been replaced by the village associations. Gatherings of neighbours at the present time are, of course, marked by conversation which reflects the interest of the speakers, but the man who is especially fond of, say, wrestling, football, joinery, or amateur dramatics meets kindred spirits more particularly at classes or matches held in the village.

Farmers and their families form a very small proportion of the membership of village associations, and tend to regard them with good natured contempt. The bonds uniting each farmer to the village are strong and lasting, but this does not prevent him from regarding the village associations with detachment and a certain degree of apathy.

The village of Gosforth is unusually large for this area of West Cumberland. The only other large village in the six surrounding parishes is the seaside resort of Seascale—and this, like Gosforth itself, is a product of the nineteenth century. Two of these parishes have tiny villages of twenty to thirty houses, and the only nucleated settlements in the other three are hamlets of six to twelve houses. The area generally has, therefore, clung to its traditional diffused social life which links up the scattered farms. Even in Gosforth the farmers tend to depend upon one another for fellowship, and this self-contained life of the countryside has impeded the development of the village as a social centre.

For its size Cumberland has comparatively few old-established towns, and the nearest of these to Gosforth, i.e. Egremont, is now the centre of a declining iron ore mining area, and is only rarely visited by people from the parish. Urban centres have few attractions for the countryfolk, and apart from a small number who go to Whitehaven once a week on market day, visits to towns are confined to 'special occasions'.[11]

Earlier in this chapter a brief reference was made to the incumbent of the parish. The discussion of the religious life in the parish is left to a later chapter, but some mention must be made here of the role of the Church in maintaining the unity of the parish, and the relationship between it and the neighbour groups. The history of the Church in West Cumberland as a whole, up until the end of the nineteenth century, is one of poverty and mismanagement and from existing diocesan records Gosforth does not seem to have been exceptional. On the other hand, the purely local evidence suggests that the ecclesiastical administration of the parish was at least tolerably efficient, since the Parish Registers and Churchwardens' Accounts are fairly complete.[12]

Moreover the Church has always been an essential part of parish life, for whatever abuses may have occurred it gave the parish its existence in the first place and unified at least one aspect of its life. Baptism, marriage, burials, the payment of tithes, moduses and Easter dues, the election of churchwardens—in all these things the people belonged to Gosforth Church and through her, to one another.

Very significant in this context is the fact that many people born in the parish who have gone to live elsewhere are brought to Gosforth for burial, often over long distances. It was not uncommon for someone to remark that there was 'an understanding' in his or her family that such and such a relative, who lived some distance away, would be buried in 'in t'Church' when the time came.

The tenacity of this sense of 'belonging' to a particular Church is illustrated by the custom in one family, which has lived in Gosforth for at least three generations, of having all its male children christened in another parish 'because our fore-elders were from there'.[13]

The relationship between the Church and neighbourliness is manifest in the concept of 't'priest' as the neighbour of every man and woman in the parish, irrespective of social status or religious beliefs. This concept is clearly expressed in the following entries in the Parish Magazine:

Nov. 1950. 'The Rector of Gosforth must needs be a broad-minded person and provide roads for all users. Quarry Brow and Row Lane have been in a bad state through the recent floods, and are now being repaired with the kind help of Messrs. Sherwen and Park. . . .'[14]

Sept. 1950. 'The words of the Collect are a true description of the work of the women and men who have cleaned the Church and done the Churchyard paths.'

Sept. 1950. 'During August I had the privilege of helping in hay and harvest fields instead of looking after two acres of my own garden.'

July 1951. 'Four members . . . have almost finished the work of spraying the yard with weed-killer.'

—and in such remarks as, 'If it wasn't for t'parson there'd be a whole lock o' folks in Gosfer' wouldn't have paid their rates this year' and 'he's helped most on us some time or another. It's a straight-backed job is t'priest's but he gives more than he gets likely.'

Moreover, this feeling of neighbourliness is emphasized by the teaching of the Church. 'Love thy neighbour' is a text that appears in the Parish Magazine almost every month in some form or other. There can be little doubt that this constant emphasis helps to reinforce the individual's sense of responsibility towards the other members of the community, despite the fact that the majority appear to be indifferent to the Church and its teaching. This is exemplified in the close connection which exists between the Church and the Gosforth Charities. All the bequests which have been made with a view to helping the children, the aged, and the poor of the parish, came from persons who attended the Church regularly. Assisting those members of the community who are least able to fend for themselves is one of the most concrete expressions of neighbourliness, and in this respect the influence of the Church is extended beyond the minority who attend services regularly.

The affairs of the Church are parish affairs in every sense, and for this reason no one saw anything unusual in the presence of Methodists and Roman Catholics at Church fêtes, garden parties, and whist drives, often as stall holders and officials. In the same way, children and adults who sing in the Church choir on Sunday morning and evening attend the Methodist Sunday School in the afternoon without causing any popular comment. The secular aspects of Church life, are, then, matters which concern every parishioner, directly or indirectly; the religious aspects of Church life are very much more limited in scope (see Chapter X, 'Religion').

CHAPTER IX

GOSFORTH AND THE OUTSIDE WORLD

THE people of Gosforth make a sharp distinction between 'Gosfer' folk' and those who live outside the parish. The precise location of the parish boundary is very widely known and a very real difference is recognized between the people who live on either side of it, even where the actual distance is a matter of a few yards. There are several farms situated just inside the parish limits and the families who occupy them make full use of the services and amenities of Gosforth village, despite the fact that all of them could use other centres much more conveniently. In one case the extra distance involved is as much as two miles. On the other hand, there is one farm situated less than ten yards outside the parish boundary: its occupants are rarely seen in Gosforth and seldom mentioned in everyday conversation, although the farmhouse is a mile nearer to Gosforth village than to the hamlet which is the focus of their activities.

This feeling of membership of a social unit with well-defined territorial limits and the accompanying distinctions applied to non-members are very apparent in attitudes towards 'offcomers'. When a stranger comes to live in the parish, his period of 'settling down' is never a very comfortable one. Several families who had recently arrived felt that 'they were not wanted' or that 'people want to know the in's and out's of all your business'. One farmer's wife remarked, 'I don't know anyone in the village yet, and no one speaks to me, but they all know the colour of my wallpaper.'

More often than not the new family's first few months in the parish are marked by a combination of hospitality and hostility, of co-operation and criticism. Interviews with farmers who had recently arrived in the district suggest that the sequence is very much the same in all cases. When a family comes to start farming, their first day is notable for visits from neighbours, who offer to help them in moving in, promise the loan of machinery and make suggestions or supply information about local conditions. The newcomers find in due course that the offers of co-operation are well-meant, and it comes as a severe shock to them to discover that, say, the farmer who had been so obliging about lending a manure drill has consistently been making highly derogatory remarks about them to an appreciative audience in the local public house. One farmer, who thought himself to be on excellent terms with his neighbours, heard that one of them had told several people that the 'offcomer' had ruined many of his hedges because he was unaware of the function of the hydraulic lift on his tractor.[1]

The apparent ambivalence in the attitude of local people is very puzzling to newcomers, many of whom describe it in such terms as 'stabbing you in the back' or 'being two-faced'. Their resentment is frequently increased by the great interest shown in their affairs by their neighbours, particularly if they have come from an urban area where neighbour relationships are poorly developed. Sometimes too the conflict of emotions is heightened when a newcomer confronts a neighbour concerning his behaviour, since the country folk are unable to offer a satisfactory explanation. Not one of the people I questioned about this matter could explain why they behaved so inconsistently, and were very embarrassed when the subject was mentioned.

This seemingly paradoxical behaviour is an expression of the country people's sense of identity and difference. The initial acts of friendship and the offers of co-operation represent, as it were, an invitation to the offcomer to become a member of the community. The derogatory remarks and the stories about the shortcomings of the stranger express the sense of difference from the outside world, of which the stranger is the immediate representative. Thus in offering a newly-arrived neighbour the loan of his machinery a farmer is in effect accepting him as 'one of us'; in criticizing his use of the machinery, the farmer is classifying him as 'someone from elsewhere and therefore different from us'.

As the process of settling down goes on the criticism and hostility usually diminishes. Eventually the newcomer is regarded as having settled down, although—as we have seen already—he will always be to some extent an offcomer.

The length and nature of the period of settling down varies from one person to another according to a complex series of factors. If, for example, the newcomer is a Cumbrian by birth and upbringing who speaks with the local dialect his acceptance takes much less time than that of the 'Southerner'. Among farmers, previous experience of farming considerably reduces the 'settling down' period. Failure to accept certain approved forms of behaviour, albeit unwittingly, is likely to postpone acceptance, while alternatively, relationship by blood or marriage—however remote —with an established member of the community decreases the time taken to settle down very much indeed.

The two extremes in the process of acceptance are illustrated by a comparison of two farmers who came to the parish at about the same time. The first, who had previously farmed a holding some twenty-five miles away from Gosforth, is a second cousin to two local farmers and more distantly related to several other people in the parish. Although not personally known to the majority of people this farmer appears to have been accepted very rapidly indeed, and the process of settling in seems to have taken place with very little criticism and hostility. The second farmer was born in the South of England, had never farmed before he came to Gosforth, and was not related or known to anyone in the parish. He speaks with what is locally termed a 'la-ti-posh' accent and retains a great many of the urban habits and values he acquired before coming to Cumberland. After nearly seven years this farmer has clearly not 'settled down'. He is the subject of slanderous stories by a large number of people and is still in many ways as much an offcomer as on the day he came.

The variation in the length and nature of the period of acceptance of these two men and their families is directly related to the degree to which they are identified locally as being 'one of us' or 'different from us'. (The recognition of degree of difference is, of course, the underlying factor in the local attitude to 'other people' in general. Applied, *mutatis mutandis*, in varying contexts it explains the differences in attitude towards 'folk in t'district', 'Cumbrians', 'Northerners', 'Southerners', 'town folk' and so on.) In particular, blood relationship with several parishioners in the case of the first farmer made identification easy, while the second farmer was immediately recognized as 'different'. This 'difference' was emphasized by the fact that the social class of the second farmer was difficult to determine. His wealth, his accent, his general appearance and behaviour, and his ancestry qualified him for membership of the Upper-Upper class: his occupation and the fact that he sent his children to the village school were characteristics associated with the Medial class. (He was, as perhaps might be expected, placed eventually in the Lower-Upper class.)

In addition to the small number of people who come to live in Gosforth, the inhabitants meet many representatives of the outside world in the numerous officials of county and national agencies who visit (or live in) the parish. In all cases the attitudes and behaviour of the Gosforthians reflect to greater or lesser extent the loyalty of the individual to the community and resentment of external interference in any form. These feelings are often developed to a degree that astonishes officials new to the district.

For example; much of the hostility and suspicion I encountered in the early stages of the field-work were due to the fact that I was believed to be variously an Inspector of the Ministry of Agriculture, an official of the Inland Revenue, a Rates Assessor for the Rural District Council, or simply an unspecified 'bloody Nosey Parker from some office'. Instances of the way these officials are treated are plentiful. Some farmers regularly refused to open the door to them and others always demand to see the credentials of officials they have met many times before. Even officials who are well known locally are generally received with either open hostility or a formality that contrasts markedly with the hospitality accorded to other visitors. Several people told me of the farmer who took a representative of 't'Ministry' up on horseback to a very remote fell pasture to see some of his animals, and then returned alone, leaving the unfortunate man to walk back. This was locally regarded as very amusing and its telling was normally garnished with such remarks as, 'Ah doubt he nivver learnt about that at College.'

In all such stories the local inhabitant outwits the visiting official and the greater the discomfiture of the latter, the better the story. Another example is the account of the farmer who, when the time came for payment of sheep subsidy, brought down his own flock as well as the sheep belonging to several of his neighbours, and thus collected over twice the amount of subsidy to which he was entitled. This story was one I heard many times, presumably because it not only illustrated the ignorance of the official in being unable to distinguish between the various flocks, but also showed how the farmer had gained financially at the expense of 't'Ministry'.[2]

A similar attitude to external authority has already been mentioned in connection with cock-fighting, a matter which intimately concerns the village policeman. This officer lives in the parish and is friendly with a number of the inhabitants, but there is evidence that a great many people make a distinction between his personal qualities and those implied by his work. It was said of him, for example, 'Aye, he's a nice enough lad when he's not on t'job' and 'You'd a' thowt a decent laal feller like him would be in another job'.

It is significant that in his off-duty hours the policeman patronizes a public house some miles away in a neighbouring parish, and rarely, if ever, spends an evening in the village 'pubs'. It seems likely that this expresses an awareness of the difficulties and embarrassment that might arise. A very intelligent villager commented 'Folk isn't all that keen to have a good crack or a drink with a feller whose job is to run thee in if tha's had a sup too many'. Also important is the fact that informants who clearly looked on the policeman as 'a nice enough lad' were astonished and even somewhat horrified when I asked if many people reported misdemeanours to him. Again and again the reply was that 'Folk hereabouts settle their differences among themselves, maister'. It seems possible that this reluctance to refer to external authority is in part responsible for the general absence of litigation which is so characteristic of parish life. The only lawsuit which occurred while the field-work was in progress concerned a local farmer and the Forestry Commission, and it need hardly be said that public opinion supported the farmer almost unanimously. Recourse to the machinery of the law is, then, only considered justifiable and necessary in exceptional circumstances or when the dispute involves an external agency or individual.

This reluctance to accept external controls is extended to include even such agencies as the Ministry of National Insurance. A few people in the parish refused to pay N.I. contributions until threatened with legal action, and a great many more still look on the scheme with great disfavour. Several families, particularly those on farmsteads, have continued as fee-paying patients, despite the added expense and the fact that they are entitled to the services of the same doctor under the National Health Act. To justify this it was said that 'You get better treatment for it if you pay for it' and 'You gets better medicine if you're a private patient'.

Equally interesting was the reaction to the 1951 Census. Some difficulty was experienced in finding enumerators, and this was followed by even greater difficulty in persuading people to fill in the Census forms. Since the field-work included the collection of material very similar to that required for the Census, I was often taken to be 'one of them Census folk' and was therefore able to discuss it at some length with a great many people. Many regarded it as pointless and quite a number as a devious method of obtaining information for tax purposes. If many of the statements made concerning it by informants were true, then not a few of the returns were deliberately falsified 'to give 'em summat to puzzle on'. My attempts at explaining the uses of the Census were often regarded with open disbelief or dismissed in such terms as, 'Well it's time they found something more useful to spend their money on I fancy.' It was quite clear that a large number of people looked on the Census as an unwarranted intrusion into their affairs, and in some vague and unforeseeable way as a threat to the well-being of the individual and the community. As one housewife remarked, 'I still can't see why them London folk wants to know ivveryything about ivverbody in Gosfer." Similar attitudes were frequently met with during the earlier stages of my own field-work and it was not uncommon to discover deliberate misstatements from time to time. (Unfortunately I was never able to discover what the local reaction was to the fact that I appeared to accept these as true.)

The way the Gosforth people look upon the representatives of the local governing bodies—the County Council and the Rural District Council—are largely similar to those described in respect of national agencies. These local institutions may be less remote—in the geographical sense, and in the fact that their officials may be men born and bred in the region—but in many ways this tends to increase local resentment rather than diminish it. 'When one of them laal College fellers (i.e. official of the Ministry of Agriculture) tells me what to do on t'spot' (farm), said one farmer, 'I think to mesel', "He'll know no better likely." But when one o' t'lads from t'district comes and tells me what to do I feel fit to bust.' The failure of 'them chaps from t'Ministry' to take local conditions into account (or so it seems locally) is considered excusable on the grounds of ignorance. Officials from local bodies, on the other hand, are expected to appreciate the country folk's viewpoint, and their apparent failure to take this into account is often deeply resented.

In the case of the County Council and the Rural District Council, however, much of their contact with the parish is effected through the Parish Council, unlike, for example, the Ministry of National Insurance which deals directly with the individual. This, combined with the fact that many of the functions of local government are poorly developed in the parish, reduces the impact of the C.C. and R.D.C. to a minimum.

It is one of the more important characteristics of Gosforth that the close-knit social organization enables daily life to proceed with very little interference or help from local governing bodies. Until very recently, there were no 'Council' houses in the parish, and the majority of the inhabitants pay no 'direct' rates. The village school was, until a year or so ago, a Church of England school administered by the Rector and the School Managers—all members of the community. Again, only two stretches of road in the parish network are controlled and maintained by the County Council.

On the somewhat rare occasions when matters arise which

involve the local authority and the parish, the details tend to be settled by the Parish Council with little or no reference to the majority of the inhabitants. Most of the issues are routine in nature and it is only very rarely that anything controversial occurs.[3] For example, the provision of street lighting for the village has been the subject of correspondence between the Parish Council and the R.D.C. over a long period. Surprisingly few of the inhabitants knew of this and those who did were largely indifferent. The consensus of opinion among farmers was that 'It's darker in our lonning (lane) than in t'village and we always find our way home without necking ourselves' (i.e. breaking our necks). Among villagers typical attitudes were 'It would be handy for kids likely, but most on them's at home when it's dark', 'there's plenty o' light from windows and such' and 'a waste o' good money'.

Since the C.C. and the R.D.C. affect life in Gosforth only slightly, the Parish Council has few functions and very little power. Its influence on parish life is very small and this must largely account for the absence of competition for seats during elections. There has in fact been no election for a number of years. Moreover, the members of the Parish Council are 'non-political'. This is because the people of Gosforth are almost entirely supporters of the Conservative Party. This means that they vote for the Conservative candidate at election time, but this is in effect the only occasion when politics assume any importance in local life. The political affairs of the parish were succinctly described by the informant who said, 'Folks just isn't interested in politics.' Political matters hardly ever came up in conversation during my stay in Gosforth, unless I introduced them, in which case it was clearly regarded as uninteresting. People voted for the Conservatives because 'we all do' or because 'me father did', and practically no one thought it necessary to give reasons in terms of national policy.

This indifference to politics is clearly related to the remoteness of the parish and its long history as a relatively self-sufficient unit. The people of Gosforth regard the issues discussed at Westminster as mainly irrelevant to the life of the community and, as this implies, are seemingly unaware of the connection between the political party in office and the activities of the various government officials they meet from day to day. The opinion of the farmers—who as a group have probably been affected more by changes in government than the remainder of the community—is summed up in the words of one who said, 'I've been on this spot a good lock of years now and there's been Labour Governments, and Conservative Governments, and National Governments, but none on them has stopped maggot fly in me sheep. It'll make a difference to them big farmers down South likely, but this farm is the same now as it was in me father's time.' Another commented, 'Some folks say these subsidies is because of one party or t'other, but way I looks at it if folk want more meat they pays more for it and that's that. What do them politicians know about Herdwick hoggs and suchlike anyhow?'

The feeling of belonging to a community which is different from, and independent of, the outside world is equally well developed in attitudes to the numerous national organizations which have members in Gosforth. Most farmers, for example, belong to the National Farmers' Union, but the stock reason which was given for joining was that it enabled them to insure their equipment and buildings at preferential rates. The majority attended few meetings because 'we have better things to do'. Again, as we have seen earlier, the traditional relationship between farmers and their hired men contrasts sharply with the policy of the Agricultural Wages Board.

In the same way, such parish organizations as the Women's Institute are regarded as essentially local in scope, and their regional and national affiliations as more or less incidental. The success of the various appeals by the Red Cross and the National Savings Movement in wartime, and the numerous 'flag days' in more recent years, has varied according to the extent to which they could be seen to have a purely local application. The 'Comforts Fund' during the War was highly successful because it was the organized expression of the community's desire to assist those of its members in the Forces. The other wartime appeals were successful because they were thought of as directly benefiting '*our* lads' and because of the prestige considerations involved.

The latter are particularly important in the success of the 'flag days'. People accept the task of selling flags, or buy them, because 'If you don't, people will think you're mean' or because 'We don't want to look stand-offish'. Many bought flags without knowing what charity they represented. There is a common feeling that flag days are 'a damn nuisance', but even the most hostile of critics continue to contribute rather than face the possible charge of niggardliness.

CHAPTER X

RELIGION

THE origins of the Christian Church in Cumberland are shrouded in obscurity and there is still considerable controversy among historians as to when Christianity first became firmly established in this area. The choice of dates varies from the period of the Roman occupation (St. Ninian) to the sixth and seventh centuries (St. Kentigern and St. Herbert).[1]

The first evidence of early Christian worship in the Gosforth area is provided by the Norse Cross and hog-back tombstones in the churchyard, which most authorities date about the end of the tenth century.[2] Part of the Church is of Norman origin, dating from the twelfth century, but most historians of the area accept the archaeological remains as signs of an earlier church on the site. Early documentary evidence of a church in Gosforth occurs in a deed of gift to Calder Abbey in 1180,[3] which mentions 'Jurdanus persona de Goseford' and Gosforth is among the churches listed in the *Taxatio Ecclesiastica* of Pope Nicholas the Fourth (1291).[4] These and later records offer some documentation of the prosperity of the Church in Pre-Reformation times, but otherwise gave little indication of the state of religious life. For example, the subsidy rolls of the Diocese of York for the years 1523-5 show that Gosforth had a rector, a canon, a curate and three chaplains at that time, while most of the surrounding parishes had one curate only.[5]

Sources dating from early Post-Reformation times supply details of a Church in which ignorance, corruption and laxity were not uncommon, a state of affairs that was to last for centuries. The records of the 1578 Visitation of the Diocese of Chester [6] show that in West Cumberland the ordinands were almost always men of local birth, most of whom had apparently been educated at the village school. Many of the churches were in an advanced state of decay and much of the church equipment was missing. Several parishes had absentee clergymen, while at others, Gosforth among them, the priest gave no sermons and often attended no services. Just over twenty years later a letter from Bishop Robinson of Carlisle to Secretary Cecil described the state of religious feeling as a matter of concern:

'I find here more Popish recusants than I thought, yet the number within my diocese is far less than within ... the deanery of Copland in Cumberland ... belonging to the jurisdiction of Chester.

Most part of the ... gentlemen of the county are sound in religion, and the poorer sort generally willing to hear, but pitifully ignorant of the foundations of Christianity; ... many of them are without all fear of God, adulterers, thieves, murderers. The chief spring of all this weakness and carelessness of the ministry in divers places of the Borders ... others (i.e. clergy) there are that might do much good if they had half that delight in discharging their function which they have in idleness, in vain pleasures, and worldly cares. The far greater number of them is utterly unlearned, unable to read English truly and distinctly....'[7]

The Civil War further impoverished the spiritual condition of the Border Counties, and after the Restoration there were numerous cases of incumbents being found guilty of drunkenness and gambling. Seventeenth-century records of the Western Deaneries (i.e. including Gosforth) state that many of the churches were still in decay and lacking in equipment, and many priests are noted as failing to carry out their routine obligations.[8]

During the following century more than half the church livings in Copeland were worth less than £10 a year in value, and of the second half of this period a modern church historian remarks: '... apart from the period immediately following the Reformation, the Church was in a worse condition at this time than at any other period in its history.'[9] Pluralism was rife—over a third of the parishes were held by pluralists—and the bishops showed little interest in this remote corner of Northern England. As late as 1794 there were instances of priests being deprived of their livings for habitual and excessive drunkenness, indecency, and swearing.

Matters had improved only a little by the time the *Report* of the Commissioners on Ecclesiastical Revenues was submitted to Parliament in 1835. Of the 112 livings in the diocese, 33, including Gosforth, were held by pluralists,[10] but the parish was one of the 49 which were graced with a parsonage fit for residence; 53 had no house for the incumbent at all.

Over twenty years later clergymen in West Cumberland were still being suspended for perpetual drunkenness and many still lived in extreme poverty. By the time the Parish Magazine begins in Gosforth in 1887 there had been some improvement in the religious life of the district, but there was still much which caused concern amongst the higher ranks of the clergy. Quarterly communion was not unknown, and the general neglect of this ritual by church-goers was described by the Bishop of Carlisle as 'scandalous'.

Although Gosforth has apparently a better record than most West Cumberland parishes during the eighteenth and nineteenth centuries, inasmuch as it was better endowed than most and from about 1875 onwards had resident rectors with University degrees,[11] the evidence of the Parish Magazine suggests very strongly that the majority of parishioners were completely apathetic to the Church and its services. In the five-year period beginning January 1890, an average of 9·3 persons attended communion every Sunday. When Easter is excluded the average drops to 7·5 and when the three festivals of Easter, Whitsun and Christmas are omitted the average for the remaining forty-nine Sundays is 6·9. Corresponding figures for later periods are:

1900: 11·4	9·8	9·0
1910: 12·4	10·2	9·6

while throughout the period under review there were many days on which the number of communicants was less than that prescribed by the canons of the Church. Expressed as a percentage of the total population these figures mean that the average attendance at communion barely exceeded one person in every hundred during these years.

Comparable figures could not be obtained for later years, but occasional references in the Parish Magazine and statistics collected during the field-work for 1950 give the impression that, if anything, attendance at the communion ritual has decreased in the last forty years. Thus in 1914 the average attendance was 8·1 persons, as compared with 7·6 in 1950, and the consensus of opinion was that this last figure is representative of the period between the end of the first World War and the present.

Apart from attendance at this fundamental ritual of the Church, the Parish Magazine shows clearly that Gosforth is not a pious community, at least as far as the formal aspects of religious life are concerned. The following is a brief but representative selection of items from the monthly issues of the magazine through the years:

(i) November 1890. 'The Rector remonstrates against the young men "who congregate around the Church doors in winter while the people are entering, making it uncomfortable for those who have to pass through".'

(ii) December 1891. 'The Churchwardens post a notice concerning "hymn books being wantonly destroyed, the coverings of seats cut, and the threads pulled out".'

(iii) April 1897. 'The Communicants of the Parish are growing very slack.'

(iv) May 1912. 'Ascension Day is much neglected, the collection was six shillings (nine coins).'

(v) August 1921. 'The Rector complains of non-communicants leaving in the middle of the monthly Choral Communion; "it is irreverent and unnecessary".'

(vi) May 1925. 'Only the officials and two others, out of an Electoral Roll of two hundred, were present at the Vestry Meeting.'

(vii) January 1926. 'The Church would have been undecorated at Christmas if the senior school girls had not come forward.'

(viii) June 1926. 'We were astounded by the total lack of response to the Service of Prayer and Intercession for the settlement of the General Strike; surely there must be some in the Parish who believe in the power of United Prayer.'

(ix) May 1927. 'The men were absent as usual on Good Friday.'
(x) July 1928. 'No one came to the service on Ascension Day.'
(xi) May 1933. '... the Church was almost empty on Good Friday in accordance with Tradition.'
(xii) July 1950. 'The Bishop of Penrith confirmed 35 candidates ... six only of the newly-confirmed made their first Communion on the following Sunday.'
(xiii) September 1951. 'We appreciate your friendliness ... though I must not hide from you my conviction that your attendance at Holy Communion could be better than it is.'[12]

Furthermore it appears that some of the clergy who have held the living of Gosforth were not entirely free from the habits which caused the Bishops so much alarm. Apart from pluralism, which was a regular part of Church administration,[13] intemperance and laxity were characteristic of some local parsons. An eighteenth century entry in the Churchwardens' Accounts mentions 't'priest' being late at service 'owing to Saturday night potations'. Even during the last ninety years there have apparently been examples of secular habits interfering with the conduct considered to be appropriate to representatives of the Church. It was said of some of the clergymen who have served in the Parish during the life of its oldest inhabitant that they were 'far too fond of a glass of port', 'could and would swear better and longer than any farmer', and were 'keen on everything except t'Church'. Also mentioned were constant failure to hold Early Communion and to visit the sick.

The history of the Church in Gosforth has been reviewed in some detail to show that the present lack of interest in many of the formal aspects of religion is not a new phenomenon. This is important to an understanding of much of the attitude of parishioners to the Church and its representatives. There is good reason to suppose that in societies where religious instruction is weakly developed or ignored the majority of people will be indifferent to religion; Gosforth has rarely been characterized by clergymen who have devoted much effort to disseminating religious knowledge.[14]

RELIGION

In spite of the above evidence to the contrary, it is widely believed that the poor attendance at Church dates from the arrival of the present Rector [15] and that it would immediately improve on the induction of a new incumbent. This is symptomatic of a general tendency to use the shortcomings of the parson as an excuse for the worldliness of his flock. Many people were very reluctant to admit that they only went to Church rarely or did not go at all, and seemed very embarrassed at questions directed at this point. In particular they found it difficult to explain why they did not go to Church when a clergyman other than the Rector was holding the service. Almost always people rationalized the discrepancy between their own behaviour and the ideal pattern of attendance by describing at length the faults which they and their friends attributed to the Rector.

One of the most common criticisms directed at the Rector was that of the woman who said, 'Every time he comes here he's wanting summat; if it's not money then it's clothes for t'Rummage Sale or prizes for t'Whist Drive. He thinks we've got nowt better to do with our money likely.' There can be little doubt that this aspect of the Rector's duties results in a considerable lowering of his prestige. This in turn is aggravated by the fact that his stipend is insufficient to meet the expenses implied by a large parsonage (it has eighteen rooms) and the ideal conception of a Rector's status which is held in Gosforth. The maintenance of the Church fabric and equipment is a problem that has caused increasing concern throughout the English Church in this century. So grave has it become that a distinguished Churchman, writing of the onus which this difficulty has placed on the parish priest, has written, 'Mendicancy has grown to a fine art.'[16] As we have seen, the problem has been particularly acute in West Cumberland, and in Gosforth the Parish Magazine provides ample documentation of the continuous struggle for funds. There is hardly one issue that does not contain at least one appeal for money or the result of a previous appeal.[17]

Moreover, until very recently the maintenance of the village school and its equipment was partly the concern of the parson and this, combined with a low stipend, has made his position an exceedingly difficult one. The clergy of Gosforth have been more fortunate in this respect than many of the incumbents in other West Cumberland parishes, but their income from the Church can hardly be considered munificent. In 1950 the value of the living was £350.[18]

The Rector made it quite clear to me that he was unable to live on his stipend, let alone maintain the Rectory, and this seems to have been true of many of his predecessors, as the following quotations show:

Parish Magazine, July 1905. 'Easter Dues. I must thank all those who have paid me their debts ... I cannot very well ask for these small sums and yet they are due to me by law and right.'

(The amount was three half-pence for every parishioner over sixteen years of age.)

Parish Magazine, September 1923. 'The living is a poor one with a large and expensive Rectory to keep up. ... I have to pay very much out of my own pocket. No one in the parish has offered to help me in this matter.'

The parishioners expect the parson to maintain a standard of living worthy of his position as a leading member of the community, living in one of the largest and most imposing houses in the parish, speaking to the 'Upper Ten' on equal terms and living a life that appears to the average man to be free from the hard work and uncertainty and that is so much a part of his own life. This concept conflicts very sharply with the Rector's incessant appeals for funds and gives rise to much resentment in the parish. It would seem therefore that the apathy towards the Church, which has characterized this area for so many centuries, is increased by an ecclesiastical financial system, also a legacy from the past, which places the burden of maintaining the parish church upon the inhabitants. This forces the parson to fill the dual roles of priest and beggar, positions which in a great many societies are at opposite extremes of the class hierarchy.[19] The indifference to the Church results in an unwillingness to contribute to its upkeep —the Parish Magazine is full of such phrases as 'miserable offering' and 'shockingly poor response'—and this means that the incumbent has to increase his efforts and the urgency of his appeals for funds; this in turn lowers the status of the parson and induces further indifference—a classic example of the 'vicious circle'.

The Church then is regarded locally with a marked lack of interest, clearly expressed in the saying, 'If he won't mak a farmer, mak him a parson.' People object to the Rector as a man and as a collector of money to maintain the Church, but they do not, however, question his fitness to conduct church services. They unconsciously accept as part of the natural order of things the religious rites which punctuate the life-cycle of the individual, but seem to have no conscious interest in religion. The rite in which they have no interest is the central one which has no *physical* correlations like birth, marriage and death. It celebrates a happening long long ago, too far into the remote past to be apprehended. People frequently remarked that they never went to Church 'except of course when we have to' or 'except when we're forced to go'. In the second part of this chapter an attempt will be made to account for the compulsive character of the few occasions when the inhabitants of the parish feel they are 'forced' to go to Church.

The rites which accompany birth, marriage and death are inevitably associated with changes in social status. The one remaining initiation ceremony, that is Confirmation, marks a change in religious status, and in Gosforth people do not think of it in the same terms as baptism and the like.

Confirmation is looked upon as a ceremony which everyone who has been baptized in the Church *must* go through sooner or later. I could find no one who questioned its inevitability and a comparison of the Baptismal and Confirmation Registers showed that the only names which did not occur in both were those of people who had died or left the parish during childhood.[20] It is noteworthy that the vast majority of the people attend church services for a few weeks after their confirmation, before reverting to the general practice of 'going when we have to'. Many indeed do not enter the Church for several years after Confirmation.

From this it is clear that the local attitude to this rite is almost diametrically opposed to that of the Church. From the ecclesiastical viewpoint, Confirmation, the rite which transforms the individual into a full member of the Church, is essentially a beginning. In local eyes, however, it is a ceremony preceded by several months of preparation and church-going, which for the average person is the most intensive period of religious activity he will experience during his entire life, and of which the confirmation ceremony is the climax and the end.

Being confirmed also has social implications. Confirmation Day is anticipated weeks beforehand; new clothes are bought and on the day itself kinship solidarity is manifest in the numerous relatives of the 'candidates' who fill the Church. Fear of criticism and what may be termed 'traditional momentum' are potent influences in assisting to perpetuate the importance of this ritual. People remarked, 'What would folk say if we didn't send our lass to t'Class? T'parson would tell ivverybody about it soon enough, I doubt', and 'I nivver thowt nowt about going mesel', neither did me brothers and sisters. Me father and me fore-elders was all confirmed, and me mother and her folk, so our lad can go like t'rest on us.'

As for the young candidates, their reason was most often, 'Me Dad tellt me to go.' There was apparently complete ignorance of the underlying significance of the ritual, a conclusion which is supported by the poor attendance at Church which is typical of its aftermath. It would seem, therefore, that the motives which impel parents to have their children confirmed are very similar to those which cause people to be married in Church. In both cases the rites are preceded and followed by almost complete indifference to the Church, so that the sacred aspect of these ceremonies is of minor, or even negligible, importance. If the confirmation service has any 'religious' value at all attached to it, then the limited evidence available suggests that it is essentially a fear of the consequences which attend failing to follow exactly the pattern prescribed and sanctioned by tradition.

The ritual observance of Easter appears to lie somewhere between the two extremes of baptism etc. on the one hand and the 'normal' Sunday service on the other. As the figures quoted earlier suggest, Easter is marked by larger congregations at Church that an almost any other time during the year. In the years 1890–1911, the average number of communicants at Easter was nearly twenty-five times the average number of communicants at other occasions during this period. A large number of people, who otherwise never enter the Church for years on end, appear regularly at the Easter Communion, an occasion which, like the Confirmation Service, is invested with considerable social importance. The women make every effort to buy new clothes for this event, or at least take particular care over their appearance. The men wear sober suits of black or dark blue, many of which are afterwards returned to wardrobes to remain unworn for another year. This gathering provides sufficient material for conversation between friends and relatives for many weeks afterwards and—since the same people tend to be present each year—gaps in their number are the subject of much speculation and comment.

Other religious festivals in the year at which there are more communicants than on most Sundays are, in descending order, the Harvest Festival, Christmas, Whitsun, the Feast of All Saints (November 1st), and the Feast of the Circumcision (New Year's Day). In former years the numbers of people taking communion on these occasions were of the order 50, 40, 25, 20, 15, respectively; the number of communicants on Good Friday and Easter were of the order 15 and 100 respectively. Nowadays November 1st and New Year's Day are marked by only slightly better attendance at Church than on most Sundays and it would seem therefore that the majority of parishioners do not consider them as especially important.

The Harvest Festival is only slightly less significant (in terms of numbers) than Easter as a social occasion and there is considerable rivalry in the giving of fruit, vegetables, etc. This aspect of the Festival is so pronounced that the Church has devoted much effort to minimizing its importance: 'Although we know the Harvest Festival is popular, it is not a great Christian Festival' (Parish Magazine, December 1921).

Feast days, however, have a significance in Gosforth quite distinct from the services held in the Church. Candlemas, Lady Day, Whitsun, Michaelmas and Martinmas are, as we have already seen, landmarks in the farmer's year around which the cycle of agricultural activity is organized. Similarly, Christmas is the time for an exchange of gifts and a whole complex of customary behaviour which are quite independent of its sacred aspect. Easter is characterized by 'pace-egging', a game which is anticipated by the younger people with almost as much eagerness as Christmas-time.

Throughout West Cumberland the weeks before Easter are marked by the appearance of hard-boiled eggs, dyed in various bright colours, lined in rows along window-sills, or arranged in bowls where they can be seen by everyone.[21] On Easter Monday the eggs are taken to a traditional meeting-place and rolled down a slope or tapped against each other until the shells crack. They are then eaten and the game begins again with a fresh supply. There is much competition between households over the number of eggs they display and the variety of colours achieved, and, significantly enough, the purchase of chocolate Easter eggs—a relatively recent innovation—is regarded as 'showing off' and is likely to result in some loss of prestige.[22] Easter is also important as an occasion for the making of Simnel cake and 'Hot Cross Buns', and for a few people as a landmark in the cock-fighting season.

Formerly Easter Sunday was a fête day celebrated by the holding of 'Filly Fair' in a field near the village, at which there were races, wrestling and other contests of skill. One inhabitant said of it, 'It were a big day in Gosfer'. Ivverybody went till it and there were that many there tha could walk on people's heads. All t'lasses wore ribbons and it looked a bonny sight.'[23]

Hallow E'en is another day that the children of the parish look forward to eagerly. Once it is dark, little groups can be seen moving from house to house carrying turnips which have been hollowed out and cut to resemble faces, with lighted candles placed inside, while in the houses games of 'bob-apple' are played.

Other 'red-letter days' are New Year's Day, Collop Monday, Shrove Tuesday and Whitsun. On New Year's Eve, the ceremony known as 'first footing' is still practised to some extent, although much less than twenty years or so ago.[24] The following day is a festive occasion devoted to visiting friends and relatives, and to eating. Most families order poultry for New Year's Day as well as Christmas, and as much rum-butter is made as the family can afford. On Collop Monday the Rector holds a 'Jumble Sale and Whist Drive', and every Shrove Tuesday there is a 'Parochial Tea'. Shrove Tuesday, or 'Fassens E'en' as it is known locally, is now commemorated only by the making of pancakes and possibly the holding of a cock 'main'. It was at one time an important holiday in Cumberland. School-children paid their 'cock-penny' for months before, so that money could be staked on the annual School Cock-fight which took place on that day.

Whitsun is a general holiday and many of the people spend their day in the fair-ground at Whitehaven. Until recently, Whit Sunday in Gosforth was one of the most important days in the year, for on it was held the 'club walk' of the 'Gosforth Lodge of the Grand United Order of Oddfellows'. This association still holds monthly meetings, but it is now declining rather rapidly in importance as a result of the National Health Act, which has deprived it of its main function. A former 'Oddfellow' described the club walk as follows: 'A real day was that. All t'members walked in a great long procession right round t'village up to Wellington. Ivveryone on us had white gloves on and there was a brass band in front. After t'walk we had dinner in t'Globe or t'Wheatsheaf and then sports in t'field by Gosfer' Hall. It was t'biggest day in t'year for Gosfer' folk in them days.' The club walk died out 'just before the first War'.

While the social activities outlined in the last few paragraphs are not, of course, regarded by the Church as religious celebrations, except for the club walk, which used to begin with a Church service, it is significant that the modern holidays are old Church holy days, and conversely, that the Church festivals which to-day bring more people than usual to Church are precisely those which have also become secular festivals. This is clearly illustrated in the following table:

Church Festival.	Number of Communicants.			Secular Festival.
	1893–1903	1907–9	1936–40	
Easter *	91	138	144	Filly Fair, Pace-egg.
Christmas	33	43	73	Santa Claus, etc.
Harvest Festival	28	29	38	Kurn Supper, etc.
Whitsun	26	18	14	Club Walk, etc.
All Saints	31	15	6	Hallow E'en.
Circumcision	14	10	16	First footing, etc.
Ascension Day	5	5	4	None.
Advent	12	6	4	None.
Michaelmas	4	Nil	Nil	None.

* Good Friday and Easter Day combined.

If the other Church festivals were added to this table, in no case would the number of communicants exceed the figures given for Ascension Day, and on many Saints' days there were often none at all.

This close relationship which exists between the religious and secular festivals in Gosforth is neither recent in origin nor peculiar to this part of the country. Recent research has shown quite clearly that the Christian Church used pre-existing holy days and customs for its own sacred festivals and syncretized pagan and Christian beliefs so that the contrast between the old and new religions was minimized.[25] Candlemas, for example, was the Christian counterpart of the Roman Lupercalia and 'thus what was done before in honour of Ceres was now done to the honour of the Virgin'.[26] In this way many deep-rooted customs became intimately associated with particular Church festivals and as the Church gained in strength the religious content of the old rites was transferred to those that succeeded them. The Church, however, did not succeed in assimilating all the ancient practices and many have survived as secular customs until the present day.

When the secular customs of Gosforth are examined against this background it is clear that many of them retain traces of their early religious origins. The customs centred around eggs at Easter, for example, link the present with the Rites of Spring that were celebrated throughout Northern Europe in pre-

Christian times: the egg has been the symbol of the 'house of new life' in societies the world over in ancient and modern times. Similarly the celebrations which marked the end of the harvest were held all over Europe millenia before the Victorian Church invented the Harvest Thanksgiving, while Hallow E'en is a survival of the great feast of the first day of the ancient month of the dead and of the Celtic New Year.

Whitsun is the only important Church festival which is not associated with customs handed down from pre-Christian times, since the Pentecost was not foreshadowed in the cycle of birth, death and regeneration which was so significant in early ritual. The club walk is the successor of the 'Whitsun Ale', a parish holiday which some authorities derive from the 'Agapae' or love-feasts of the primitive Church,[27] and is therefore of considerable antiquity, but is characteristically lacking in the symbolism which is so fundamental in the popular practices which accompany the other major holy days. Significantly, Whitsun has never been accorded the reverence which is given to Christmas and Easter, and it has been suggested that its popularity was in fact derived from the social customs that accompanied it.[28] Unfortunately there is no evidence as to the importance of this festival in Gosforth before the club walk rose to prominence in the late eighteenth century, but certainly the number of communicants has declined steadily since the perambulation of the village ended, and at present it is little more than a public holiday devoid of any religious significance.

The Harvest Festival, on the other hand, has grown in importance in recent years despite the fact that kurn suppers ended at the outbreak of the last war. In this case the Thanksgiving Service may be regarded as a deliberate invention designed to absorb the sentiments centred around the traditional festivities, in much the same way as the early Christians used pagan temples as churches in order to facilitate the transference of the reverence associated with them. In most of the counties of England 'harvest homes' were dying out in the latter half of the nineteenth century, so that the Church Thanksgiving appeared at a time when traditional values could most easily be diverted to religious channels. This was not the case in Cumberland, where the kurn supper flourished until about 1940, and this possibly accounts for the fact that the Harvest Festivals have always been looked upon as social events to a much greater degree than any other Church festival. This is clear from the following entries in the Parish Magazine:

September 1894. 'The Harvest Festivals in the Deanery were held simultaneously to prevent attendance at these Services for the sake of comparing the decoration at one Church with those of another, and other unworthy motives, which the Clergy have reason to believe, have arisen from the flocking of young people from Church to Church.'

October 1924. 'Many people will have read the opinion of our Bishop on Harvest Festivals, as expressed in the Diocesan Gazette. He made us all think seriously whether Harvest Festivals, in spite of their popularity, do any lasting good. They mean, for most districts, large congregations, drawn from people who do not usually attend a place of worship, bright services, and a round of visits to the Churches of friends. And so, the question should be faced, how can we keep alive something of this Festival spirit ... The Cross must enter *even into the keeping of Harvest Festivals*, if they are to be acceptable to God' (italics mine).

The origins of the religious and secular festivals have been considered at some length in order to render their inter-dependence intelligible. When considered in relation to the present social life it would seem that the social importance of the various religious festivals is closely related to deep-rooted traditional values and also to the extent to which each festival can be expressed in concrete everyday terms. Thus the Harvest Festival is popular partly because people feel it in some vague way to be important and partly because their participation can be reduced to actually doing something—decorating the Church, giving fruit and flowers and so forth—which is intimately connected with their everyday lives.

In this way it can be said that religious festivals are observed when they punctuate the life-cycle of (*a*) the individual and (*b*) the year. In either case the religious ceremony corresponds to secular events which can be seen and experienced. So, briefly:

Baptism = birth; Confirmation = adolescence; Marriage = cohabitation; Burial = death; Easter = pace-egging; Christmas = feasting, giving presents; and so forth.

This is seen very clearly in connection with the less well-known Church festivals. A very large proportion of the people I spoke to had never heard of St. Barnabas, St. Bartholomew, St. Stephen and others whose feast days are given prominence in the Book of Common Prayer. Candlemas, Michaelmas and Martinmas, on the contrary, were readily identified by their relationship to matters of everyday life. This is perhaps to be expected in a region where the clergy have not devoted a great deal of energy to religious teaching.

The analysis of the formal aspects of religious life which has occupied the first two parts of this chapter is, of course, only one aspect of the role of religion in the local way of life. In this section an attempt will be made to describe the influence of religion on the behaviour and mores of the community.

The most striking feature of this problem is the contrast which exists between the mores of the community generally and what is held to be appropriate by the Rector. The attitude of the Church is expressed in the following quotations, taken from the sermons and writings of Rectors who have held the living of Gosforth during the past sixty years:

'Sorrow is good for us if we accept it from God in the right spirit. Sorrow is meant by God to have a purifying effect on our lives. Sorrow which is a part of repentance will bring us back again into the sunshine of God's love. In this sense it is a good thing.'

Following an attack on adultery, based on the text Leviticus xviii 20 and Deuteronomy xxii 22:

'Is there not just cause why this terrible crime should be mentioned, a crime which all God-fearing, clean-living, men and women will ever detest and denounce.'

RELIGION

Concerning non-attendance at Church:

'The finger of shame will be pointed at him by saints and angels.'

'We cannot be saved against our will, but we certainly will be judged whether we wish it or not. . . . If we wilfully choose to be foolish and unwise, we shall have no one to blame but ourselves if the Judgment Day goes against us.'

'Why God in Heaven should allow such a terrible catastrophe to happen, over which human power has no control, we cannot tell. There is, no doubt, a wise purpose in it beyond our human comprehension. It should be a warning to all of us who call ourselves Christians to be prepared for a sudden and unexpected end to our earthly lives.'

'We are often asked if Church people should go to Dances or Whist Drives or any of the lighter sides of life. The answer is not easy, because Lent means not only self-denial but also turning to God in Prayer. The giving up of amusements will lead to little without trying to be better Christians at heart. And so we will keep a good Lent for at least these three reason [*sic*] (i) because it is the Churche's [*sic*] Rule and Discipline and we are loyal. This way we shall at all events with an [*sic*] healthy self control over the body. (ii) Because self-denial is the only outward expression of sorrow for the harm done to ourselves others and God by sins and failures. (iii) Because we want to know Christ better as He died and rose again and lives in and for us.'

'I must protest against the holding of Saturday night dances during Lent, particularly after the Public Hall Committee have decided to give them up.'

This emphasis on supernatural retribution through sermons of the 'hell-fire and brimstone' variety, and the asceticism which is the ideal implied in some of the passages quoted above, have no counterpart in the life of the community. The intolerance and negatory moralizing characteristic of the Puritan is conspicuously absent in Gosforth. In matters relating to sexual morals, for example, there is a broad-mindedness which in the eyes of the Church verges on the libidinous. As far as it was possible for an outsider to judge, illegitimacy was regarded with considerable tolerance and, although unmarried mothers were thought to be very unfortunate, the consensus of opinion was to the effect that 'Any on us could mak the same mistake likely' and any loss of prestige was slight and temporary. The number of illegitimate children and those born very soon after marriage is evidence that the ideal of pre-marital chastity is very largely disregarded in the parish, and several people thought that 'such carrying on' had increased in recent years.

There is, however, some degree of realization that the popular attitude to sexual behaviour differs considerably from that of the clergy and there are numerous stories which symbolize this. One I heard often, and stated to be true, relates that the father of a large number of children was asked by one parson if he thought his family would ever stop increasing: he replied, perhaps ambiguously, 'Not while there's the likes of thee around likely.'[29]

Adultery seems to have been rare in Gosforth and divorce and broken marriages are almost unknown. I could find only two cases of divorce during this century. The one case of infidelity which came to my notice during the field-work was, characteristically, judged entirely in terms of social class: 'Tha can't expect much else from that mak o' folk' was the comment most often made. It seems possible that the high degree of development of family loyalty has reduced adultery to the status of a contingency too remote to be even considered by the average man and woman. The normal reaction to questions on this matter was 'Folks up here nivver do things like that, maister.'[30]

The record provided by the Parish Registers of relative laxity in sexual behaviour before marriage and its absence afterwards suggests that the community has successfully resisted the ideals put forward by the Church. The same is true of visiting public houses, drunkenness and indulgence in any of the 'lighter sides of life'. The tolerance applied to sexual conduct is extended to these leisure time activities; drunkenness is regarded more as a sign of weak character or inferior social status than as sinful in any way. Religious beliefs are not strong enough to prevent the holding of dances during Lent, although the attendance of parishioners, as distinct from 'offcomers', tends to decline somewhat during this period.

Until almost the end of the last century Lent fell within one of the three periods in the year which, from ancient times, the Church had regarded as unsuitable for the celebration of marriage.[31] Although the restrictions were abolished in 1888, Lent has been thought of as a 'closed season' for marriage by the Rectors of Gosforth up until the present day; anyone wishing to be married during this period faces considerable opposition from the incumbent. Entries in the Marriage Registers show that very few marriages have in fact taken place in Lent, although it is of course impossible to say if this has been due to the attitude of the clergy alone, or resulted from a general acceptance of the restriction by the community as a whole. But in recent years some marriages have taken place during this time in spite of the hostility of the Rector. Thus, of 436 marriages solemnized between 1572 and 1785, only one occurred in March (a month that fell within the prohibited period irrespective of the date of Easter), while of the 364 marriages recorded for the period 1887 to 1950 there were 21 which took place in March.[32]

Percentage of marriages occurring in each month.

Period.	Jan.	Feb.	Mar.	Apr.	May	June	July	Aug.	Sept.	Oct.	Nov.	Dec.
1572–1887	9·1	9·0	0·9	7·4	9·0	11·6	8·0	6·9	6·9	7·0	13·9	10·3
1887–1950	8·8	6·9	5·8	10·7	5·5	9·9	6·6	6·0	11·0	10·7	8·2	9·9
1920–1950	7·4	8·0	6·0	12·3	6·0	8·5	6·5	4·4	12·9	13·4	5·4	9·2
1572–1950	9·0	8·2	2·8	8·7	7·6	10·9	7·6	6·7	8·3	8·9	11·5	9·8

This flouting of the authority of the Rector is a clear indication that the power of the Church is very weak in Gosforth, possibly even weaker than it was in the past. Furthermore certain traditional practices relating to marriage and burial have persisted in spite of a great deal of clerical opposition. For example, marriages on Christmas Day and Boxing Day are found quite frequently in the Registers despite the remonstrances of the incumbent. The same is true of burial on Sunday, a practice much favoured in Gosforth and disapproved of by the Church. The divergence

RELIGION

between popular and ecclesiastical attitudes towards marriage is reflected in the entry in the Parish Magazine of July 1934, which reads, 'The intention and mind of the Church is that marriages should be followed by the Sacrament, but we have never yet been asked for this complete service.'

The persistence of long established traditions has, therefore, been sufficiently powerful to force the incumbent to sanction practices which conflict with the canons of the Church. This is probably the explanation of the local custom of burying suicides in the churchyard with the rites accorded to natural deaths.[33] Suicide appears to have been as rare in Gosforth as adultery, but three cases have occurred within living memory, each being buried according to the usual rites of the Church. The reason given by informants was that 'his folk wouldn't have anything else' and there is every justification for assuming that the Rector of the time was fully aware of the circumstances. Burial in unconsecrated ground without the rites of the Church is thought of in much the same way as the burial of unbaptized children. People regarded it as horrible and frightening without being able to say why they did so.

In general, therefore, religious beliefs have little restrictive effect on social life. Indeed Sunday is the most important day of the week for those interested in football and cricket, for all through the year a game of one or the other takes place on the playing field on Sunday afternoon. Since the great majority neither attend Church services nor practise personal or family devotions, they have really only a very superficial apprehension of Christian doctrine and ethics. The average man only remembers the supernatural at baptisms and the like and in certain crisis situations,[34] and it has little discernible influence upon the conduct of everyday affairs. Nevertheless one cannot say that the ideal pattern for a 'proper' religious life is not recognized at all. Most people admitted that they did not go to church 'like we ought to', and conceded that the few regular churchgoers 'are better folk than us likely'.

In addition to the members of the Church of England, who

form the bulk of the population of the parish, there are a few who belong to other religious denominations:

Wesleyan Methodists	10
Roman Catholics	18
Quakers	5
Christian Scientists	2
Presbyterians	1

Of these, only the Methodists have a chapel in the parish. This was built in 1874 and has been aptly described as 'a red-sandstone building with little architectural beauty'.[35]

Although there are very few Methodists in Gosforth their influence greatly exceeds their numbers. In recent years more and more children have been attending the Chapel Sunday School, thereby decreasing the already meagre attendance at the Church Sunday School. These children, whose parents are almost invariably 'Church folk', were unanimous in agreeing that 't'Chapel is much more fun. You have plenty of singing, not like in t'Church where you sings "There is a Green Hill Far Away" all the time, and the teachers are nice and tell lots of good stories'.[36] Significantly enough, the teachers are not inhabitants of the parish but resident teachers at a girls' boarding-school in Seascale who know the art of making the Sunday School lessons interesting and attractive. It is a reflection of the attitude of the majority to the Church that none of the parents objected to their children attending the Sunday School of another denomination. Indeed two families who were nominally Church people now regularly attend services at the Chapel, after spending their Sundays for several years in purely secular activities.

Methodism, for reasons we need not discuss here, is firmly established in the towns of Cumberland and, like other Nonconformist sects, its influence becomes progressively weaker as the way of life becomes more rural. Gosforth is an outpost of a 'circuit' centred on Whitehaven, but its relative isolation is more than compensated by the energy and zeal of its members. Unlike the Church of England, West Cumberland Methodism is markedly proselytic in character and the rapid rise in popularity

RELIGION

of its Sunday Schools in Gosforth and other rural parishes testifies to the success of the efforts of its ministers and members.

The two Quaker families in the parish also attend the Methodist services, a practice common in South Cumberland where the members of this sect are too scattered to make regular meetings convenient. Quite a number of people spoke of these families in a very hostile way and accused them of using their religious beliefs to avoid conscription during the last war. Among their critics were farmers and villagers who were not themselves conscripted and who did not in general appear to be zealously patriotic. It seems very probable that the hostility towards the Quaker families results not from any concern about national affairs, but rather from the fact that their religious beliefs set them apart from their neighbours and emphasize their status as strangers.

The Roman Catholic families in the parish attend the services at the Catholic Church in Egremont. They are all descendants of the Irish immigrants who settled in industrial West Cumberland in such large numbers during the last century, and not, as one might have reason to suppose, members of the families of the recusants who figure so largely in the history of the County in Post-Reformation times.

CONCLUSION

IN this survey, selective emphasis has been placed on those aspects of the culture which distinguish Gosforth, as a representative parish of rural West Cumberland, from that of the 'champion' country, and also from that of the large urban centres. Attention has been given to the farmsteads which is out of proportion to their numerical importance in comparison with the village, because the traditional aspects of community life have survived among farm families to a much greater degree than among village families.

Although handicapped as an 'offcomer', the analysis of the social structure was much facilitated by the fact that I approached it as a Welshman who had lived for some time in Southern England. The contrast between the latter and much of the social life of Gosforth, and the numerous similarities which exist between it and Wales is particularly striking. The weak development of kinship, the high degree of nucleation in the settlement pattern, the relative isolation of the individual family, and the economic and social subordination of the lower strata of society—all of which have been marked features of much of Southern England from medieval times, are noticeably absent in Gosforth. Their opposites—extensive social relationships based on kinship, dispersal of habitations, and a diffuseness in the social structure as a result of this—which are so well developed locally, are equally characteristic of Wales.

Unlike Wales, however, the social class structure is in many ways similar to that of Southern England, largely because both areas were under the manorial system for a large part of their history. But even in this respect the independence of the lower social classes is more in keeping with Wales than it is with the Midlands and South of England. The introduction of the manorial system and its associated class structure was never successfully completed in Coupland, where the pre-existing way of life survived to a considerable degree. In contrast with most of medieval

CONCLUSION

England, where half the population was unfree, in Coupland there was a very large class of free farmers who clearly belonged to an intermediate group between the free tenants and the serfs.[1] Some centuries later it was observed that 'There are probably few counties, where property in land is divided into such small parcels as in Cumberland; and these small properties so universally occupied by their owners'.[2] In the same way, the tied cottage is virtually unknown in this part of West Cumberland, and the hired man has for centuries been free to move from one master to another without any material loss, and with every prospect of a relationship with his employer which is largely devoid of any overtones of dominance and submission.

Unlike Wales also, the religious life of the community is similar to that of Southern England. In Gosforth the Church of England is predominant and Nonconformists are a very small minority. This is, of course, because Cumberland did not experience the Religious Revival which so transformed the Welsh way of life. Sabbatarianism is unknown, and sports and games are much more important in the life of the people than they are to the Welsh countryman. Moreover, religion is a far less potent factor in determining what the average man does and thinks.

Nevertheless, the similarity between Gosforth and rural Wales, which extends from such minor matters as the occasional use of a word [3] to the important role of kindred in the life of the parish, is so widespread and striking that it appears to harmonize very neatly with the concepts of the 'Celtic fringe' and the 'Highland Zone' put forward in recent years by Sir Cyril Fox and others.[4] It is, of course, impossible to say to what extent these similarities result from a common origin, and it is relevant to recall here that Cumberland was that part of England characterized by the most intensive development of Norse culture following the Viking Invasions, and that many of the most distinctive features of the present way of life may be likened with equally striking results to that of the Norsemen of the Saga times. Failing the discovery of additional evidence, we must then be content with noting that in early medieval times the social life of West Cumberland was characterized by features which it possessed in common with the

CONCLUSION

Norseman and the Celt, both of whom had previously occupied the area, and that many of these features have survived in some form or another to the present day, thereby giving rise to the contrast with the remainder of England.

The term 't'old days' has appeared again and again in different chapters, and its use epitomizes the tendency of the Gosforthian to look on the present life of the parish as an impoverished edition of what it was in his youth. So marked was this tendency that one could not but regret that the study was apparently made twenty or thirty years too late.

Gosforth has changed more in the past two or three decades than it did in the two previous centuries, largely as a result of the increasing influence of urban culture. The change had begun much earlier than twenty years ago, when the economy, based essentially on subsistence agriculture, was transformed into one dependent on national and international economic trends. Until recently, however, the traditional way of life has been strong enough to minimize the extent of the change-over.

During the last two decades urban culture has been accepted to such a degree that it now appears to threaten the whole social framework. This has largely resulted from improvements in methods of transportation, the introduction of new industries into the locality and the influx of population which accompanied it. Also important are the widening of the social horizon of many of the inhabitants who served in the Armed Forces, and the change in outlook that accompanied this; and the fact that countrymen can only rarely read a book or newspaper, or listen to the wireless, without being brought into contact with urban culture in all its aspects.[5]

As yet, this new influence has not completely overshadowed the traditional way of life, but the possibility that it will do so is a very real one. It is not without significance that what was once part of the most isolated and self-contained region in England now stands in the shadow of the most modern development of technological civilization, the Atomic Energy Station. Every new feature of parochial life is a reflection of an urban outlook. The

CONCLUSION

last six houses to be built in the parish were located in the village, and in the last twenty years the only other important building erected in Gosforth was the Public Hall, also in the village. Newly formed organizations are specialized in function and cater for some of the inhabitants, and not for the community as a whole. The number of people employed in 'modern' industries is increasing, and so forth.

All in all, every development that has taken place in parish affairs in recent years has emphasized and reflected an urban way of life in various ways. Against this the traditional way of life is static and can offer nothing to replace the loss in community feeling which is a result of these developments. The social structure, an inheritance from the past, was not designed for a world where every individual is conceived of as a highly mobile unit, and does not seem capable of adaption to suit this concept. If the present change continues to its logical conclusion, then the sociologist of fifty years hence may well find it difficult to distinguish Gosforth from any other rural parish in England.

APPENDIX I

TABLE I

PLACE OF BIRTH OF OCCUPIERS, THEIR WIVES, AND PARENTS

	Gosforth.	Adjoining Parishes.	Neighbouring Parishes.	Cumberland.	Other Districts.
All occupiers	74	21	61	30	44
Farmers	9	6	16	10	2
Others	65	15	45	20	42
All wives	41	18	40	31	44
Farmers' wives	6	6	10	8	7
Others' wives	35	12	30	23	37
Farmers' father	5	4	20	9	4
Others' father	45	12	51	22	55
Farmers' mother	8	6	15	9	5
Others' mother	39	22	46	24	56
Farmers' wives' father	4	4	12	4	13
Others' wives' father	27	11	32	21	44
Farmers' wives' mother	3	3	14	9	8
Others' wives' mother	21	13	39	18	43
All occupiers' father	50	16	71	31	59
All occupiers' mother	47	28	61	33	61
All wives' father	31	15	44	25	57
All wives' mother	24	16	53	27	51

Neighbouring parishes within a ten-mile radius are: Rottington; St. Bees; Egremont; Cleator Moor; Weddicar; Arlecdon and Frizington; Lamplugh; Loweswater; Eskdale; Ulpha; Waberthwaite; Bootle; Muncaster; St. John Beckermet; St. Bridget Beckermet; Haile; Lowside Quarter.

Adjoining parishes are: Irton with Santon; Drigg and Carleton; Seascale; Ponsonby; Ennerdale and Kinniside; Nether Wasdale.

APPENDIX I

Table 2

Demographic Statistics

(a) Census Figures for Gosforth and Cumberland:

Year.	Gosforth.	Cumberland.
1801	652	117,230
1811	685	133,665
1821	888	156,124
1831	935	169,262
1841	1113	178,038
1851	1116	195,492
1861	1146	205,276
1871	1149	250,647
1881	1127	250,647
1891	1017	266,549
1901	935	266,933
1911	931	265,746
1921	922	273,173
1931	786	263,151
1951	723*	285,358

* According to a count made by the author; no official statistics were available: the 1951 Census volume for Cumberland, published at the end of 1954, gives the total population as 772; this presumably includes the boys and masters at the preparatory school. (See Note 1 to the Introduction.)

Not all the migrants from the rural parishes went to the industrial areas of the Cumberland coast, hence the decline in the county totals for 1911 and 1931. Many people from Gosforth went to other parts of England, and a fairly large number emigrated to widely scattered parts of the world.

According to a well known method of estimating the population for past centuries, the population of Gosforth in 1600 was 650. This figure has a possible error of ten per cent either way.

(b) Percentage of the Population in Different Age Groups, 1951:

Age Group.	Total Population.	Males.	Females.
0–9	14·0	16·4	11·7
10–19	11·7	13·2	11·4
20–29	15·7	14·0	16·6
30–39	12·6	12·9	12·6
40–49	13·3	14·0	12·6
50–59	16·2	15·7	16·6
60–69	9·0	8·9	9·1
70–79	4·7	2·3	7·2
80+	2·8	3·6	3·2

APPENDIX I

(c) Percentage of Males and Females in Different Age Groups, 1951:

Age Group.	Males.	Females.
0–9	56·5	43·5
10–19	54·1	45·9
20–29	44·1	55·9
30–39	48·9	51·1
40–49	51·1	48·9
50–59	47·0	53·0
60–69	47·7	52·3
70–79	22·9	77·1
80+	43·0	57·0

(d) Age and Marital Condition, 1951:

Age Group.	Total Population.	Males Married.	Males Single.	Males Widowed.	Females Married.	Females Single.	Females Widowed.
0–9	101	—	57	—	—	44	—
10–19	85	—	46	—	1	38	—
20–29	111	24	24	1	34	28	—
30–39	92	36	9	—	35	12	—
40–49	96	41	8	—	43	4	—
50–59	117	50	4	1	38	14	10
60–69	65	19	6	6	19	10	5
70–79	35	4	3	1	4	11	12
80–88	20	4	1	3	2	2	8
90+	1	—	—	1	—	—	—
Total	723	178	158	13	176	163	35

APPENDIX II

TABLE I

SIZE OF HOLDINGS

Acreage.	1870.	1914.	1918.	1939.	1949.
1–5	3	13	14	8	5
5–20	7	16	15	14	12
20–50	2	11	12	9	10
50–100	4	22	21	24	19
150–300	—	4	6	5	5
Over 300	—	1	—	—	—
Total number of holdings.	19	76	77	67	59
Holdings consisting of rough grazings only.	NR	2	2	—	4

It should be noted that the figures in Table 1 are those given by the Ministry of Agriculture and Fisheries. From the local evidence the figures given for 1870 are completely incorrect, while those for 1949 do not correspond with data collected during the field-work. According to the results of a farm-to-farm survey made in 1950 which was checked by plotting on a series of 6″ maps, the analysis of holdings for 1949–50 should read:

0–5	7
5–20	14
20–50	7
50–100	24
100–150	7
150–300	9
Over 300	1
	69

APPENDIX II

TABLE 2

OCCUPATIONS OF PERSONS OVER SIXTEEN GAINFULLY EMPLOYED (1951)

Farmers (incl. female occupiers)	45
Farmers' sons working at home	23
Farm labourers	28
Forestry workers	8
Iron-ore miners	3
Quarryman	1
Unskilled labourers (Sellafield)	23
Semi-skilled labourers ,,	12
Estate workers and gardeners	14
Domestic servants (full-time)	13
,, ,, (part-time)	10
Joiners	8
Blacksmiths	2
Mason	1
Shoemaker	1
Plasterers	2
Painters	4
Craftsmen's labourers	7
Teachers	9
Doctors	2
Dentist	1
Innkeepers	5
Clerical workers	12
Nurses	2
Dressmaker	1
Mole catcher	1
Drivers	6
Retail trades	28
Canteen workers	4
Garage and engineering	5
Other fully occupied individuals	37
Total	318

TABLE 3

OCCUPATIONS OF SMALL-HOLDERS

	Under 20 acres.	20–50 acres.
Full time farming	1	3
Postmen	2	–
Estate workers	2	2
Road worker, miner, innkeeper, caretaker, engineer (1 each)	4	1
Persons retired from full-time occupations	3	1
Total	12	7

APPENDIX III

Table 1

Male Labour on Farms

Age Group.	Occupier.	Sons. M.	Sons. S.	Other Relatives.	Non-Relatives. M.	Non-Relatives. S.
14–19	–	–	5	3	–	7
20–29	3	2	6	2	3	7
30–39	3	2	2	–	3	2
40–49	9	–	3	3	1	–
50–59	16	–	–	–	1	1
60–69	6	–	–	3	–	1
70+	1	–	–	2	–	–
Total	38	4	16	13	8	18

Table 2

Female Labour on Farms

Age Group.	Occupier.	Occupiers' Wives.	Daughters. M.	Daughters. S.	Other Relatives.	Non-Relatives.
14–19	–	–	–	2	–	–
20–29	–	4	2	3	–	3
30–39	–	8	1	2	–	–
40–49	–	9	–	–	1	–
50–59	–	9	–	1	1	–
60–69	1	5	–	–	2	–
70+	3	–	–	–	2	–
Total	4	35	3	8	6	3

Table 3

Acreage and Rent of Farms in Selected Years

Farm.	Acreage, 1921.	Rent, 1921. £	Acreage, 1951.	Rent, 1951. £
A	158	91	180	73–3–11
B	362	225–3–0	275	163*
C	149	105	149	69
D	202	250–1–0	155	90
E	109	120	94	60–8–0
F	100	120	119	65

* The arable acreage of this farm has remained the same.

APPENDIX IV

SOME METHODOLOGICAL CONSIDERATIONS IN THE STUDY OF SOCIAL CLASS

Two techniques were employed to determine the composition of the social classes in Gosforth. The first, as far as I am aware, is original; the second is based largely on the work of the American sociologist W. Lloyd Warner, particularly on his essay 'A Methodology for the Study of Social Class' (in Fortes, M. (Ed.), *Social Structure* (Oxford, 1949), pp. 2-17), which is described more fully in his *Social Class in America*, a work that was not available when I did the field-work. The second method was not employed until the use of the first was more or less completed, because I wished to test the validity and usefulness of my own method.

Method 1

(1) Once the existence of social classes had been observed early in the field-work, a working hypothesis was formulated, based on the following assumptions:

(a) That social classes were fixed in membership at any given point in time.
(b) That members of any particular class would associate more with people in their own class than with those in other classes.
(c) That people who had lived in the parish long enough to become acquainted with the local way of life were aware of the social class of their immediate neighbours.

(2) During the house-to-house interviews which formed the first part of the field-work, people were asked to name their 'close friends' in the area (the parish boundary was ignored) and to list regular visitors to the house, who could normally be expected to call over a period of three to six weeks. The distinction between 'close friends' and visitors was made as a means of cross-checking, and also because it ensured that people who were for any reason unable to visit their friends were not omitted. People were also asked for information about their neighbours. This was deliberately framed in terms that did not suggest an interest in social class—for example, 'Who lives in that house over there?' or 'Will the people next door be in now?' since it was very soon evident that most people automatically evaluated their neighbours in class terms without being asked to do so.

APPENDIX IV

(3) Any statement that contained a class evaluation, or reference in any form to the social classes was noted—whenever possible in the exact words of the speaker.

(4) Gatherings of any number of people were observed and a note made of the people present and the way they behaved.

(5) When the interviews were far advanced, the material collected was analysed to determine the number and size of groups of individuals who were interconnected as 'close friends' or as visitors to each other's homes. A distinction was made between those who were related by blood or marriage and those who were not.

It was discovered from the analysis that the population could be split up into several internally interconnected groups, with a number of people remaining who either had no friends within the parish, or who professed to have no friends or visitors at all.

(6) The social rank of each person was then added, using the evaluations given by informants regarding their neighbours. When people had lived in Gosforth for two years or less, this fact was noted. The result was that for the vast majority of parishioners there were at least two rank evaluations, and often five or more.

(7) It was clear that:

(a) The assumption that the social classes were fixed in membership at any given time was very probably true.
(b) The assumption that class members found their friends within their own class was only true of the topmost class.
(c) All the evidence suggested that social classes were firmly established in the parish.

(8) Selected informants from each class were interviewed again to obtain further information about those people whose status was unknown or was assessed differently by different men and women.

(9) Other material gathered during the field-work was examined to see if it was significant in this context.

(10) From this method it was possible to formulate a series of concepts regarding the social classes in Gosforth.

Method 2

The techniques developed by Lloyd Warner were tested in the final stage of the field-work. In their original form they are not suited to Gosforth and were therefore modified before applying them in the field. The details of the method are well enough known to make detailed recapitulation here unnecessary. Very briefly, the following procedure was adopted:

(1) Fifteen men and women, who represented a variety of ages, occupations and class levels (determined by Method 1) were selected:

APPENDIX IV

Class.	Number.	Age.	Sex. M. F.		Occupation.	Living in village.
U.U.	2	70: 62	1	1	Nil	Nil
L.U.	1	58	–	1	Nil	Nil
INT.	2	68: 53	1	1	Teachers	2
U.M.	1	47	–	1	Housewife	1
M.	5	22: 30: 32: 19: 51	2	3	1 craftsman; 4 in farm families	1
L.M.	4	48: 37: 32: 18.	2	2	1 labourer; 2 housewives; 1 nil	4

(2) These people were asked to 'explicitly divide the population ... into several social class categories, which cross-cut the whole community and distribute people into superior and inferior general social strata'.

(3) The names given by each informant were grouped in their specific classes and any disagreements regarding a person's rank were noted. The total number of disagreements was small (9) and applied only to one or two people.

(4) The results obtained by this method were compared with those of Method 1 and were found to be almost identical in content but not in scope.

(5) An attempt was also made to apply the methods of Warner's Index of Status Characteristics which, it is claimed, 'Measures the socio-economic levels of the community, and when related to Evaluated Participation (i.e. Method 2) makes it possible to say what is meant in socio-economic terms by such class concepts as upper-middle or lower class'. It was soon clear, however, that the methods of rating to determine an Index were unworkable in Gosforth, and indeed appeared quite unsuitable for rural areas anywhere. Several unsuccessful attempts were made to modify the categories to suit local conditions, and, to ensure that Gosforth was not exceptional, the I.S.C. techniques were tested on a housing estate some ten miles away, where their failure was even more conspicuous.

Assessment of the Value of the two Methods

(1) Method 1 is far more time-consuming and laborious than Method 2, both during the actual field-work and at the analytical stage. Warner's method is suitable for a general survey of the class system of a large urban community, but is unsuitable for detailed analysis. It is not clear from his work how the class of the selected informants is determined *before* the field-work begins and the informants are selected. Method 1 is completely unsuited for large concentrations of population, but is suitable for the intensive study of a small area.

(2) Unlike Method 1, much of the validity of the results obtained by Method 2 depends on the selection of informants. This can only be done after much of the field-work has been completed. It is, therefore, in many ways a supplementary rather than a basic method.

APPENDIX IV

(3) Method 1 has all the advantages and disadvantages inherent in the 'indirect' approach, while Method 2 has the strengths and weaknesses of the 'direct' approach. In the former, direct questions on the social classes were avoided, and every effort was made to give the impression that they were not particularly important or interesting. The spontaneous nature of the information thus obtained more than compensated for the fact that it varied considerably in value and content. Method 2 involves a conscious effort on the part of the informant to verbalize facts and concepts which are normally never thought of in a logical or rational manner. The whole procedure seemed 'odd' or 'pointless' to most people, and it was regarded either as a difficult and eccentric mental exercise, or as an opportunity to demonstrate the superiority of the informant. From this point of view the results can be considered much more artificial than those obtained by Method 1.

(4) When the results from the two methods were compared, it was seen that a great many people had been omitted in Method 2. This might perhaps be expected, but, much more important, many of the missing people were those whose status was sociologically the most interesting, for example newcomers.

These omissions probably result from the artificiality of the interview situation described above. The fifteen informants named more or less the same people and omitted the same people. What seems to have occurred was that the informant, unconsciously or otherwise, selected those whose class position was the most evident and rejected or avoided those about whom he was doubtful.

Even so, this method provides very valuable material, and suggests that the class boundaries are not as rigid as they are locally supposed to be.

(5) The failure of the I.S.C. method was due to the fact that it was obviously intended for urban areas of a highly specialized type—despite the claim that 'it can be used anywhere'. The index is determined for each family on the basis of four characteristics—occupation, source of income, house type, and area lived in—chosen because 'they correlate highly with class'. In Gosforth they do not correlate highly with class, and in any case the range is far too small to be of any use. When applied to the housing estate, every family received exactly the same rating in housing and area lived in, and all but a few had the same rating in the other categories as well. It would appear therefore that the people of this housing estate are of the same 'socio-economic level', and that 'in socio-economic terms' one class is exactly equivalent to another, so that the concept is valueless to an understanding of the social class system of this very common type of community. In fact the housing estate examined showed every evidence of possessing a highly developed form of class distinction.

(6) There can be no doubt that much was gained by the use and comparison of the two methods. In very general terms, Method 2 outlined the way in which the people of Gosforth regarded the social class system as an abstraction; the social classes came first, the individual came after. Method 1 showed how

APPENDIX IV

people fitted into the class system, and how the latter affected day-to-day social relationships.

A great deal of attention has been given by social scientists in recent years to the problems of the nature of the social classes. For this reason it is perhaps worth outlining the background to the use of the term 'class' in this work. The term 'class' (and its derivatives) has been used here because it is the term in use in Gosforth. The 'social classes' of the Gosforthian may not be classes in the sense defined by various sociologists—indeed, with the exception of the Upper-Upper class, they would probably be called 'status groups'. However 'class' means something specific to the people of the parish, and the various 'classes' have an undeniable social reality of their own. This local meaning is, of course, only intelligible when considered in the correct context. One of the major problems of the study of social class is the relationship between what may be called 'local' class systems and 'national' class systems.

It seems very likely that people apply the standards of their own local class system when evaluating the status of individuals and groups outside it. Thus to the average man in Gosforth 'upper class' means people like Mr. 'A'; to the Londoner it means something completely different. The problem that remains to be investigated is the relationship between these different meanings and applications. And the best method of doing it is to start with the local classes and not with the national class system.

APPENDIX V

Statistics relating to the Study of the Social Classes

Table 1

Place of Birth of the Population—by Social Class

Birth-place.	U.U.	L.U.	INT.	U.M.	M.	L.M.	L.	Not Known.
Gosforth	3	1	2	22	111	194	17	2
Adjoining parish	—	—	—	—	16	21	—	3
Neighbouring parish	—	9	1	1	45	72	3	5
Elsewhere in Cumberland	1	—	2	4	31	28	8	8
Outside Cumberland	19	12	5	3	12	48	3	11

Table 2

Distribution of Population in the Social Classes by Age and Sex

Class.	0–9 M. F.	10–19 M. F.	20–29 M. F.	30–39 M. F.	40–49 M. F.	50–59 M. F.	60–69 M. F.	70+ M. F.
U.U.	— —	— —	— 3	— 1	1 2	1 2	5 3	2 2
L.U.	1 2	1 1	1 1	1 2	5 1	2 2	— 1	1 —
INT.	1 —	— —	— —	2 —	— 1	2 2	1 1	1 —
U.M.	1 1	1 3	3 7	1 3	2 3	1 1	1 2	— —
M.	21 14	18 12	19 13	11 15	13 11	21 18	11 8	4 6
L.M.	23 26	19 18	16 30	25 23	28 26	26 36	13 18	9 27
L.	7 1	3 4	3 3	2 2	— —	2 1	— 1	— 2
N.K.	3 —	4 —	7 5	3 1	— 3	— —	— —	1 2
All classes	57 44	46 38	49 62	45 47	49 47	55 62	31 34	18 39

S.E.V.—P 215

APPENDIX V

TABLE 3

Housing, Occupation and Area Lived in—By Social Class

Class.	Occupiers. (Total)	Owners.	Tenants.	In Village.	Outside Village.	A.	B.	C.
U.U.	9	6	3	Nil	9	6	3	—
L.U.	9	5	4	Nil	8	3	3	3
INT.	5	3	2	5	Nil	1	2	2
U.M.	13	6	7	13	Nil	—	2	11
M.	52	26	26	10	42	—	40	12
L.M.	131	36	95	105	27	2	35	94
L.	6	Nil	6	6	Nil	—	1	5
N.K.	5	1	4	Nil	5	—	5	—
Total	230	83	147	139	91	12	91	127

A.—Large detached houses, standing in their own grounds.
B.—Small detached houses, standing in their own grounds.
C.—Attached houses, including semi-detached dwellings.

TABLE 4

Occupations and Social Class

Class.	I.	II.	III.	IV.	V.	VI.	VII.	VIII.	IX.	X.
U.U.	—	—	—	2	—	—	21	—	—	—
L.U.	2	—	—	—	—	—	10	—	—	—
INT.	—	—	—	4*	—	—	5	—	—	—
U.M.	—	—	—	2*	3	3	12	—	1	5†
M.	67	—	2	1	4	3	82‡	—	—	—
L.M.	—	46	26	—	34	3	115	25	22	23
L.	1	4	—	—	—	—	5	3	3	3
N.K.	—	17	—	2	—	—	3	—	1	2

* School teachers.
† Including three owners of small business concerns.
‡ Including 46 farmers' wives and daughters, and bachelor farmers' sisters.

I. Farmers, including joint owners and female occupiers; also farmers' sons working at home.

II. Farm labourers, forestry workers, quarrymen, ore miners and others in primary industries not working on their own account.

III. Village craftsmen and their apprentices.

IV. Professional workers, including teachers.

V. Clerical workers and retail trades.

VI. Small-holders.

VII. Those with no paid occupation.

VIII. Unskilled labour (night watchman, roadman, etc.).

IX. Domestic servants, full- and part-time.

X. Miscellaneous (chemists, policemen, lorry drivers, etc.).

APPENDIX V

TABLE 5

SEX AND MARITAL STATUS OF THE SOCIAL CLASSES

Class.	Total.	Male.	Female.	Married. M.	F.	Single. M.	F.	Widowed. M.	F.
U.U.	23	9	14	5	7	2	5	2	2
L.U.	22	12	10	8	7	4	3	—	—
INT.	10	6	4	4	4	2	—	—	—
U.M.	30	10	20	4	8	6	12	—	—
M.	215	118	97	52	50	64	39	2	8
L.M.	363	159	204	91	88	60	95	8	21
L.	31	17	14	6	5	11	7	—	2
N.K.	29	18	11	8	7	9	2	1	2
Total	723	349	374	178	176	158	168	13	35

APPENDIX VI

'Familiar' Names as Symbols of Class Position

The names by which people are known in everyday speech are highly symbolic of relative position in the class system. Everyone has several 'names', the use of which depend on whether the speaker is a relative, a close friend, a casual acquaintance and so on. For the purpose of this Appendix, names used only within the family are ignored.

The men of the Upper-Upper class are usually referred to in their absence by the people in other classes by the use of the initials of their Christian names or by a nick-name based on an individual peculiarity, for example 'J.B.', 'Gallopity', etc. The use of the surnames with the prefix 'Mr.' is uncommon, and usually denotes disrespect or hostility. Surnames used without this prefix are sometimes heard, and this normally indicates that the subject has fairly low prestige. The women in this class are usually referred to as 'Mrs. X' or 'Miss Y', but in one or two cases a single Christian name is used on its own, for example 'Marguerite was down in t'village.'

People in the Lower-Upper class are usually known by the prefix appropriate to their sex followed by a surname, or—in the case of one or two of the men in this class who have high prestige—by using a diminutive form of a Christian name with the accompanying surname, for example, 'Mrs. Everson', 'Johnny Davies'.

The remaining classes of the parish share their methods of naming, and what difference there is depends on sex and personal prestige within each class. This can be represented schematically as follows:

High prestige within a class.	*Low prestige within a class.*
Male:	Male:
Diminutive Christian name with or without a surname, e.g. Jake, Harry, Tom Moore, Bobby Pattinson.	Surname alone or used with a place name, e.g. Edwards, Robertson Black End.
Nicknames, e.g. Pop, Spanjy, Backer, Tarry, etc.	Surname used with 'Mr.'.
Female:	Female:
Full or diminutive Christian name with a surname, e.g. May Moore, Margaret Simpson.	Surname used with 'Mrs.'.

The effectiveness of this system of symbols may be judged from the fact that, after a year's residence in the area, I found it possible to forecast the class and

APPENDIX VI

status of people who were unknown to me, by the way they were referred to by informants. When, for example, someone spoke of 'Johnny Dawson' he was probably referring to a man with high prestige in one of the lower classes, or (less probably) in the Lower-Upper class. If someone spoke of 'R. S. Herbertson' I knew he was referring to someone definitely in the Upper-Upper class.

The use of a prefix to denote disrespect and the use of familiar forms of reference for Upper-Upper class people is widespread in Cumberland. The second of these may be a method of symbolizing the fact that the traditional relationship between 'lord and man' was essentially reciprocal in its nature.

APPENDIX VII

Parochial Organizations

Organization.	Membership.	Sex.	Entry Qualifications.	Officers.
Agricultural Society	342	Both	Ten-shilling subscription	105
Wrestling Academy	128	Both	Nil	55
British Legion	367*	Male.	Service in Forces	11
W.I.	61	F.	Nil	13
Conservatives	200†	Both	Nil	38
Angling Club	29	Male‡	Residence in parish	11
Football Club	26	Male	Nil	8
Tennis Club	38	Both	Nil	3
Men's Cricket	32	Male	Residence in parish	6
Ladies' Cricket	17	F.	,, ,, ,,	3
Evening Classes	93	Both	Nil	12
Dramatic Society	29	Both	Nil	6
Oddfellows	169	Male	Nil	6
Mothers' Union	37	F.	Confirmed in Church; married with Child(ren)	6
Girls' Friendly Society	88	F.	Confirmed in Church	3
Sports Club	22	Both	Nil	10
School Outing	29	Both	Nil	29§
Parish Council	12	Male‡	Residence in parish	12§
Public Hall	40	Both	,, ,, ,,	40§
Reading Room	18	Male‡	,, ,, ,,	18§
Playing Field	20	Both	,, ,, ,,	20§
Further Education	17	Both	,, ,, ,,	17§
Fox Hounds	11	Both	Nil	—
Beagles	7	Both	Nil	2
Charity Trustees	6	Male‡	Residence in parish; confirmed in Church	6§
Girl Guides	12	F.	Nil	1
Church	689‖	Both	Baptism and Confirmation	—
Chapel	10¶	Both	Nil	3

* Only 114 of these live in Gosforth.
† Number estimated by Secretary: not confirmed.
‡ Those associations with only male members which are theoretically open to both sexes.
§ Organizations which are 'Committees' having no 'ordinary' members.
‖ The number of people who have been confirmed, not the number who attend the Church services.
¶ Number of people who attend regularly.

APPENDIX VIII

Part I. The Settlement Pattern of Medieval Gosforth

The four vills into which the ancient parish of Gosforth was divided, Neuton, Gosford, Seschalis and Boulton, were units which must have included, respectively, the areas known to-day as Newton and Newton Manor, Gosforth Village, Seascale and Bolton. The few identifiable place-names add a little to our knowledge of the extent of these vills. In Neuton, for example, were Fleming-hall [1] and Lingbank,[2] and other evidence suggests that the area lying between the present road from Gosforth village to New Mill and New Mill Beck, which forms the north-west boundary of the present parish, also lay in this vill.[3] In the vill of Boulton are Morthweyt Bec,[4] Boltonheued,[5] and Thornbanc,[6] while there are no place-names in the vill of Gosford which have survived the centuries.

Each deed in the Chartulary of St. Bees concerning a grant of land includes details of the lands surrounding it. When people whose land adjoined made grants, it is possible to form an approximate idea of the distance separating each portion, and the dwellings stated to be upon them. From this it appears certain that in each vill the settlements were dispersed over their total area. This is admittedly based on the assumption that the pieces of land mentioned in the Chartulary were at least roughly equivalent in length and breadth. It is possible that they were, in fact, elongated strips, and that, say, a grant of land thirty acres in area referred to a strip forty yards wide and nearly a mile and a half long. Such strips, if arranged side by side, with dwellings at one end, could result in a form of settlement similar to the 'line village' of the type found in France and Louisiana.[7] Such an arrangement is, of course, completely alien to the history of the area, and it would require an almost cataclysmic transformation from this form to the dispersed type to agree with the evidence which exists for the area at a later date.

Scattered evidence from the fourteenth century make the probability of the dispersed type of settlement even greater. A document dated 1303 mentions a dwelling at 'Briggepeting',[8] and there are references to others at 'Sevenhoues' in 1310,[9] 'Thystilton'[10] in 1318, 'Todobrig in Boulton' in 1363,[11] 'Pyel', 'Julianholm' and 'Scale' in 1365,[12] and 'Keldebank' in 1376.[13]

Part II. Township, Vill, and Manor

It has proved impossible to determine the exact relationship between the vill, the township, and the manor, and I have been unable to find more than a few scattered references to the boundaries of manors in this area, and to the operation of the manorial system.[14] The information available gives little indication of the characteristics of the Gosforth manors, but fortunately the manorial system appears to have little or no importance in an understanding of the present

APPENDIX VIII

social life of the parish. Manorial rights were in the hands of freeholders in the parish over a century ago at least.

Of greater importance, but almost as obscure, is the relationship between the vill and the township which succeeded it as the unit of local administration. The vill of Gosford had no counterpart in the townships when the latter are first mentioned in local documents, and presumably must have been divided up between them when the township system was adopted. Further evidence that the boundaries of the vills and the townships were not identical is given in tabular form below.

Place-name.	In the Vill of:	In the Township of:
Lyngbank	Neuton	Boonwood
Flemynghall	Neuton	Boonwood
Briggepeting	Gosford	Boonwood
Gillbanc [15]	Gosford	Boonwood
Helewynherge [16]	Gosford	Boonwood
Morthweyt	Boulton	Bolton High
Boltonheued	Boulton	Bolton High
Thornbanc	Boulton	Bolton Low
Toddelryg [17]	Boulton	Bolton High
Stubsat [18]	Boulton	Bolton Low
Thystilton	Boulton	Bolton High
Julian Holm	Boulton	Bolton High
Sevenhoues	Boulton	Bolton Low
Scar green [19]	Gosford	Ponsonby

The method which was used to determine boundaries, and the reason for the disappearance of 'Gosford' as an administrative unit are unknown. It is, however, important to note that the division into townships reflected the dispersed type of settlement already characteristic of the vill, in that it was not considered necessary to make a township of what we may describe as the 'embryonic' village of Gosforth.

Once established, the townships did not remain unchanged throughout the centuries. In 1600, three churchwardens witnessed the Rector's signature in the Parish Register. In 1697, when the Churchwardens' Accounts begin, there are four churchwardens, each living in his own township, which were given as Seascale, Boonwood, Crook of Bleng, and Bolton. An entry of May 3, 1780, names ten members of the newly instituted church jury, two each for the five divisions of Gosforth, High End of Bolton, Low End of Bolton, Boonwood, and Seascale.[20]

Moreover, the boundaries of the townships vary considerably in local documents, and several places are given as first in one township and then in another. For this reason the map of townships (Fig. 12) based on three sources [21] of roughly the same date, which do not differ from each other in any significant detail, shows only the boundaries in 1850. Sources of an earlier [22] or later [23] date would give maps with different boundaries.

NOTES

INTRODUCTION (*pages 1–4*)

1. Excluding a boy's preparatory school with a transient population of about 50 masters and pupils.
2. A letter from Grindal, Bishop of London, to Secretary Cecil. Quoted in Gay, E. F., 'The Midland Revolt and the Inquisitions of Depopulation', *Trans. Roy. Hist. Soc.* (N.S.), XVIII (1902), p. 210n.
3. See map accompanying Nicolson, J., and Burn, R., *The History and Antiquities of the Counties of Westmorland and Cumberland* (London, 1777).

CHAPTER I (*pages 5–33*)

1. Wilson, J., *The Register of the Priory of St. Bees*, Surtees Society, Vol. CXXVI (London, 1915).
2. In the custody of the Rector of Gosforth.
3. In the custody of the Parish Clerk of Gosforth.
4. The maps, which are constructed on several different scales, are, in accordance with the provisions of the Enclosure Act, of the common land only. None of the holdings are shown, but the surveyors printed the names of the owners of those holdings which adjoined the common, and indicated the point on the edge of the common where any two holdings met.
5. Records exist for five holdings (respectively 92, 90, 65, 64 and 36 acres) which show that there has been no significant change in their arable acreage since the beginning of the nineteenth century. From the evidence there is no reason to suppose that there has been any important redistribution of the arable land of those farms which have survived from 1800 to the present day, excluding of course additions from amalgamation.
6. From a comparison of the Parish Award and the Parish Registers.
7. This is clear from the specific nature of the entries relating to the waste in the Chartulary of St. Bees. For example, a grant of land to the Priory by John the Falconer in 1247–8 mentions common pasture for 12 oxen, 2 mares, 1 horse, 50 sheep, 20 goats, and 4 pigs, with their young of one year. See Thompson, W. N., 'Gosforth in the Chartulary of St. Bees', *Transactions Cumberland and Westmorland Antiquarian and Archaeological Society* (N.S.), II (Kendal, 1902), p. 310 *et seq.*
8. See Dudley Stamp, L. (Ed.), *The Land of Britain*, Pt. 49, 'Cumberland' (London, 1943), p. 319.
9. In 1921 one estate attempted to sell its holding of nearly 2,000 acres in Gosforth: one rather small field alone was sold.
10. This fragmentation has made it impossible to produce an adequate map of land-holding in the parish as a whole on a reasonably small scale, since anything under 6 inches to the mile proved far too congested to be worthwhile.

NOTES

Moreover, there is not enough evidence for the construction of a map showing earlier conditions within any degree of completeness.

11. See, for example, Dudley Stamp, *op. cit., passim*: Bainbridge, T. H., 'Eighteenth Century Agriculture in Cumberland', *T.C.W.A.A.S.* (N.S.), XLII (1942), 56–66; and 'Land Utilisation in Cumbria in the mid-Nineteenth Century as revealed by a Study of the Tithe Returns', *T.C.W.A.A.S.* (N.S.), XLIII (1943), 87–95; Grainger, F., 'Agriculture in Cumberland in Ancient Times', *T.C.W.A.A.S.* (N.S.), IX (1909), 120–46; Bailey, J., and Culley, G., *General View of the Agriculture of the County of Cumberland* (London, 1794), *passim*: Tate, W. E., 'A Handlist of English Enclosure Acts and Awards', *T.C.W.A.A.S.* (N.S.), XLIII (1943), 175–98; and Gray, H. L., *English Field Systems* (Cambridge, Mass., 1915), 227–41 and 267–71.

12. The Agricultural Revolution did not reach Cumberland until the mid-eighteenth century, when wheat, clover, and turnips were all introduced, the two latter by Philip Howard of Corby Castle in 1752 and 1755 respectively. This was nearly a hundred years after their general introduction into Eastern England. The remoteness of the Gosforth area is emphasized by the fact that turnips were unknown in the parish at least twenty-five years after they had reached other parts of Cumberland.

13. The cattle at this time were a small breed of longhorns, with some Galloways: Shorthorns were introduced into Cumberland in the early nineteenth century.

14. This account was written in 1780.

15. Including those rented by parishioners: holdings farmed by people not resident in the parish are excluded.

16. There is mutual agreement only in a limited legal sense. In practice the tenants strongly resented the increase in rents, but agreed to it because they thought the increase smaller than that which would result if the landlord sought arbitration through official channels.

17. The names of the farms are fictitious.

18. These are not mixed farms in the sense that they have substantial arable as well as grass. They are mixed in the sense that they do not specialize in any one branch of stock husbandry.

19. One farmer remarked of Friesians, 'They're nobbut blasted milking machines.'

20. 'Hogg' is the term used for a lamb for twelve months after weaning. It is only applied to Herdwick sheep.

21. Wilson, T., *The New Shepherd's Guide* (Lancaster, 1913), *passim*. According to this book there were eleven Gosforth farms with fell stocks of Herdwick sheep. Then, as now, the sheep were regarded as inseparable from the 'heaf' (fell pasture) on which they were reared, and the exchange of a particular tract of rough grazing automatically implied the exchange of the sheep that grazed it. Thus in the various 'Shepherd's Guides' the different marks by which sheep are identified are always given in reference to a particular 'park', and a farmer might well have three different 'smits' (painted markings) and ear-croppings for the one holding.

22. As in many other parts of the country the ploughing programmes of recent years have caused an increase in the amount of temporary grass and a corresponding decrease in the area under permanent grass. The heavier stocking

NOTES

of cattle has resulted in a greater demand for winter fodder, so that mowing grass far exceeds the acreage reserved for grazing.

23. 'Dry' stone walls are found only in the north-west of the parish (above 600 feet) and in the north-east (above 300 feet). Elsewhere boundaries are marked by earth and stone walling, surmounted by a thin hedge.

24. On those farms which provide winterage, the land cannot be put up for hay until the sheep have been returned to the fells. Differences in fertilizing policy also make for variation in the date on which the hay is ready for cutting.

25. On all rented farms tenancies are on a yearly basis, dating from February 2nd or March 25th.

26. Lowland farmers who accept very small numbers of sheep for winterage are paid weekly at 9d. or 10d. a head, but normally 15s. to £1 is paid at the end of the wintering period for every sheep returning to the fell pastures. Increased tillage during war-time and the fact that lowland farmers no longer need the income derived from this source have together made wintering a severe problem for the fell farmer, and raised winterage charges to almost treble the 1939 figure.

27. A Wool Board has now been formed which will probably supersede local organizations in the buying of wool.

28. Hiring fairs are still important at Cockermouth and Carlisle. Gosforth was served until three or four years ago by the hiring fairs at Egremont, now replaced by advertisement in the *Whitehaven News* and other local newspapers.

29. Homans, G. C., *English Villagers of the Thirteenth Century* (Harvard, 1942), pp. 353–72.

30. 'Swills' are baskets made by weaving thin oak laths on an oval framework of the same material; they resemble a flattened inverted dome in section, and are produced in a great many sizes.

31. Rush candles, as far as can be traced, vanished completely from the parish towards the end of the first decade of this century. Shortages during the last war resulted in a revival of candle-making on a few remote farms, an interesting illustration of the fact that a culture trait can survive the interruption of its expression in overt behaviour.

32. King's College, Newcastle, an institution responsible for many innovations in agriculture in West Cumberland.

33. It is also the nearest source for clogs, the everyday footwear of the farmer and his family.

34. There are at least five farms which produce butter in quantities far in excess of their own needs. No details could be obtained as to its disposal.

35. Farmers whose rent was less than £100 a year were not required to keep accounts until April 1949.

36. The fact that some farmers do not pay income tax does not mean that their income is below the taxable limit. Allowances for children and for the rather large sums spent on machinery—to mention only two examples—make the payment of income tax a very unreliable index of a farmer's true financial position.

37. The generalizations in the last two paragraphs are based on: (1) Information supplied by a few farmers regarding their income and expenditure. These (atypical) individuals were the only ones who were prepared to discuss their financial affairs in any detail. (2) Isolated facts and figures mentioned from time

NOTES

to time by farmers, which have been confirmed by different informants wherever possible. (3) Analysis of the results obtained from a series of selected questions. The method devised was based on the fact that there were no tractors in the parish until 1940, and on the assumption that only one farmer bought machinery on the hire-purchase system. (No farmer admitted buying equipment on hire-purchase, but several informants who have lived in the parish all their lives, and whose opinion I consider reliable, named one farmer who bought by this means.) The procedure was to obtain details of items of major equipment (including cars, lorries, etc.) bought since 1940, on as many farms as possible. Each item was then given a value determined by averaging its price in 1945 and 1950. From this an approximate total value of equipment bought in the last ten years was obtained. This then offered some index of farm profits during the ten year period, or more accurately during the last five years, since most of the equipment has been bought after 1945.

In addition, questions were asked about the amount of feeding stuffs purchased annually, the average amount of milk sold to the M.M.B., the quantity of potatoes produced for sale, farm rent, subsidies, wintering charges, seed bills, and the profit made on selling different types of livestock. These were then converted into terms of money, by using 1950 prices and the present stocking of farms, in an attempt to obtain an approximation of major farm expenditure and income.

This method was used only after several attempts to construct a farm balance-sheet had proved abortive—mainly because precise details were never given.

38. The mole catcher must not be confused with the Pest Officer of the Agricultural Executive Committee. In Gosforth he is a former farm-worker who lives largely off the proceeds of trapping moles and rabbits and selling their skins.

39. Estate workers included game-keepers, foresters, 'beck-watchers' (i.e. water-bailiffs), gardeners, handy-men, etc.

40. The analysis is based on the previous occupations of native parishioners, and the statements of informants concerning the village as they remembered it in the inter-war period. No figures can be quoted because the 1931 Census deals only with the Rural District, which is a predominantly industrial area, and because less than a third of the present occupiers were born in the parish.

41. Married men were paid weekly at the beginning of this century.

CHAPTER II (*pages 34–58*)

1. The evolution of the West Cumberland farmhouse is an interesting topic in itself. Some descriptions of the older houses in the district are given in the *Transactions* of the Cumberland and Westmorland Antiquarian and Archaeological Society (for example 'Gosforth Hall' by C. A. Parker and J. F. Curwen in Vol. III (1903), N.S.) and the author has written a detailed study of Gosforth farmsteads, which is shortly to be published in the same series.

2. Peat fires are more characteristic of the fell farms, where they are still fairly common. The importance of the hearth as the focus of the main room of the house is too well known to need discussion here, but it is of interest to note that one of the earliest references to a house in Gosforth, in a deed dating from the early part of the thirteenth century, describes it as 'edificia ignem habencia cum

NOTES

pertinenciis'—that is as a 'fire house' (Wilson, *op. cit.*, p. 153, Deed No. 110). The term 'fire house' was used of a dwelling house, as distinct from the outbuildings, in many parts of Cumberland during the latter part of the nineteenth century.

3. Cf. Miner, H., *St. Denis. A French Canadian Parish* (Chicago, 1939), p. 141.

4. See Addy, S. O., *The Evolution of the English House* (London, 1933), p. 79, and Rees, A. D., *Life in a Welsh Countryside* (Cardiff, 1950), p. 45.

5. This is fed to the best milk cow on Christmas morning or New Year's Day. The custom of the 'last cut' is widespread in Northern Europe and is of very great antiquity. For the distribution and significance of this custom see Homans, *op. cit.*, p. 372; Whistler, L., *The English Festivals* (London, 1947), pp. 59–60 and 184–90; Sir J. G. Frazer, *The Golden Bough*, Abridged Edition (London, 1947), Chap. XLV. The local characteristics of the custom in Cumberland are described in an article in the *Cumberland Pacquet* of Sept. 7, 1893.

6. 'Rum butter' made of butter and sugar mixed into a paste and flavoured with rum is invariably made for the festivities that accompany *rites de passage* and for any other occasions of note. Much of the success of, say, a birthday party or christening depends on the quality and amount of rum butter available. Rum is also much used in other dishes prepared on special occasions, for example rum sauce to accompany the Christmas pudding. This might possibly be a legacy from the time when smuggling was rife on the lonely Cumberland coast.

7. On one occasion I was told it was 'insulting' to knock at the front door.

8. No comparisons have been made with the rural and urban districts of Cumberland, or with the county as a whole, for reasons which are given on p. 65.

9. See Homans, *op. cit.*, pp. 111–20, and 'Partible Inheritance of Villagers' Holdings', *Economic History Review*, VIII (1937), 48–56.

10. See Homans, *op. cit.*, *passim*.

11. See Arensberg and Kimball, *Family and Community in Ireland* (New York, 1939), *passim*.

12. See Spiegel, N. W., 'The Altenteil: German Farmers' Old Age Security', *Rural Sociology*, IV, No. 2 (1939), 203–18.

13. See Homans, *op. cit.*, p. 145.

CHAPTER III (*pages 59–68*)

1. It is interesting to note that these old women—the last of whom died in 1949—were also famous for miles around for their ability to cure serious illnesses, and were accredited with secret remedies which cured such intractable diseases as erysipelas and psoriasis. For an account of the role of these 'oald weaves' in Cumberland villages during the last century, see Carrick, T., 'Scraps of English Folklore', XVIII, *Folklore*, XL (1929), p. 278. Similarly gifted 'wise women' are well known in Ireland. See O'Suilleabhain, S., *A Handbook of Irish Folklore* (Wexford, 1942), pp. 214–15.

2. Very significantly it is the north wall of the churchyard which is used. There is no patch of unconsecrated ground used for burial in Gosforth, and in burying the children under the wall in this way, a compromise is effected between the canons of the Church and the popular fear of being buried 'in any old place'.

NOTES

The north is, of course, traditionally associated with Hell and the lairs of fiends and giants: see Hardwick, C., *Traditions, Superstitions and Folklore* (Manchester, 1872), p. 28, and Langland's *Piers Plowman*, II, lines 122 ff.

3. Most of the beliefs concerning the care of babies are found in many parts of England and Northern Europe. See, for example, Radford, M.A. and E., *An Encyclopaedia of Superstitions* (London, 1947), *passim*: Balfour, M. C., and Thomas, N. W., *Examples of Printed Folklore concerning Northumberland*, County Folklore Series IV (London, 1904), pp. 89–91; Hardy, J. (Ed.), *The Denham Tracts* (London, 1892), I, Section IV, pp. 141–86; and Leach, M. (Ed.), *Dictionary of Folklore, Mythology and Legend* (New York, 1949–50), I, 217–18.

4. See Rees, A. D., *op. cit.*, p. 82.

5. See Loomis, C. P., and Beegle, J. A., *Rural Sociology* (New York, 1950), Part One.

6. These marriages included all the married couples living in the parish in 1951, whose first child was born in Gosforth, supplemented by others abstracted from the Parish Registers (for the period 1920–50) to make the sample statistically valid.

7. Leffingwell, A., *Illegitimacy & The Influence of the Seasons Upon Conduct* (London, 1892), pp. 6–21.

8. See Leffingwell, *op. cit.*, *passim*, and Myrdal, A., *Nation and Family* (London, 1945), *passim*.

9. The number of children who are stated to be illegitimate in the Parish Registers is greatly exceeded by those whose exact status is extremely doubtful, and for this reason no figures have been quoted for previous centuries. In numerous cases, for example, only the father's *or* the mother's name has been recorded, and only infrequently is it possible to discover whether or not the parent referred to was married when the entry was made. Thus during the period 1581–1669 the number of children stated to be illegitimate gives a rate of 47 per thousand births. When the number of doubtful births is added the figure rises to 63. W. E. Tate has noted in his valuable book on Parish Registers (p. 213) that the birth of an illegitimate child was apparently an unusual event in most country parishes during the sixteenth century, became rather more common during the seventeenth century and was very frequent from 1750 onwards. Gosforth therefore had a comparatively high illegitimacy rate during the time under consideration. In this area at least, it is no new phenomenon and was not, as Tate suggests, one which appeared in the late eighteenth century.

10. Several of the younger married women in the parish stated that, as far as they knew, none of their friends or members of their families had ever visited the Family Planning Association Clinic at Carlisle. Many of them were unaware that this organization existed.

11. See Stagg, J., 'The Bridewain', in *Minstrel of the North* (London, 1810).

12. Sometimes the corpse is moved into the 'best bedroom' because the period before burial is marked by a constant procession of friends and relatives calling to 'have a last look' at the deceased.

13. The magical properties of the rowan tree are mentioned in the folklore of many countries, suggesting therefore that the last of these stories is a 'folktale' rather than an actual event. The first, on the other hand, was apparently witnessed by several informants.

NOTES
CHAPTER IV (*pages 69–85*)

1. Until a few years ago, when the building of the Atomic Energy Station at Sellafield resulted in a large influx of population from other parts of the country to the neighbouring parish of Seascale, where a new town is rapidly growing.
2. It is, of course, a commonplace in sociological literature that while consanguinity is a prerequisite for the development of extensive social relationships based on kinship, a high degree of biological interconnectedness does not, *per se*, result in the use of this base for a system of social relations. See, for example, Loomis, C. P., and Beegle, J. A., *Rural Social Systems* (New York, 1950), pp. 39–63.
3. This is an inversion of the normal order of surname and place-name. Souty How was a small-holding now absorbed into another farmstead.
4. In 1600 there were 9 families living in separate homesteads who were surnamed Moscroppe; 9 named Gunson; 9 named Poole; 11 named Benson; and 9 named Wilson. In 1800 there were 10 separate families named Tyson; 11 named Mossop; 11 named Mawson; 10 named Hartley; 10 named Steele; and 8 named Dixon.
5. Cf. Arensberg, C., *The Irish Countryman* (London, 1937), p. 100.
6. The term 'kin-group' is used here instead of 'family' because kinsmen other than members of the 'family', as understood in this chapter, occupied the holdings in the past.
7. These examples are particularly striking when considered in relation to the general unreliability of local 'folk memory'. See MacCulloch, J. A., 'Folk Memory in Folk Tales', *Folklore*, LX (September 1949), 307–15.
8. I was able to identify several of the younger members of this kin-group quite easily without knowing who they were.
9. The genealogy of this family is complicated by the fact that there are children by both marriages, and the two brothers were children of a widow, still alive, who married three times, two of these marriages resulting in children. All of the surviving members of this group live on two farms close together which are worked as a unit.
10. Mossop is the modern form of the older Moscrop or Moscroppe.
11. The use of more than one Christian name also became common during the latter half of the nineteenth century. The only people with more than one Christian name before this time were members of the 'gentry', which suggests that the idea spread downwards from the uppermost social level to the remainder of the community.
12. Of 134 eldest sons living at present in the parish, for whom full genealogies are available, 33 inherited their paternal grandfather's name alone, but 15 of these also bear the same name as their father. In all, 27 eldest sons are named 'after' their father. Six eldest sons are named after their maternal grandfather, the same number after their paternal grandfather combined with that of their father, and two after their paternal grandfather combined with that of their mother. Two are named after their father combined with that of their maternal grandmother, two after their father with that of their maternal grandfather, and three after their maternal grandmother. Three inherited their mother's maiden surname, and five their father's name and mother's maiden surname. There were

NOTES

12 others named after their parents or grandparents in different combinations. The remainder are either named after more distant relatives (in one case a man with three rather unusual Christian names bears exactly the same name as his paternal grandfather's brother's wife's brother!) or, in the case of younger people, are given names which only appear in the Parish Registers during the last twenty to thirty years, for example Brian, Vincent, Geoffrey, etc.

Of 47 eldest daughters, 17 are named after their maternal grandmother, but 9 of these bear the same name as their mother. In all, 14 daughters are named 'after' their mother. Three are named after their paternal grandmother, and one after her maternal grandmother and mother together. The remainder have all been given names that were alien to the parish until recently, for example Celia, Patricia, Daphne, Hilary, Sandra, etc.

13. It is interesting to note that these names correspond very closely in frequency to those which appear in the *Birth* columns of *The Times* and the *Daily Telegraph*, and that the introduction of any new name into the Baptismal Register in Gosforth is quite often coincident with a spate of the same name in the columns of these papers. The people who put birth notices in newspapers of this type are, of course, generally upper-middle or upper class in status, and therefore it seems reasonable to conclude that the same process is in operation as that noted for the introduction of 'second' Christian names in the last century.

14. For a note on alternate generations in another part of north-western England see Myres, J. L., *Man* (1938), 169: alternate generations in other parts of the world are discussed in Hocart, A. M., *Man* (1931), 214 (Fiji), and (1938), 31 (Egypt); and Rees, A. D., *Man* (1938), 168 (Wales).

15. As in other parts of Northern England, where the name of a deceased relative is only given normally as a 'second' name, to be used solely on formal occasions.

16. Similar examples are also known in Ireland. See O'Suilleabhain, *op. cit.*, p. 146.

17. There are dozens of examples of 'emergency' baptisms in the Registers; see, however, pp. 59–60.

18. The inter-relationship between the social class system and the kinship system involves complex values and motives which make it more appropriately the field of study of the social psychologist. As far as Gosforth is concerned the conflict between the two systems—which appear in some ways to be incompatible—did not manifest itself sufficiently in overt behaviour to make its examination much more than mere guesswork.

19. *Catalogue of Ancient Deeds* (London, 1902), IV. Deed A.8591.
20. *Ibid.* Deed A.9235.
21. *Ibid.* Deed A.8591.
22. *Ibid.* Deed A.9707.
23. *Ibid.* Deed A.10272.
24. *Calendar of Patent Rolls. Edward I, 1301–7* (London, 1898), p. 181.
25. See Homans, *op. cit.*, pp. 119–20.
26. For Celtic society see Ellis, T. P., *Welsh Tribal Law and Custom in the Middle Ages* (Oxford, 1926): for consanguine families in Western Norway see Olsen, M., *Farms and Fanes of Ancient Norway*, Instituttet for Sammenlignende Kulturforskning, IX (Oslo, 1928), pp. 44–9. Olsen's description of co-operation between

NOTES

farmers, based on ties of kinship, which lasted in Western Norway from the Saga times until the late nineteenth century, corresponds in remarkable fashion to the conditions in Gosforth described in this chapter.

27. The extent and permanence of the Viking Invasions are best illustrated in the distribution of place-names, personal names and dialect terms of Norse origin, many of which are to be found in the Gosforth district. See, for example, Armstrong, A. M., Mawer, A., Stenton, F. M., and Dickins, B., *The Place-Names of Cumberland*, English Place-Name Society, Vol. XXI, Pts. II and III.

W. G. Collingwood in his *Lake District History* (Kendal, 1928, p. 135) shows how many of the larger landowners in the twelfth century, when the manorial system was well established, bore old Norse names, and elsewhere (*Scandinavian Britain*, London, 1908, p. 219) comments: 'Situated on the shore of the Irish Sea, which was a Viking lake, and on the main road from the English East to the Celtic West, the neighbourhood of Gosforth was indeed geographically the focus of all the influences which fostered the birth of the Edda poems. Wherever they were composed, it was here that they were illustrated almost at the moment of their production.'

Other historians quote documents to show that the introduction of Anglo-Norman administration did not greatly affect the social organization of the Norsemen. See, for example, Bouch, C. M. L., *People and Prelates of the Lake Counties* (Kendal, 1948), pp. 17-18.

CHAPTER V (*pages 86-120*)

1. For a discussion of the terminology used in this chapter, see Appendix V.
2. These methods are discussed in Appendix V.
3. Since this is typical of most of the members of this class, the average age of the 'Upper Ten' is much higher than that of the other classes. See Appendix V, Tables 1 and 2.
4. Calculations based on the stated wage earned by this family and current rates of mortgage and interest on the price of the house give a figure of twelve shillings and ninepence per head to cover all weekly living costs—apart from any savings they may have.
5. People in Gosforth are generally well aware of the class to which they belong, although they usually have considerable difficulty in putting their thoughts into words concerning this. This was easily proved in the later stages of the field-work by coupling the person to whom I was speaking with the name of someone in an inferior social position. Their reactions seldom left any doubt that I was sociologically correct and socially indiscreet.
6. This interpretation could possibly lead to the hypothesis that the social structure, of which the class system is a part, operates independently of the people who compose it. I do not hold this view, and it is, moreover, one which goes beyond the evidence available here.
7. This does not include those people who have relatives living in the parish.
8. Why the upper class buy antiques at all, and why they buy certain kinds of antiques rather than others is a matter involving such relatively unexplored

NOTES

topics (at least to the anthropologist) as aesthetic values. A partial explanation is given in a later section of the chapter.

9. Exact figures on cinema attendance and reading habits were not collected. As a rule, however, farmers go to the cinema about once in two months if they have young children, and not at all if childless. Villagers attend from several times a week to once in ten years, depending on their age, sex, marital status, etc.

Farmers buy farming periodicals in some quantity, but little else. Villagers read a wide range of magazines, from cheap 'sensational' fiction to *Hansard* and *The Times Literary Supplement*.

10. See Wilson, J., *op. cit.*, *Elenchus Contentorum*, pp. 6–8, and Deeds 109–133 (pp. 151–73), and 308–26 (pp. 316–22). The first grants were made in the years 1150–70, by which time the Anglo-Norman administration was well established.

11. For example the Senhouse family, which held land in Gosforth from 1271 to 1707, and owned property in the parish until the present century.

12. There were free tenants, tenants at will, and bond tenants. The differences in their status, which were considerable, are not taken into account here.

13. Burial in wool was common in this area during the latter part of the seventeenth century and was enforced by an Act passed in 1667—'For the Encouragement of the Woollen and Paper Manufacture of the Kingdom'. This law was abolished in 1814, having been long in disuse.

14. Mannix and Whellan, *History, Gazetteer, and Directory of Cumberland* (Beverley, 1847), p. 340.

15. In Cumberland as a whole the decline of the statesman had begun at a much earlier date, and was especially marked during the years 1770–1830. In Gosforth, on the other hand, the change took place much later. The Parish Registers and the Glebe Terrier of 1778 reveal that the number of statesmen in that year was almost the same as that in 1829.

16. Evidence of the prosperity of the statesmen of this period is fairly abundant. The will of William Poole of Hall Senna, for example, dating from the first decade of the nineteenth century, mentions 'My Dressing Chest made of Mayhogany and now standed in the room over the Parler . . . together with my two dining tables made of Oake standing in the house, and the other made of Mayhogany now standing in the Parler'. Among other bequests was the sum of £600 to a relative, a large amount of money in those days.

17. See Hocart, A. M., *Kings and Councillors* (Cairo, 1936), pp. 256 *et seq.*

CHAPTER VI (*pages 121–39*)

1. Cf. Warner, W. L., and Lunt, P. S., *The Social Life of a Modern Community* (New Haven, 1941), pp. 307–8 and 349–50.

2. The Church is not shown in this diagram because Church membership has special features which are dealt with elsewhere. (See below, Chapter X, 'Religion'.)

3. This definition of an office-holder in an association is taken from a long conversation with a member of the Lower class, in which he condemned *all* associations.

NOTES

4. The numbers given for each association apply only to members who live in the parish.

5. This divergence—between ideal patterns and actual behaviour—is very widely recognized in anthropological literature. See, for example, Linton, R., *The Study of Man* (New York, 1936), pp. 100–2; McIver, R. M., and Page, C. H., *Society: An Introductory Analysis* (London, 1950), pp. 443–6; and Hoebel, E. A., *Man in the Primitive World* (New York, 1949), p. 432—'There are always gaps between what a people think they do, say they do, and actually do'.

6. In all there are five charities—the Hartley Charity (1858), the High School Charity, the Hearse House, the Unknown Donor, and the Poor Stock. For further details see Loftie, A. G. (Ed.), *The Rural Deanery of Gosforth* (Kendal, 1889), p. 55.

7. A village on the border of Cumberland and Northumberland, sited about sixteen miles E.N.E. of Carlisle.

8. Muscular skills of this type are very difficult to describe in words, but an account of the main features of this kind of wrestling is given in *Encyclopaedia Britannica* (Chicago, 1947), Vol. 23, p. 806.

9. See Robinson, J., and Gilpin, G., *Wrestling and Wrestlers* (London, 1893), *passim*.

10. The initial position is as follows: The contestants stand facing each other with legs apart: each leans forward so that his chin rests in his opponent's right shoulder. Each clasps his arms about the other's back, so that the right arm is above and the left arm below the adversary's.

11. If, during a round, the wrestlers leave the mat or fall to the ground simultaneously (a 'dog-fall') the round is re-started.

12. For example in the *Cumberland Pacquet*, May 20, 1786, concerning a wedding in the nearby parish of Lamplugh.

13. Details of these competitions fill several pages of the Parish Magazine for July 1887. For a consideration of ritual contests in a wider context see Huizinga, J., *Homo Ludens* (London, 1949), p. 18, and Chap. III, 'Play and Contest as Civilizing Functions'; and Hocart, A. M., *Kingship* (London, 1941), pp. 15–17.

14. The origins of 'backhold wrestling' appear to be very obscure. For an account of this sport in nineteenth-century Cumberland, see Litt, W., *Wrestliana* (Whitehaven, 1823), *passim*.

15. According to Dickinson (*A Glossary of the Dialect of Cumberland*, Carlisle, 1899) cock-loaf was made of white flour, eggs, sugar and 'other ingredients'. No yeast was used. It was baked in an oven and 'murled' (crumbled between the fingers) as wanted.

The use of closely guarded secret recipes is also typical of hound-trailing, another popular Cumberland sport. Among the ingredients used are reported the following: sheep's brains, eggs, hares, and port wine.

16. The same is largely true of poaching, which seems to be at least moderately prevalent in Gosforth. Salmon finds its way to the tables of many people who belong to no known Angling Club.

17. For the purpose of this analysis 'fairly regular intervals' is defined as being within the range of once a day to once a fortnight. Sporadic visits at longer intervals are not included.

18. The behaviour of one of the regular visitors to Kellbank is interesting for

NOTES

reasons not connected with the subject of this chapter, but which may most conveniently be considered here. One day I saw this man leave the inn and go to a shop in the village, where he bought one currant bun. He returned to Kellbank, ate the bun, and then repeated the performance six or seven times. Later, many people told me that this man was 'moon-struck'. The day on which the incident occurred was that following the full moon, and this was said to account for his odd behaviour. The belief that the moon can affect a person's sanity is firmly held in Gosforth, and many stories are told to support it. Cf. Bayne-Powell, R., *English Country Life in the Eighteenth Century* (London, 1935), p. 269.

19. In 1857, 'Gosforth' included the present parish of Seascale, but the figure quoted refers only to the present parish of Gosforth. In 1829 there were six inns in the parish, and a petition of 1774 refers to two licensed public houses near the Church, but it is not known if there were any more elsewhere in the parish at that time.

20. In 1885–6 the present school was built on the site of 'Kirk Style', as the inn was known. It is interesting to note that according to local tradition the ruined farm of High Guards was once an inn, known as 'Sheepshank Hall', and many of the older parishioners firmly believed that their fathers had visited it. The evidence of the Parish Registers and of other local records proves conclusively that there never was an inn at this site. And it is extremely unlikely that the fathers of the present parishioners ever visited it while it was inhabited, since it was unoccupied when the Parish Award Survey was made in 1806, and has remained so since then. The name 'Sheepshank Hall' does not appear in any local document I examined. This seems to be an example of 'folk memory' based on false information, and it is also illustrative of the concept of time, especially past time, held in Gosforth.

The measurement of past time is based almost entirely on living memory, and on very many occasions people spoke of events that occurred two hundred years ago or more as happening 'in me father's time'. Conversely, when people were told that three houses, which have now completely disappeared, existed and were inhabited near the village in the decade 1830–40, they flatly refused to believe this—'because me father nivver said nowt about them'.

A striking example of this concept of time is that of the farmer who stated that his family had farmed the holding for 'a gay long time', because he remembered his grandfather saying that he had come to this farm with the rest of the family 'when he were a laal lad'. According to the Parish Registers this farmer's family have been in uninterrupted possession since 1697.

For an interesting discussion of 'folk memory' and time sense, see Lord Raglan, *The Hero* (London, 1949), pp. 30–45.

21. See, for example, Ian Hay's *The British Infantryman* (1942), pp. 152–5 and 201–2.

CHAPTER VII (*pages 140–54*)

1. For example in Japan, where the system of rights and duties involved in an obligatory action is particularly well developed. See Benedict, R., *The Chrysanthemum and the Sword* (London, 1947), pp. 99 ff.

2. See, for example, the Gosforth Parish Magazine for January 1934: 'the formal quadrille was a great success'.

NOTES

3. A most noticeable feature of the dialect is the use of the verb 'to want' especially with prepositions and past participles. Such constructions as 'The dog wants out', 'The clothes want washed', 'He wants nowt (nothing) going there' (i.e. he should not go there), were very common indeed.

4. See Homans, *op. cit.*, pp. 264-7, and Wilson, *op. cit.*, p. 179, Deed 141.

5. The sheep are sheared in the barn, using a 'sheep stool', a device unknown in many parts of England. There are two traditional methods of shearing. The most common is to start at the breast below the neck, open down the underside of the sheep and then work outwards on the shearer's right side. The sheep is then turned over, its legs are tied and the left side is sheared, the process being completed by cutting down the back and ending at the tail. The less common method is to start at the shoulder, open down the side and shear to the right and left, ending at the opposite shoulder. Both these styles differ considerably from parts of England where sheep are sheared on the ground, although the method of folding the fleece afterwards is identical (see Hennell, T., *Change in the Farm* (Cambridge, 1934), pp. 13-14). After being clipped the sheep are 'smitted' with the mark of the 'heaf' from which they come, using a mixture of Venetian Red and oil.

6. For descriptions of kurn suppers similar to those held in Gosforth, see Henderson, W., *Notes on the Folklore of the Northern Counties of England and the Border* (London, 1879), pp. 87-9, and Carrick, T. W., 'Scraps of English Folklore', XVIII (Cumberland), *Folklore*, XL (1929), p. 286.

7. This occurs on several farms which have a threshing machine installed, particularly those with a large area under oats.

8. Cf. Embree, F. J., *A Japanese Village. Suye Mura* (London, 1946), 74-7 and 84 *et seq.*, Munch, P. A., *Sociology of Tristan Da Cunha* (Oslo, 1945), pp. 271-2, and Pryde, G. S., *Social Life in Scotland since 1707*, Historical Association Pamphlet No. 98 (London, 1934), p. 17.

9. For a further discussion of the decline in co-operative practices in West Cumberland generally, see my 'Some Social Aspects of Recent Changes in Agriculture in West Cumberland', *Sociological Review*, (N.S.), Vol. I, No. 2 (December, 1953), pp. 93-100.

10. Cf. Lord Raglan, 'The Scope of Folklore', *Folklore*, LVII (1946), p. 101— 'It is not unusual to find a farmer's wife who has never set foot inside the next farmhouse' (Monmouthshire).

11. In this respect the farm family differs from most of those in the village, where the husband frequently puts the children to bed and performs other tasks usually assigned to women, while his wife visits friends or attends a whist-drive in the Public Hall.

CHAPTER VIII (*pages 155-67*)

1. The present hamlet of Hall Senna was known as 'Sevenhoues' or 'Sevenhouse' in medieval times (St. Bees, *c.* 1225), so this might possibly have been a hamlet as early as the thirteenth century.

2. For example, Bolton (Old Norse *Bud*—a booth, or dwelling) and Laconby

NOTES

(Old Scandinavian *byr*—a homestead). See Lindkvist, H., *Middle-English Place-Names of Scandinavian Origin* (Uppsala, 1912). I. Introduction, pp. xlix ff. and *passim*.

3. It should be noted that the use of the dot method in this map tends to over-emphasize the importance of the hamlet. Each large dot represents one elementary family, and not one dwelling, and it is, of course, possible that several families lived in the same house. In most cases it was possible to pick out the families of occupiers from the use of such terms as 'husbandman', 'yeoman', 'taylor', etc., but this does not eliminate the possibility of error. A husbandman and a tailor might, for example, share the same dwelling, while the fact that two families occupying the same site have different surnames might disguise the existence of a close blood relationship between them, for example by a marriage not recorded in the Register. Also since the actual sites of sixteenth-century homesteads are not known, it has been necessary to group all the families together near the contemporary place-name, so that some of the hamlets may appear far more compact than they were in fact. It is possible, for example, that the six families living at Above-wood inhabited the sites of the three farms that exist there now (represented on the map by small dots).

4. The tendency to over-emphasize the importance of hamlets was still unavoidable despite the amount of additional information that is available for the beginning of the nineteenth century. In some cases a site occupied by six or more families in 1810 is now marked by a single farmstead, and there is no evidence at all of other building—at Peel Place, for example. In other instances, for example at Hall Senna and Boonwood, the dwelling sites are known but there is no distinction made between them in the documents of the nineteenth century.

5. This probably encouraged compilers of the nineteenth-century 'directories' to perpetuate the mistake made by Denton two centuries earlier, since all those I have examined correspond with this early source—a case of 'aide toi, le ciel t'aidera'.

6. The predominance of the scattered habitat is equally evident in the history of the larger units of which Gosforth is a part. Unlike those parts of England where nucleated settlements were dominant, none of the larger territorial divisions have been named after towns. Gosforth was in the barony of Copeland and later in the Ward of Allerdale above Derwent. It is now part of Ennerdale Rural District.

7. There is a lowland proverb which says 'Sheep make bad neighbours'.

8. Cf. Frazer, J. G., *Folklore in the Old Testament* (London, 1923), pp. 307–13. The same belief is found in much of Africa, Lapland, the Scottish Highlands, Lincolnshire, Worcestershire, etc.

9. None of the hill farmers in Gosforth own a motor car or motor cycle, and only one, a newcomer, owns a bicycle. None ride horses.

10. The prevalence of this practice is reflected in the large number of dialect terms used to describe it, and the numerous references to it in the literature of the county. See, for example, Dickinson, *op. cit.*, pp. 127, 131, 133, 265, etc., and *Cumbriana, passim*.

11. Approximately a third of the farmers in the parish visited Whitehaven three times or less during 1950; another third went every two months, and the remainder ranged from this to a maximum of once a fortnight. A sample of a

NOTES

hundred villagers of both sexes, aged 20 to 60, said they normally visited Whitehaven as follows: 14 once a week; 7 once in three weeks; 18 once a month; 42 once every two to three months; 19 once in four months or less.

12. Apart from isolated years there is a fairly complete record of baptisms and burials; there are several gaps in the Marriage Register, including those from 1612–35; 1643–50; 1753–68; and 1774–91.

13. In each generation of this family, which has the unusual surname of Pharoah, one son is invariably named Crispin. This is a family tradition arising from the belief that 'hundreds of years ago' a farmer found a baby boy on Hardknott Pass and named him Crispin Pharoah—Crispin because he was found on St. Crispin's Day, and Pharoah because this was the first name which the farmer found in the Bible that lay open on the table when he returned with the infant.

The 'Foundling motif' in this tale is, of course, a familiar one in the folklore and mythology of many lands.

14. Significantly, one of these farmers is a Methodist and the other is not a regular Church-goer. Assisting the Rector is not correlated in any way with regular attendance at Church, and many of the people who are notable for the help they give him go to Church perhaps once or twice a year at most.

CHAPTER IX (pages 168–77)

1. This story of the hydraulic lift was heard with every evidence of belief by a number of people who must have known it was untrue. Overtly at least, people accepted the fabrication as a 'social truth'.

2. Stories of much the same kind are told of the visits of 'Professors', experts, etc. For example, on one occasion, it is said, a visiting 'Professor' who came to give a lecture was unable to answer many of the questions put by his audience and was further embarrassed by having his mistakes pointed out to him. Other stories are told of the outwitting and confounding of 'experts', and of the failure of travelling salesmen to sell inferior goods by using scientific jargon. The theme of the patronizing well-educated stranger being made to look foolish by the quick-witted countryman is, of course, very common in folklore.

3. According to the Clerk to the Parish Council, the following matters have been considered by the Council in recent years:

(a) Street Lighting. 'Application to the R.D.C. and North Western Electricity Board for the extension of street lighting to the Wellington end of the village has been going on at approx. 6 months intervals since 1947—still without success. . . . The matter now rests with R.D.C.'

(b) War Memorial. 'Originally erected in memory of the men of the Parish who gave their lives in the 1914–18 War. Through the initiative of the Parish Council, by the addition of a suitable inscription it has now been made to serve as a Memorial to the men of the 1939–45 war.'

(c) Further Education Committee. 'The Parish Council is authorized to appoint this local Committee. In recent years it has consisted of the entire Parish Council with the addition of three members of the Gosforth Women's Institute—elected annually.'

NOTES

(d) Gift Food Parcels. 'Since 1947 a number of Gift Food Parcels from Australia have been received by us through the R.D.C., each allocation varying in number from 26 in 1947 to 8 this year.... We distribute ours to widows and Old Age Pensioners in the village.'

(e) Parish Seats. 'Only three of these in the village situated at various points on the roadside.... Two years ago a brass plate bearing (an) inscription was fixed to each of these seats.... Parish Council is authorized to maintain these. Maintenance has been carried out by way of painting and minor repairs from time to time during the past fifty years.'

(f) Survey of Footpaths. ('This proved to be one of the biggest jobs in my experience as Clerk.) In 1950 all Parish Councils were asked to assist in the National Survey of Public Rights of Way.... A sub-committee from members of the Parish Council was formed to deal with this. The survey of our Parish took about 4 months to complete.'

(g) Post Collection (Sundays). 'At a Parish Council meeting in March 1951 it was resolved that application be made for the Mail to be collected on Sundays at the Whitecroft and Wellington Post Boxes—this was granted. Hitherto, Mail had been collected on Sundays at the Post Office only.'

CHAPTER X (pages 178–99)

1. See Nicholson, N., *Cumberland and Westmorland* (London, 1949), pp. 136–42.
2. See, for example, Calverley, W. S., Parker, C. A., and Petersen, M., 'The Sculptured Cross at Gosforth, West Cumberland', *T.C.W.A.A.S.* (O.S.), VI (Kendal, 1883), pp. 373–404; Calverley, W. S., 'Shrine-shaped or Coped Tombstones at Gosforth, Cumberland', *T.C.W.A.A.S.* (O.S.), XV (1889), pp. 239–46.
3. Quoted in Loftie, *op. cit.*, p. 57.
4. There were 25 parishes in the Deanery of Coupland at that time; this suggests the parochial system was already well established in the area.
5. Quoted in Bouch, *op. cit.*, pp. 154–5.
6. *Ibid.*, pp. 210–11. Gosforth was successively part of the Dioceses of York, Chester and Carlisle.
7. *Calendar of State Papers. Domestic. 1598–1601* (London, 1869), pp. 362–3. Letter dated December 26, 1599.
8. Bouch, *op. cit.*, p. 328.
9. *Ibid.*, pp. 367–8.
10. The living of Gosforth was held at that time by the Rev. James Lowther Senhouse, Rector of Sawley in Derbyshire.
11. In the eighteenth century the value of the living was £35, more than twice that found in the majority of local parishes.
12. This was written by a visiting clergyman from Newcastle.
13. The Rector of Gosforth in 1772 has been described as 'a pluralist and very careless about the Register'—Phillimore, W. P. W., and Ruston-Harrison, C. W., *Cumberland Parish Registers*, II (Marriages), (London, 1912), p. 143.
14. Cf. Lord Raglan's view: 'Nowadays the Devil has taken a back seat, and ignorance is usually urged by the clergy as the cause of indifference. It may well be that if there were more religious teaching there would be more religion....

NOTES

Such evidence as there is suggests that children brought up without religion do not acquire it' (*The Origins of Religion*, p. 18).

15. This chapter has been written about the parish in 1950-1. Since then the Rector has retired, and when I visited Gosforth in the summer of 1953 there was no incumbent and apparently no likelihood of one in the near future.

16. Henson, H. H., *Bishoprick Papers* (London, 1946), p. 86.

17. Some indication of the decline in Church revenue during the past 150 years is given by the fall in glebe rents during this time. In 1813 they were worth £100; in 1845—£68; in 1886—£38; in 1903—£16; and in 1929 their value was £8.

18. The value of the living (including glebe revenue) at different times was as follows: 1291—£20; 1318—£4; 1535—£17; 1714—£35; 1835—£140; 1925—£270.

19. For a work which convincingly equates priest and king see Hocart, A. M., *Kingship* (London, 1925), pp. 119-29.

20. There were also a few entries in the Confirmation Register which do not appear in the Baptismal Register, that is of young people not baptized in the parish.

21. Onion skins and whin flowers are the most common materials used for dyeing eggs in Gosforth.

22. According to many authorities, pace-egging, a very old custom, is more characteristic of Cumberland than of any other English county. For a full description of pace-egg practices and also customs in other countries in which the egg is prominent, see Wright, A. R., *British Calendar Customs. England*, Vol. I, *Movable Festivals* (London, 1936), pp. 90-1, and Calvert, W. R., *The Hungry Hills* (London, 1933), pp. 148-50. It may be noted in passing that Whistler (*op. cit.*, p. 118) is wrong in stating that pace-egging has now died out completely.

23. This died out some time between 1900 and 1915. The name is reminiscent of a festival known as 'Ffair Ffyliaid' which is held on the first Tuesday in May in the Welsh hamlet of Llanerfyl in Montgomeryshire (Rees, *op. cit.*, p. 134). References to the Cumbrian feast are rare in local literature, although Palm Sunday was celebrated in the same way under this name in the village of Arlecdon, about ten miles away from Gosforth. See the *Cumberland Pacquet* for November 2, 1893, p. 6, col. 1.

24. The details of this custom are so well known it is not thought necessary to repeat them here. Descriptions of it are given in Whistler, *op. cit.*, pp. 73-5, and in *Folklore*, XL (1929), p. 283.

25. See James, E. O., *The Social Function of Religion* (London, 1940), Chaps. I, II and III.

26. From a statement attributed to the Pope, quoted in Hone, W., *The Everyday Book* (London, 1826), I, p. 202.

27. See Hocart, *op. cit., passim*.

28. See Whistler, *op. cit.*, pp. 158-9 and 163.

29. The 'tone' of this anecdote is characteristic of many told about the local clergy, and may possibly be an inheritance from the days when the Cumberland parson was not always a model of good and pious living.

30. This is, of course, by no means a complete explanation. The incidence of adultery in different societies (or different regions within any one society) is, like the incidence of illegitimacy, still in many ways an unexplored problem.

NOTES

31. These were, respectively, Advent to St. Hilary's Day (i.e. at most from November 27 to January 13 of the following year); Septuagesima to Low Sunday (i.e. the period falling between the two extremes of January 19—March 30 and February 21—May 2, depending on the date of Easter); and Rogation Sunday to Trinity Sunday (i.e. the period between the two extremes April 27—May 18 and May 30—June 13, depending on the date of Easter). These restrictions were generally observed in England during the sixteenth and seventeenth centuries.

32. The other two periods of restriction do not appear to have been enforced in Gosforth during the time covered by the Parish Registers.

33. The Church has not always ignored the cause of death in this way. Among the burials in 1600 is recorded the following: 'Ricardus et Johannes Sowyarde felones de se tumulati fuere.' 'Tumulati' cannot mean Christian burial.

34. A striking example of a crisis situation is the drought which occurred within living memory; this was so prolonged that the Prayer for Rain was used in a crowded Church. The Parish Magazine records that 'several showers fell, and the Prayer of Thanksgiving was made on the following Sunday'.

35. Bulmer, T., *History, Topography and Directory of West Cumberland* (Preston, 1883), p. 130.

36. Children and adolescents in large towns are apparently being attracted, by exactly the same things, from the Church of England to the Methodist chapels. See Jephcott, A. P., *Girls Growing Up* (London, 1949), pp. 56-7.

CONCLUSION (*pages 200-3*)

1. See Bouch, *op. cit.*, p. 20 *et seq.*
2. Bailey and Culley, *op. cit.*, p. 11.
3. For example in the phrase 'carters in Gosforth always wore a white brat'. (Cf. Welsh *brat*—an apron.)
4. See, for example, Fox's *The Personality of Britain* (Cardiff, 1938), *passim* and Childe, V. G., *Prehistoric Communities of the British Isles* (London, 1949), pp. 4-7.
5. For an indication of the importance of the Press, wireless, and cinema as media in influencing public opinion, see Lazarsfeld, P. F., and Knupfer, G., 'Communications Research and International Co-operation', in *The Science of Man in the World Crisis*, Linton, R. (Ed.), (New York, 1945).

APPENDIX VIII (*pages 221-2*)

1. Wilson, *op. cit.* (St. Bees) Deed 134, p. 173 (1271).
2. *Ibid.*, p. 153*n*., 'Nethergwhynbanke alias lyngbanke in Newtona in Gosford'.
3. See Thompson, W. N., *op. cit.*, pp. 312-17.
4. Wilson, *op. cit.* Deed 271, p. 287, dated 1235.
5. *Ibid.* Deed 287, p. 298, dated 1282.
6. *Ibid.* Deed 275, p. 290, dated 1230.
7. See Loomis and Beegle, *op. cit.*, pp. 232-4.

NOTES

8. *Calendar of Patent Rolls. Edward 1 1301–7* (London, 1898), p. 181.

9. *Historical Manuscripts Commission. Tenth Report*, Appendix, Pt. IV. A release of seven acres of land in 'Sevenhoues and Bowelton', p. 224.

10. *Cat. Ancient Deeds*, IV (London, 1902). Deed A.9573, p. 437.

11. *Ibid.* Deed A.9241, p. 405.

12. *Ibid.* Deed A.9707, p. 451.

13. *Ibid.* Deed A.9498, p. 430.

14. The few documents available suggest that the manors were fragmented, particularly the manor of Newton and Seascale. See Parker, C. A., 'Some Medieval Crosses, Cross Sites, and Cross Names in West Cumberland', *T.C.W.A.A.S.* (N.S.), IX (1909), 84; Magrath, J. R., 'Fresh Light on the Family of Robert de Eglesfeld, Founder of the Queen's College, Oxford', *T.C.W.A.A.S.* (N.S.), XVI (1916), 241–2; and documents relating to the Court Baron and Customary Court of Divisions of Henry Lutwidge, Lord of the Manor of Newton and Seascale (1788) (in the custody of the Rector of Gosforth).

15. Thompson, W. N., *op. cit.*, p. 308.

16. *Ibid.* and Magrath, *op. cit.*, p. 242.

17. *Cat. Ancient Deeds*, IV (1902), Deed A.9235, p. 404.

18. *Ibid.* Deed A.9573, p. 437.

19. 'Scarth in the vills of Gosford and Ponsonby', *H.M.C.*, X, Appendix IV, p. 225 (fourteenth century). Scar Green is now in the parish of Ponsonby.

20. Crook of Bleng became High End of Bolton, and Bolton became Low End of Bolton.

21. Land Tax Assessment (1850) in the custody of Mr. William Poole, Hall Senna, Gosforth: A document entitled 'James L. Senhouse, Gosforth' in the custody of the Rector of Gosforth; Mannix and Whellan, *op. cit.*, pp. 322–4.

22. For example, Parson, W., and White, W., *History, Directory, and Gazetteer of the Counties of Cumberland and Westmorland* (Leeds, 1829), pp. 209–10.

23. For example Bulmer, T., *op. cit.*, 132–3. The directories seem to be based on John Denton's *Accompt*, an unreliable source which describes Gosforth as 'Above Dregg lies the parish, mannor and town of Gosford'. See Denton, J., *Accompt* (c. 1610), *C.W.A.A.S.*, Tract Series II (Kendal, 1887).

INDEX

Adultery, 195, 197, 239
Agapae, 191
Agricultural Revolution, 224
Agricultural Society, 121, 123, 127, 220
Alternate generations, 80, 230
Ascension Day, 181, 182, 190

Bank End, 77
Baptism, 59–60, 102, 143, 197, 230
Beagling, 134
Benbank, 156
Benson, 79, 229
Birth, 59, 68
  place of, 2, 204
Blacksmith, 74, 135, 141, 158, 163, 208
Bolton, 221, 222, 235
Bolton Head, 76, 221
Boon day, 147–50
Boonwood, 158, 160, 236
Boonwood Fair, 21
Borrowing and lending, 141–2, 144–7
Boxing Day, 196
Braithwaite, 80
Bridewain, 66
British Legion, 19, 121, 123, 125–6, 220
Brocklebank, 116
Buchanan, 76
Bundling, 63
Bunker, 77

Calder Abbey, 178
Candlemas, 16, 17, 18, 19, 188, 190, 193
Census, attitudes to, 173
Chartulary of St. Bees, 4, 5, 155, 221, 223
Christian Scientists, 198
Christmas, 135, 180, 181, 187, 188, 190, 191, 196
Church of England, 59, 67, 68, 103, 130, 165–7, 174, 178–97, 201, 232, 237
  communion in, 180–1, 182, 187
  Confirmation in, 185–6
  revenue, 179 ff., 183–4, 238, 239
  churchwardens, 158, 165, 181
Churchwardens' Accounts, 4, 165, 182, 222
Cinema attendance, 232
Clements, 80
Clippin' Day, 82, 148
Clogs, 113–14, 225
Club walk, 189, 191
Cock-fighting, 131–4, 172, 189, 233
Cock-loaf, 133, 233
Cockermouth, 18, 24, 225
Collop Monday, 189
Common land, 6–7, 159, 223
Contraception, 54, 66
Co-operation, among farmers, 144–55, 235
  among villagers, 141–4
Copley, 115
Coupland, 3, 115, 179, 200, 201, 238
Courtship, 61–3, 64
Craftsmen, 20–1, 54–5, 59, 158, 163, 216
Cumberland County Council, 174 ff.

Death and burial, 67–8, 102, 142, 151, 227, 228, 232
Divorce, 195
Dramatic Society, 123, 124, 127, 220

Easter, 19, 165, 180, 184, 186–7, 188, 190, 191
Easter Monday, 131
Egremont, 9, 24, 25, 164, 225
Enclosure Act, 6, 223
Eskdale, 1, 75, 132
Estates, 7, 116, 118, 223
Experts, attitudes to, 237

Families, elementary, 52–3, 56
  size of, 40, 50, 52–3, 57
  three generation, 53–6

243

INDEX

Family Planning Association, 228
Farm accounts, 26 ff., 41–2, 225
Farmers and villagers, division between, 160–2
Farm-houses, 22, 23, 34–6, 226
Farming, calendar of, 16–19
 division of labour in, 40–1
 mechanization of, 16, 20, 21–4, 44, 160
 types of, 13–14
Farms, fragmentation of, 7–8, 223
 hired workers on, 35, 37, 38, 39–40, 209
 inheritance of, 49–52
 rents of, 10–11, 17, 18, 209, 224, 225
 sales of, 11–12
 size of, 5–7, 9–10, 207, 209, 223
 turnover of, 28–30, 225–6
Filly Fair, 188, 239
Fleming Hall, 221, 222
Folk memory, 229, 234
Football Club, 121, 123, 129, 220
Forestry Commission, 15, 31, 172
Forthneet, 164
Forty-second cousin, 71, 72, 74
Foundling motif, 237
Fox hunting, 134, 220
Furniture, 34–7, 97, 112, 113

Ghosts, 68
Girl Guides, 61, 220
Girls' Friendly Society, 61, 220
Glebe Terrier, 5, 232, 233
Good Friday, 182, 187
Gosforth Bottom, 120
Gosforth Charities, 128–9, 166, 233
Gosforth Show, 18, 19, 85
Government officials, attitudes to, 171 ff.
Guards Lonning, 63
Gunson, 229

Hall Senna, 76, 156, 232, 235, 236
Hallow E'en, 188, 191
Hartley, 229
Harvest Festival, 103, 187, 190, 191–2
Herbert, 79
Herdwick sheep, 1, 14, 160, 224

High Guards, 234
Hinde, 80
Hiring fairs, 225
Hog-back tombstones, 178
Honeymoon, 66
Hound trailing, 124, 135, 233
Howesbarrowe, 156

Illegitimacy, 65, 110, 195, 228, 239
Inheritance, 49–52, 55, 57
 partible, 50–7

Johnson, 85

Kemplerigg, 77
Kinship, 69–85
 'claiming kin', 69 ff.
 collective attributes, 77–8
 and co-operation, 82–3
 and land-holding, 76–7
 and marriage, 74, 78
 and names, 76–7, 78–82, 85, 229–30
 and location, 70
 and social class, 83–4, 230
 and social stability, 76, 84
Kitchen, 34 ff.
Kitchin, 85
Kirk Style, 234
Kirkby, 85
Kurn supper, 148, 154, 235

Laconby, 236
Lady Day, 16, 18, 19, 188
Land-holding, 5–8, 201, 223
Last cut, 36
Lent, 194, 196
Ling Bank, 221, 222
Litigation, absence of, 172
Lupercalia, 190

Mariage de convenance, 63
Marriage, 45–9, 50, 55–6, 64, 66, 68, 102, 110, 111, 143, 228
 age difference in, 49
 and first birth, 64
Martinmas, 18, 19, 39, 154, 188, 193
Mawson, 229
Methodism, 167, 198, 237

244

INDEX

Michaelmas, 188, 190, 193
Mid-summer Day, 131
Milk Marketing Board, 10, 18, 24, 28, 226
Mole catcher, 30, 226
Moon, affecting sanity, 234
Moore, 79
Moscroppe or Mossop, 79, 229
Mothers' Union, 121, 123, 220

Names, inheritance of, 79–80, 229–30
and social status, 39, 218–19
Neighbours, 140–55
New Mill, 221
New Year's Day, 131, 187, 189
Newton, 221, 222
Newton Manor, 221
Nicholson, 79
Noble, 80
Norse Cross, 3, 178

Occupations, 30–3, 208, 226

Pace-egging, 188, 239
Palm Sunday, 239
Parental authority, 42–4, 57–8
Parish Award, 5, 7, 223, 234
Parish Council, 126, 128, 174–5, 237–8
   Magazine, 117, 166, 180, 181–2, 183, 184, 197, 233
   organizations, 220
   Registers, 4, 65, 72, 74, 78, 79, 81, 82, 83, 85, 115, 152, 155, 165, 222, 223, 232
Park, 166
Parlour, 36–7
Peel Place, 236
Pharoah, 237
Pin money, 41
Plough Sunday, 19
Poaching, 233
Policeman, 172
Politics, 175–6
Poole, 76, 79, 82, 85, 229, 232
Population, 1–3, 205–6
   movements of, 2, 229
Postlethwaite, 85
Presbyterians, 198

Prestige, 37, 66, 80, 111–15, 126, 130
Public Hall, 61, 66, 104, 131, 135, 203
Public houses, 124, 135–9, 234
Pyel, 156, 221

Quakers, 198, 199
Quarry Brow, 166

Ravenglass, 9
Reading habits, 232
Rector, 6, 60, 138, 166, 174, 180, 181, 183–5, 222, 223, 237, 238–9
Roman Catholicism, 65, 167, 198, 199
Rough grazing, 9, 10, 11, 12, 22, 23
Row Lane, 166
Rum butter, 36, 59, 227
Rural District Council, 171, 174 ff.
Rush candles, 20, 225
Russell, 85

St. Herbert, 178
St. Ninian, 178
St. Kentigern, 178
School, 60–1, 160, 183
Seascale, 5, 158, 164, 221, 222, 234
Sellafield, 31, 229
Senhouse, 117, 232
Sermons, 193–4
Settlement pattern, 155–6, 200, 221, 237
Sevenhoues, 156, 221, 222
Sheepshank Hall, 234
Sheep shearing, 235
Shepherd's Guide, 224
Sherwen, 76, 79, 115, 116, 166
Shrove Tuesday, 133, 189
Skelton, 85
Social class, 86–120, 231–2
   and behaviour, 97, 99, 103–4
   'profiles' of, 89–99
   and economic status, 90–1, 93, 98
   and education, 91, 94, 95
   and friendship, 100 ff.
   historical changes in, 115–19
   methodology, 210–14
   and occupation, 91–2
   and the 'old standards', 109–11
   and parish organizations, 121–9

INDEX

Social class and pedigree, 90
    and public houses, 138
    and 'social perspective', 107–9
    statistics of, 215–17
    and strangers, 105–7
    and value judgments, 102–3
Steele, 80, 229
Strangers, attitudes to, 105–6, 151–2, 168–71
Suicide, 42–3, 197, 240
Swills, 225

Tarnhow, 76, 77
Taxatio Ecclesiatica, 178
Threshing day, 148–50
Time, measurement of, 234
Town End, 77
Townships, 156–8, 221–2
Tyson, 75, 77, 80, 229

Vikings, 3, 85, 201, 231

Wasdale, 14, 17
Wasdale Head, 19
Wellington, 119–20, 140–1, 189, 238
Wheel-barrow farms, 6, 7
Whit Saturday, 131
Whitehaven, 2, 18, 20, 22, 23, 24, 25, 26, 150, 198
    visits to, 236
Whitsun, 19, 39, 133, 180, 187, 189, 190, 191
Whitsun Ale, 191
Widows, 48, 49, 51, 52
Wilson, 80, 229
Winterage, 14, 225
Women's Institute, 121, 122, 123, 127–8, 129, 153, 163, 220, 237
Wrestling, 129–31, 233
Wrestling Academy, 61, 121, 123, 125–6, 127, 129, 131, 163

Young Farmers' Club, 61, 153
Youth organizations, 61

Printed in Great Britain
by Amazon